The Best Of Fine
WoodWorking

Traditional Woodworking
Techniques

The Best Of Fine
WoodWorking

Traditional Woodworking
Techniques

The Taunton Press

Cover photo by Roger Holmes

TAUNTON
BOOKS & VIDEOS

...by fellow enthusiasts

©1991 by The Taunton Press, Inc.
All rights reserved

First printing: February 1991
International Standard Book Number: 0-942391-94-2
Printed in the United States of America

A FINE WOODWORKING Book

FINE WOODWORKING® is a trademark of The Taunton Press, Inc.,
registered in the U.S. Patent and Trademark Office.

The Taunton Press, Inc.
63 South Main Street
Box 5506
Newtown, Connecticut 06470-5506

Library of Congress Cataloging-in-Publication Data

The Best of Fine woodworking. Traditional woodworking techniques:
    38 articles / selected by the editors of Fine woodworking magazine.
      p. cm.
      "A Fine woodworking book"—T.p. verso.
      Includes index.
      ISBN 0-942391-94-2
      1. Furniture making.   I. Fine woodworking.
    II. Title: Traditional woodworking techniques
    TT194.B47 1991
    684'.08—dc20   90-24707
                                                           CIP

Contents

Introduction

Like most middle-age woodworkers, I'm fairly attached to my little shopful of stationary power tools. Early on my teachers convinced me that "you gotta have the tools if you wanna do the work," and tools meant noisy things with electric motors and accurately machined components that required precise adjustments. I think we all secretly hoped a little skill would also be built into these mechanical marvels.

It took years for me to appreciate that the skill was really in the worker, and that tools were nothing magical by themselves. Some of the work, both contemporary and traditional, that I most admire relies heavily on hand tools and good old-fashioned skills. In this collection of 38 articles from *Fine Woodworking* magazine, some of the best technicians in the field present methods for traditional work, such as lovely inlaid tambours, barred-glass doors, dovetailed case work and multiple drawers with piston-like fit. For the carvers and those who admire traditional embellishments, there are pie-crust tables, pineapple and flame finials, scallop shells and cabriole knees. Lest we forget that woodworking doesn't always have to be serious, we've included a couple of puzzlers and things for fun, such as secret compartments and a twisted dovetail joint that appears impossible to make.

—*Dick Burrows, editor*

The "Best of *Fine Woodworking*" series spans issues 46 through 80 of *Fine Woodworking* magazine, originally published between mid-1984 and the end of 1989. There is no duplication between these books and the popular *"Fine Woodworking* on..." series. A footnote with each article gives the date of first publication; product availability, suppliers' addresses and prices may have changed since then.

Dovetails for Case Work
Strength and durability from traditional joint

by Gene Schultz

I cut my first set of carcase dovetails 12 years ago for a large toolbox. At the time, I was planning a career reproducing American furniture of the 18th and 19th century, a period in which dovetailed carcases were the norm for fine furniture. I've since expanded my business to include modern materials, methods and designs, which permit a wide variety of carcase joinery. But for unquestioned durability and strength in solid-wood construction, it's hard to beat dovetails, and I use them whenever the job warrants—and the customer will pay for them.

Traditionally, both through and lap (also called half-blind) dovetails were used for carcase work. In through dovetails, the joint is visible on the surface of both joined pieces. Lap dovetails are visible only on one surface and hidden behind a lap on the other. Through dovetails, which are faster to cut, were first choice when it didn't matter if the joint was visible; lap dovetails were selected when it did. Contemporary makers often choose through dovetails for their decorative quality, and use lap dovetails mainly for drawer work.

To illustrate the process of cutting both joints, I'll describe the making of the simple carcase shown in the drawing, lap dovetailed on top, through dovetailed on bottom. Before any joints are cut, the stock must be prepared. I usually rough cut the stock about 1 in. longer and 1 in. wider than finished dimension, then plane them to final thickness—I finish by taking light shavings with a sharp handplane to smooth the surfaces. Next, cut them to exact size on the tablesaw. I use an accurate framing square and a 12-in. combination square to check that the boards' ends are square to the edges, as well as the faces. If necessary, I handplane them square. The stock must be perfectly square and uniform in thickness for the dovetailed case to go together well, without wind or other difficult-to-correct distortions.

Next, mark each board so there is no doubt about its position in the carcase. I mark the outside and inside faces of the top, bottom, left side and right side; then on each of those pieces, I mark the front and back edges, and the top and bottom ends. This may seem redundant, but it saves a lot of time and mistakes later on.

I layout and cut the tails first, then mark the pins from the tails. Others do the reverse, but I find this sequence easier and faster. Set a marking gauge to the exact thickness of the stock and scribe a line on the faces and edges of the tail boards, and on the faces of the pin boards. If the boards are the same thickness, tails and pins of through dovetails will be the same length and all four boards can, therefore, be scribed with the same

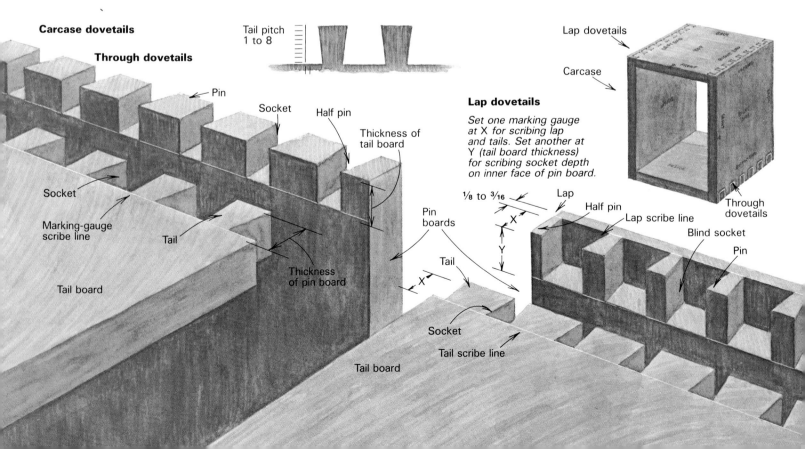

Carcase dovetails

Through dovetails

Pin

Socket Half pin

Tail pitch 1 to 8

Thickness of tail board

Socket

Marking-gauge scribe line

Tail

Thickness of pin board

Tail board

Lap dovetails

Set one marking gauge at X for scribing lap and tails. Set another at Y (tail board thickness) for scribing socket depth on inner face of pin board.

Lap dovetails

Carcase

⅛ to 3/16

Pin boards

Lap

Half pin

Lap scribe line

Blind socket

Pin

X

Y

X

Tail

Socket

Tail scribe line

Tail board

Through dovetails

marking-gauge setting. I sharpen the spur to a chisel point so it cuts rather than scratches across grain. Darken the scribed lines with a chisel-point pencil so they're easier to see.

Some craftsmen space the tails precisely and evenly, their pitch uniform. I prefer the handmade look of asymmetrical pitch and spacing. For added strength, the pins and tails should be about equal at their widest part, but there are no hard and fast rules regarding width, and pleasing appearance is certainly important.

I divide the board for the tail spacing by eye, rather than measurement. Start by marking the center, then mark a half pin in from each edge, just a bit wider than half an actual pin. Divide the spaces between the center and end pin marks in half, and continue to subdivide until the spacing looks good to you. You may want to sketch out a few tail/pin spacings on paper to find one pleasing to you, then divide the board to approximate the sketch.

Now, draw the tails using your dividing marks as centerlines. The pitch I prefer is about 1 to 8. A much higher ratio resembles a box joint; much lower and the short grain in the tails may weaken them. I draw the tails with a pencil and plastic draftsmans' square, gauging the pitch by eye. If other joints on the case are the same, use the first layout as a rough template for them. Square the pitch lines across the end with a square and knife, then darken them with a chisel-point pencil. Finally, mark an "X" on the waste between tails—a simple precaution that can save much grief.

I saw the tails with a 20-point dovetail saw or a bandsaw, cutting the layout lines in half, rather than sawing to either side of them. Handsawing is best done with the work held rigidly in a vise, the top end parallel to the floor, and at a comfortable height. The closer the end of the board is to the vise, the less chatter sawing will create. As this puts the end rather low, I prefer to sit on a stool while sawing. As you work along the end, you can switch the board from one side of the vise to the other to reduce chatter. Auxiliary clamps, fixing an unsecured edge to the bench, for example, may be useful, too.

Start the cut with the saw at about 45° to the board's face. Use your thumb as a guide as you pull backward with light downward pressure to establish a kerf. As the kerf deepens, be sure you're cutting square across the ends, following the knifed-in scribe lines. As you near the marking-gauge line, lower the saw to finish the cut at the gauge line on both faces. After sawing all the tails, remove the bulk of the waste between them with a fine-tooth coping saw, slipping it into the dovetail sawkerf and cutting about ¹⁄₁₆ in. to ⅛ in. proud of the marking-gauge lines.

I clear the rest of the waste in the sockets between the tails with a sharp ¼-in. to ½-in. bevel-edge chisel and mallet. Lay the board flat on the benchtop and clamp it securely. Place the chisel in the gauge line between two tails and chop down about halfway through the board. Chop first in the center of the socket, then in each corner; bevel-edge chisels conform to the pitch of the tails. If the waste is too thick, reduce it by making a cut or two away from the line. Chop square to the board's face or undercut slightly—this makes for much less clean-up later. Chop halfway through all the sockets on one side, turn the board over and chop from the other side to clear the remainder of the waste. Check with a square, or by eye, to make sure the socket bottoms are flat or concave (undercut), not convex, and pare any high spots with a chisel.

Dovetail saw cuts that aren't square to the board's face must be squared up before marking the pins. To do so, knife a square line on the end of the tail, then rest the chisel in the line to start a paring cut. Control the chisel by holding your arm and elbow

Determine the tail centerlines by eye, dividing the board in half, then quarters, and so on. You can freehand the tails' pitch with a straightedge as shown here, or use a sliding bevel for strictly uniform pitch.

Cut down the pitch lines for each tail. Start the cut against your thumb, the saw at an angle. Lower the saw to finish the cut at the scribed lines.

After clearing most of the waste from the sockets with a coping saw, chop to the scribe lines on both faces with a sharp chisel.

Drawing: Philip Harvey

scribe lines down to the marking-gauge lines on both faces. Darken these; and mark the waste between pins with an "X."

The procedure for sawing and chopping the pins is much the same as for the tails. Accurate sawing is especially important when cutting the pins. Try to split the knifed scribe line in half—that is, the sawkerf should fall entirely in the waste, leaving half the V of the scribe line on the pin. Removing the scribe line completely, or leaving it completely on, will make the joint either too tight or too loose. If you have difficulty controlling the dovetail saw, it is better to cut away from the line on the waste side and pare to the line with a sharp chisel. Clear the bulk of the socket waste with a coping saw, then lay the board flat on the bench and chop to the socket-bottom gauge lines, as for the tails.

Before test fitting the joint, inspect all the tails and pins for squareness and accuracy, and pare where necessary. Then, line up the tails and pins and tap them together evenly along the width of the boards with your fist, or a hammer and a scrapwood block. Keep the pieces square to each other to avoid damaging the joint. Don't force the joint together—you may break a tail or even split a board. Instead, note where the joint doesn't fit, pull the boards apart and trim where needed. I usually drive the tails all the way home on the test fit. When you knock them apart, be sure to keep the boards square to each other and tap evenly along the width.

Lap dovetails are laid out and cut in much the same way as through dovetails, the main difference being the blind sockets. When preparing the stock, remember that tail boards must be shorter than the overall width (or length) of the case by the combined thickness of the two laps on the pin boards.

When laying out lap dovetails, I find it convenient to use two marking gauges, which eliminates some confusion and possible error when resetting the gauge. Set the first gauge to the length of the tails—the thickness of pin-board stock minus the lap, usually $\frac{1}{8}$ in. to $\frac{3}{16}$ in. Set the second gauge to the thickness of the tail-board stock. With the first gauge, scribe the faces and edges of the tail board and the ends of the pin boards to establish the lap line. Scribe the inside faces of the pin boards with the second gauge for the socket depth.

I divide the board and lay out the pitch of the tails by eye, as for through dovetails. The pins of lap dovetails are customarily much smaller than those of through dovetails, though extremely slender pins reduce the joint's strength considerably. Saw and chisel the tails exactly as described for through dovetails.

When the tails are finished, scribe the pins using the previously described setup, positioning the end of the tail board exactly on the scribed lap line. After knifing around the tails, knife the pin lines square down the inside face, darken with a chisel-point pencil, and mark the waste. Split the knife lines with a fine dovetail saw, but this time, saw only to the lap line and the marking gauge line on the inside face.

Some craftsmen remove the bulk of the socket waste with a Forstner, or similar flat-bottomed drill bit or a mortising machine, others cut it out with a fine-tooth coping saw, as I do. I clamp the board flat on the benchtop for making the coping saw cuts, keeping well clear of the gauge lines on the end and face of the board. I complete the sockets with a chisel, chopping vertically and paring horizontally a little at a time ($\frac{1}{8}$ in. or less). Start the final cuts in the scribe lines and clean out the corners with a skew chisel. Undercutting slightly is okay. Take very thin slices with a very sharp chisel in difficult or reversing grain. Dry assemble the joint to check the fit.

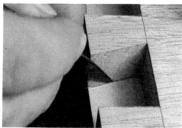

A stable, accurately aligned setup is crucial when scribing the pins from the tails. Pull any bow out of the pin board (the vertical one) by clamping it to the bench, as shown above. Scribe carefully, keeping the knife blade flush with the tail, as shown at left.

tight to your body and use "body English" to push, while manipulating the chisel slightly from side to side to guide it. Keep the chisel flat throughout the entire slice.

Now you're ready to lay out the pins. Clamp one of the pin boards in the vise, with the board's top end parallel to and just slightly above the surface of the benchtop, its outside face toward you. Place scrap blocks under the bottom end of the board so that it won't move under downward pressure. Lay the tail board on the benchtop, aligning the appropriate end (check your marks) flush with the face and edges of the pin board. When the tail board is positioned exactly, secure it to the benchtop with a hand-screw clamp to keep it from moving while you scribe around the tails.

A snug-fitting set of dovetails depends on precise positioning and scribing of the pins from the tails, as well as accurate sawing and chiseling. A board that has bowed slightly across its width—a common problem—needs to be straightened for accurate scribing. I use a series of handscrews and my vise to pull it flat, as shown at top left. I move the piece manually until the distortion is corrected, then improvise a clamping arrangement that duplicates my hand position.

I scribe with a jackknife, and one that doesn't have a super-sharp edge seems to work best. Place the blade tight against the tail and draw it toward you lightly. Then deepen the mark with a second pass under slightly more pressure—double scribing is less likely to follow the grain of the wood. When all the tails are scribed, remove the tail board and darken the knife lines with a chisel-point pencil. With a square and the knife, extend the

From *Fine Woodworking* magazine (March 1986) 57:52-55

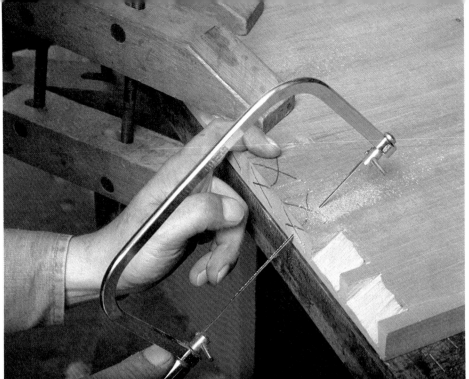

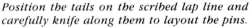

Position the tails on the scribed lap line and carefully knife along them to layout the pins.

Now you're ready to glue up. With all you've invested in cutting the joints, take the time to prepare for assembly. I make a complete dry run to uncover any problems with the clamping procedure. Once you start spreading glue, you must work extremely fast to finish before the glue sets up. I usually use white glue, which allows about 10 minutes for assembly, but if you're inexperienced in putting these joints together, you might try a much slower setting glue, such as liquid hide glue. An assistant is a big help for spreading glue and handling the clamps.

For a carcase like this, I usually use three or four bar clamps across each case end, placing a 1x2 hardwood-scrap batten under the clamps to avoid denting the work. To put pressure on only the tails, I cut a shallow relief in the batten over each pin. A strip or two of masking tape prevents excess glue from sticking to the battens. Before spreading any glue, lay the carcase parts in the correct positions on the benchtop, preset the clamps to length and place them, the battens, and some damp rags for wiping excess glue conveniently near the case parts.

Spread glue evenly on all surfaces of the tail and pin sockets. Work quickly and methodically. It's usually best to first assemble two pin boards to one tail board, pushing them together as far as you can by hand pressure, then push on the remaining tail board just far enough to hold the case together. Position the battens (tape them in place if you don't have a pair of helping hands) and apply pressure uniformly with all clamps. Tighten the clamps slowly to allow the excess glue to squeeze out. If one part of the case isn't drawing down, reposition a clamp or add an extra clamp at that point and continue tightening all the clamps evenly.

When the joints are seated, put the case on a flat surface and check the squareness of the carcase by comparing diagonals across the front and, if possible, the back openings, with a tape measure or a pair of sticks. If the diagonals aren't equal, the case is out of square. Depending on the diagonal to be shortened, move the heads or heels of the clamps away from the carcase to pull it square. Once the glue has dried, plane the joints smooth—you'll be amazed at how crisp the joinery looks. At that point, all of your hard work will indeed be worth it. □

Gene Schultz is a partner in Boston Cabinet Making, a custom shop in Boston, Mass.

Clear waste from the sockets with a coping saw (top right), staying well short of the scribed line for the socket bottoms. Then chop the remainder of the waste, making the final paring cuts on the scribed lines (above).

Using battens to protect the wood and distribute pressure, glue and clamp up the carcase. Work all the clamps down evenly to avoid straining the joints.

Fig. 1: Anatomy of a dovetailed drawer

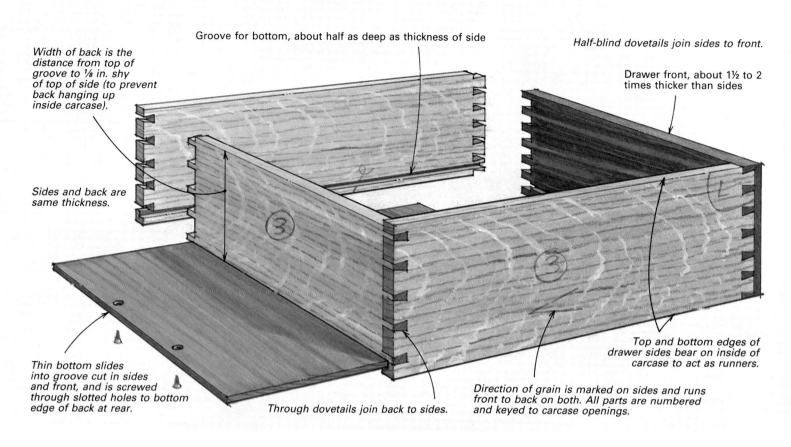

Groove for bottom, about half as deep as thickness of side

Half-blind dovetails join sides to front.

Width of back is the distance from top of groove to ⅛ in. shy of top of side (to prevent back hanging up inside carcase).

Drawer front, about 1½ to 2 times thicker than sides

Sides and back are same thickness.

Thin bottom slides into groove cut in sides and front, and is screwed through slotted holes to bottom edge of back at rear.

Through dovetails join back to sides.

Direction of grain is marked on sides and runs front to back on both. All parts are numbered and keyed to carcase openings.

Top and bottom edges of drawer sides bear on inside of carcase to act as runners.

Multiple-Drawer Construction
Pretrimming the parts makes for a piston-like fit

by Alan Peters

One disadvantage of building one-of-a-kind furniture or cabinetry is that you must constantly break new ground and develop construction methods for each and every part. This can be an exhilarating challenge, but it's very time-consuming, because you can seldom set up predictable, time-saving procedures for repetitive operations.

No matter how unique the piece though, you can always save time on a dresser or desk by employing a standardized drawer-production routine. This isn't to imply you must compromise on the quality of materials or joinery; in fact, I make drawers for most of my case pieces from solid wood and dovetail all four corners. I do this efficiently by following a systematic method for choosing drawer materials, marking, cutting and assembling the drawers into the completed carcase. The result is a simple, solid drawer with a piston fit—my shop's trademark. In this article, I'll describe how I built the drawers on the chest shown in the top photo on the facing page, but you can apply the method to most wooden drawers.

Design—My basic drawers have a front, back and two sides, all dovetailed together. The drawer bottom slides into a groove dadoed into the sides and front and is slot-screwed to the bottom edge of the back. The drawer slides in and out of a carcase that contains the drawer and also guides its movement. With this simple arrangement, you save time by not adding separate guides on the drawer sides or installing and aligning runners inside the carcase. The disadvantage is that both the carcase and the drawers must be made and fitted accurately for the drawer to slide smoothly, and these drawers are susceptible to binding or rattling if they expand or shrink.

Despite its simplicity, my system offers several design variables that can alter the appearance of a drawered carcase piece considerably. I often make my drawer fronts to fit flush with the carcase front. Alternatively, overlay fronts create a clean look, because very little carcase shows. But, they're more trouble to fit than flush fronts: In addition to fitting the drawers, you must trim the

From *Fine Woodworking* magazine (November 1988) 73:48-51

overlays so the gaps between adjacent fronts are even and equal. It's possible with either flush or overlay fronts to make an entire bank of drawers from matching boards or veneer leaves, thus creating an uninterrupted flow of grain across the front of the case piece that is visually striking.

Handles and pulls offer another design option. Applied handles, such as knobs or wire pulls, are the easiest to fit, but if they're not chosen carefully, they can look stuck on and can spoil a front's clean appearance. To avoid this, I often incorporate a wooden pull or hidden finger recess as part of the drawer front itself. This may take more time, but it's a detail that adds character to a piece. One option, as shown in the bottom photo at right, is to rout a cove with a core-box bit, then attach a short section of dowel made from a contrasting wood for the pull. Also, the fronts on this drawer are joined to their sides with through dovetails, and the exposed joinery provides another visual detail.

To give more visual interest to the walnut case piece, shown in the top photo at right, I started with regular flush-front drawers, but added a twist: I carved out curved hollows in the frame members beneath the drawer fronts. This lends an otherwise straightforward piece a curvaceous look, and the 1-in.-deep hollows provide access to finger pulls on the drawer bottoms. This does require the face frame's rails to be wider than otherwise necessary—a disadvantage if you want to get maximum drawer space in minimum carcase height.

Drawer materials—The first step toward building a solid, stable drawer is to choose the right materials. Drawer sides should only be cut from top-quality, mild-grain and preferably quartersawn timber. It's good to use lumber that planes easily and shows minimum movement or warping over time. My favorites are Honduras mahogany and quartered English oak. I like my drawer sides to contrast the fronts, so I usually use mahogany with light-color drawer fronts, such as ash or sycamore, and oak with rosewood or walnut fronts. From time to time, I've also used teak for drawer sides because of its excellent wearing properties. Wavy-grain sycamore can be nice on special cabinets where the visual quality of the sides is important, but the wood's interlocking grain planes poorly, and this can cause problems in drawer fitting.

I usually make my drawer fronts from the same wood as the carcase, and I save the highly figured sections for these most-visible parts. To make a stable front out of a wild-grain board, I may cut ⅛-in.-thick veneers and glue them to both sides of a mild-grain board of the same species. I also use this method to create grain patterns on drawer fronts, such as a book-match between adjacent fronts, or when I don't have enough figured solid wood to cover the drawer fronts for an entire piece.

For consistency of movement and sheer convenience, I use the same timber for the backs as for the sides, machined to the same thickness. Wherever possible, I use the offcuts after having cut out the sides. For drawer bottoms, I almost always use solid cedar. I love the smell, and so do my clients, but happily the moths and worms do not. If I need to make extremely thin bottoms to get the maximum depth inside a drawer, I use thin plywood, such as ⅛-in. Baltic birch, and then veneer it on both sides with cedar.

All drawer stock must be thoroughly dry and allowed to stabilize in your workshop. Sticker the planed boards in the warmest part of the shop for weeks, if possible. Allow the air to circulate around each board. If your shop is not heated or as dry as it should be, bring the boards into the house. The relevance of this advice depends on the climate where you live and the destination of the furniture piece. I live in one of the wettest parts of Britain, where central heating is needed more than half the year.

Although the author's walnut chest of drawers, above, has 19 dovetail drawers, his organized system of marking, cutting, assembling and fitting results in drawers with a piston fit. The piece has a frame-and-panel carcase and bent-laminate drawer fronts that provide a built-in pull underneath.

To achieve a pull that's integrated with the design of the drawer front, the author routs a cove in each front, then attaches a short section of dowel made from a contrasting wood for the pull. The through dovetails on the fronts provide another visual detail.

Shipping a drawered chest to a drier climate can cause even well-fit drawers to rattle, so I always take the precaution of buying my drawer stock thoroughly dry and keeping it that way.

Construction—Whether I'm building five drawers or 50, I group all my cutting, assembling and fitting work together so I complete each step on all the drawers before moving on. This exploits the fact that the more you repeat a process, the faster and more skillful you become.

Before cutting out the parts for flush-fitting drawers, I go through the stickered boards and set aside any severly warped pieces. I then joint one edge of each board and rip the boards to width. I determine the widths by measuring the height of the openings on the carcase, then rip all the sides and fronts ¹⁄₁₆ in. wider so there's extra to be trimmed later. The backs are cut as wide as the sides minus the distance from the bottom of the side to the top of the groove to be dadoed for the drawer bottom and an extra ⅛ in. for carcase clearance (see figure 1 on facing page).

I cut all the drawer parts to length on the tablesaw using a crosscut carriage and length stop, but you can use a radial saw or miter box as well. Next, I number each set of drawer parts, keying them to a particular opening in the carcase. I do this even if the drawers are all the same size, because there are inevitably small discrepancies in the carcase. I then pair up the sets of draw-

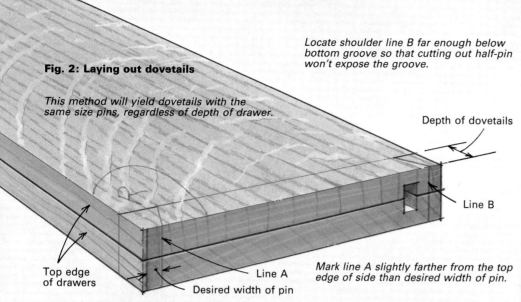

Fig. 2: Laying out dovetails

This method will yield dovetails with the same size pins, regardless of depth of drawer.

Locate shoulder line B far enough below bottom groove so that cutting out half-pin won't expose the groove.

Line A

Depth of dovetails

Line B

Line B

Top edge of drawers

Line A

Desired width of pin

Mark line A slightly farther from the top edge of side than desired width of pin.

Step 1: Lay a matching pair of drawer sides on top of one another with inside surfaces touching. On the endgrain, mark the position of the half-pins (lines A and B) with a pencil and square.

Step 2: Set a pair of dividers to the estimated width of one tail plus the desired width of one pin. Place one point of the dividers on line B. Walk the dividers across the width of the side, and by trial and error, reset the dividers until the point reaches one pin width beyond line A. Mark square lines from these divider points, except the point that fell beyond line A.

Using a plywood box as a demonstration carcase, the author shows students attending a seminar he taught at Anderson Ranch in Colorado how to fit and pretrim the sides of a drawer before assembly. This method makes it easier to achieve a close fit between drawer and carcase, and it minimizes the trimming required after the drawer is assembled.

er sides and mark rights and lefts, indicating the grain direction on each. I try to align the grain of the sides so I'll be planing with the grain, front to back, when fitting the completed drawers later.

Carcase construction—Whether you use a slab or frame-and-panel construction, a smoothly operating drawer is as dependent on a solid, square carcase as it is on good drawer construction. Build and finish the carcase before you start the drawers. During the final assembly, make sure the carcase sides and dividers are flat and free from wind, and all parts are square and true to one another. Equally important, the drawer openings should never be smaller at the rear than at the front, but preferably a fraction larger so the drawers won't bind at the rear.

After you've glued up the carcase and removed the clamps, allow the piece to settle for awhile, preferably a few weeks. This is especially important with a solid-wood piece, because the tension and moisture that can build up in a board during glue-up may distort the case later on and ruin a close drawer-to-carcase fit.

Before making the drawers, it's prudent to check each drawer opening with a straightedge: Lay it inside the drawer aperture, both vertically and horizontally, and remove any humps or dips in the frame around the opening with a shoulder or chisel plane. Leave the back of the carcase off, if possible, until after the drawers have been fit. Once the carcase's outside has been finished, wax all the inner surfaces that the drawer will contact.

Prefitting—The next step may seem unorthodox, but it will save you a lot of trouble getting a good drawer-to-carcase fit. Before cutting the corner joints and assembling the drawers, prefit each drawer piece into its respective carcase opening. Using a bench vise and a jack plane, trim each side down until it slides smoothly in and out of the carcase, as shown in the photo at left. After all the sides are done, prefit all the drawer backs, trimming both edges and ends until each back slips snugly into the carcase opening. When you trim, forget your try square and ruler: Hold the back up to the opening, reach in from the open back to mark where it is proud and plane that edge to fit. Prefit the drawer front using the already-trimmed back as a template to mark where it needs trimming. Then, trial-fit each front into its opening and make it a tight fit so it enters only about ¼ in. for final fitting after assembly. Once all the drawer parts have been prefit, plow the groove for the drawer bottom on the insides of the fronts and sides with a straight bit and router or with a dado blade and tablesaw. The groove width should allow a snug fit of the drawer bottom, and groove depth should be half the drawer side thickness.

Dovetailed corners—Dovetailing all four corners of a large batch of drawers can seem an endless task, but once again, an orderly approach speeds things up. Laying out the dovetails can be particularly tedious if you have lots of different drawer depths and need to figure out many different pin-and-tail spacings. My layout method, illustrated in figure 2 above, only requires you to pick a desired pin thickness and then follow a step-by-step procedure. If you mark the half-pin lines the same on all the drawer sides and keep the same desired pin thickness, this method will produce evenly spaced dovetails, regardless of the width of the drawer side. Mark out and cut the tails on the drawer sides, a pair at a time, until all the sides are done. Next, scribe the pins on the fronts and backs directly from the tails. I usually cut the pins for a half-blind dovetail on the drawer fronts so the joints won't show on the front of the case, and cut through dovetails on the backs. It's more efficient to cut and chisel the waste from each row of pins immediately after marking. If you could do with a refresher on the finer points of dovetailing, see the article on pp. 8-11.

Test-assemble all the drawers, but don't knock the dovetails together all the way, just ⅛ in. or so. Clean up any fitting prob-

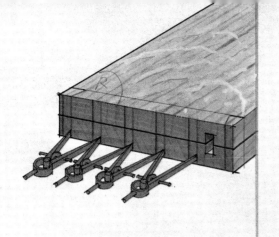

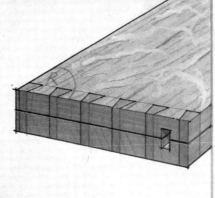

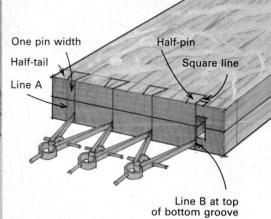

One pin width

Half-tail

Line A

Half-pin

Square line

Line B at top
of bottom groove

Step 3: *Keeping the same divider setting, plant a point on line A and walk the dividers back across the end of the drawer sides. These points mark the other side of each pin at the desired width.*

Step 4: *Using the pin lines as a guide, mark and cut out the pin waste. Using the same divider setting and line A and B positions, repeat the process to lay out the front dovetails on drawer sides of the same width.*

Step 5: *To lay out the back dovetails on the sides, mark line B at the top of the bottom groove and mark line A to reference half-tail at top. Starting with dividers on line B, set dividers to walk down and end up one pin thickness shy of line A. Mark one side of pins, then place dividers on line A and walk down to mark other side of pins. Cut out pin waste.*

lems with a chisel, and then sand and wax all interior surfaces of the drawer parts. When you're ready to glue up the drawers, coat the joints adequately but sparingly so you won't have to do a lot of cleanup inside the drawers later. Clamps should never be used when gluing dovetail drawers, because they can introduce distortion that will appear only after the clamps are removed. Simply drive the dovetails together with a hammer and hardwood block. With the drawer assembled, minus the bottom, test for wind by sighting across a pair of winding sticks layed on top of the drawer. Also check for square by measuring the drawer diagonally. The two diagonals should be the same; if not, clamp the drawer diagonally until it is square. Set the drawer aside on a flat surface until the glue sets, preferably overnight.

Final fitting—If the prefitting is done properly, the final trimming of the bottomless drawers is a breeze. You should only have to plane the dovetails true and flush on each drawer down to the pins and remove any sharp edges and corners. As you slide each drawer in and out of its opening, the wax you applied to the inside of the carcase earlier should mark the drawer enough to reveal the high spots to be planed and sanded. Carefully plane the drawer sides and bottom edges until the drawer slides smoothly, but not so much that it rattles in the carcase. Plane the sides with the grain from front to back, as previously discussed. To support the drawer while planing the sides, take a thick piece of scrap plywood as wide as the inner width of the drawer, secure it to the bench and slide the bottomless drawer over it, as shown in the photo at right. Final trimming is not a job you should rush: Work with care and patience so the shavings only come off where required. When the drawers all slide like silk, sand and wax the drawer sides and all running edges.

The drawer bottoms can be made at any stage, but don't install them until the drawers are assembled and fitted. If you make solid-wood bottoms, run the grain from side to side and make each bottom wide enough to be screwed to the underside of the back through slotted holes to allow for subsequent shrinkage. The bottom's length should make for a tight fit, but take care not to bulge out the sides. Sand and wax each bottom and slide it into the drawer. Make one final check to see that the drawer operates smoothly with the bottom in place, then glue the bottom at the front groove and set the screws at the back.

Supporting a drawer while planing the sides for a final fit can be done with a piece of scrap plywood, at least 1 in. thick and as wide as the inner width of the drawer, secured to the workbench. The bottomless drawer slides over the plywood and is held securely without clamping.

Any needed knobs or pulls can be fit after the drawer front has been sanded and finished. If your drawer-front design features built-in handles, these may need some final attention, such as rounding off any sharp edges. Also, if your carcase has built-in drawer stops, now is the time to do the last bit of trimming and fiddling so the drawer fronts will align properly. □

Alan Peters is a British furnituremaker and operates Aller Studios in Kentisbeare, Devon, England.

Cove and Pin Joint
Making a bull's-eye dovetail

by David Gray

The cove and pin joint is a real eye-catcher. It has a beautiful symmetry, is captivatingly intricate, and adds a special quality to any project. It is also a nice way of combining careful machine work with some pleasurable handfitting. I first became fascinated with the joint after seeing it on a box by Timothy McClellan of Minneapolis, Minn., in the first *Biennial Design Book* (Taunton Press, 1977). I later saw the joint on drawers in several older casepieces, but those joints were cut by machines that are no longer available. Eventually, I worked out a hand/machine method for cutting the joint with a modified plug cutter chucked in my drill press. For the maximum visual effect on things like drawers or jewelry boxes, I cut the pins in a dark wood and the coves in a light wood. My method for cutting the joint is to mill the pins by running the plug cutter into the endgrain of one board, and then use the same cutter to score the face of the mating piece to mark out the coves. Then, I bore out the pin holes and trim the outside of the cove with a saw, chisel, and knife.

Before you can cut the joint, you'll have to modify a four-fluted plug cutter to form pins and coves, as shown in figure 1 detail, regrind a bevel-edge gouge that matches the outside diameter of the coves, and build an indexing jig for your drill press. My cutter is a stock Fuller model (available from W.L. Fuller, Inc., P.O. Box 8767, 13 Cypress St., Warwick, R.I. 02888) designed to cut ⁵⁄₁₆-in.-dia. plugs. The outside diameter of the cutter, which is used to mark out the coves, is about ⁹⁄₁₆ in. The odd-looking ½-in. gouge with its edges ground back, shown in figure 2, is used to trim the roughsawn coves. A standard ²¹⁄₆₄-in.-dia. twist drill clears the pin holes.

My indexing jig is based on a 10-in.-square piece of ¼-in. aluminum plate that has ¼-in. holes drilled on ¹⁷⁄₃₂-in. centers along one side, as shown in the drawing. The joint components are clamped to an L-shaped wood tray that slides along the indexing plate. To ensure that mating pieces will interlock, I use the same jig for both the endgrain pins and the face coves, so any inaccuracies are mirrored on each piece and cancel each other out. No matter how good your setup, though, you'll still have to invest a healthy amount of time and patience to handfit the pieces together. I average about five minutes per pin for handfitting.

To make the jig, I lay out the hole locations with a 6-in. steel rule and a sharp knife, then make a punch mark to guide the drill into the aluminum. The spacing isn't terribly critical here; small variations won't show and will be duplicated on both pieces. Next, bore two holes so that you can fasten the plate to the slots on your drill-press table with flat-head machine screws, washers and wing nuts. You should have enough free play in the slots to

adjust the jig back and forth. Make sure the side with the stepping holes hangs just over the table edge to give clearance for the sliding tray. I made the pin by spinning ¼-in.-dia. brass rod in the drill-press chuck and sanding until it fits.

The sliding tray is two 9 in. by 7 in. pieces of hardwood or particleboard glued together at right angles along the 7 in. side. The tray slides along the edge of the index plate, hanging over the side with the holes. It's butted against the metal edge and the index pin each time the pin is moved to locate a new cut. To cut the pins, clamp the dark wood endgrain up on the vertical portion of the tray. The coves are cut with the pieces aligned in the same position at the corner of the tray, but this time along its horizontal surface.

In laying out the joint, you can experiment with different sizes and numbers of pins, but there's a practical limit on the width of the pieces to be joined—the more pins you use, the more handwork necessary to fit the pieces together. I lay out four to six pins on small drawers and have done up to 10 pins, but it's very difficult to accurately space so many cuts. Generally, 2³⁄₁₆-in.-wide stock is perfect for four pins and 3¼-in.-wide stock for six pins. The stock for the pin side should be at least ⅝-in. thick. The pins are cut at the inside edge of the board, thus leaving space for the ⅛-in.-wide plug-cutter groove and for the scalloped border of the coves. The cove stock is considerably thinner, usually about ¼ in. to ⁵⁄₁₆ in., because the plug cutter can't mill pins longer than that before bottoming out.

Once you've decided on the number of pins, you'll have to go through a juggling act to line everything up properly. With the tray and indexing plate in place, align the drill-press table so the plug cutter will cut at the inside corner of the pin board. Position the piece of stock with a clamp and/or change the location of the jig on the table to locate the first and last cuts equidistantly from the edges. Move the pin back and forth between the two outside step positions, adjusting until everything is symmetrical. Make sure the stock is clamped perpendicular to the press table and that the endgrain edge is perfectly flush with the tray. Once the magic position is located, mark it and tack an auxiliary fence next to the pin board to make it easy to line up the next piece to be cut. Set the drill-press depth gauge to cut the pins as deep as the stock you plan to join. Cut all the pins, stepping across each end to be joined.

Next, mill the cove stock to match the depth you have cut the pins. Again, go through the juggling act, but this time clamp the light wood to the tray's horizontal surface, with its endgrain just flush with the corner of the tray. The cove must be stepped across the jig twice, once to score the stock with the plug cutter to out-

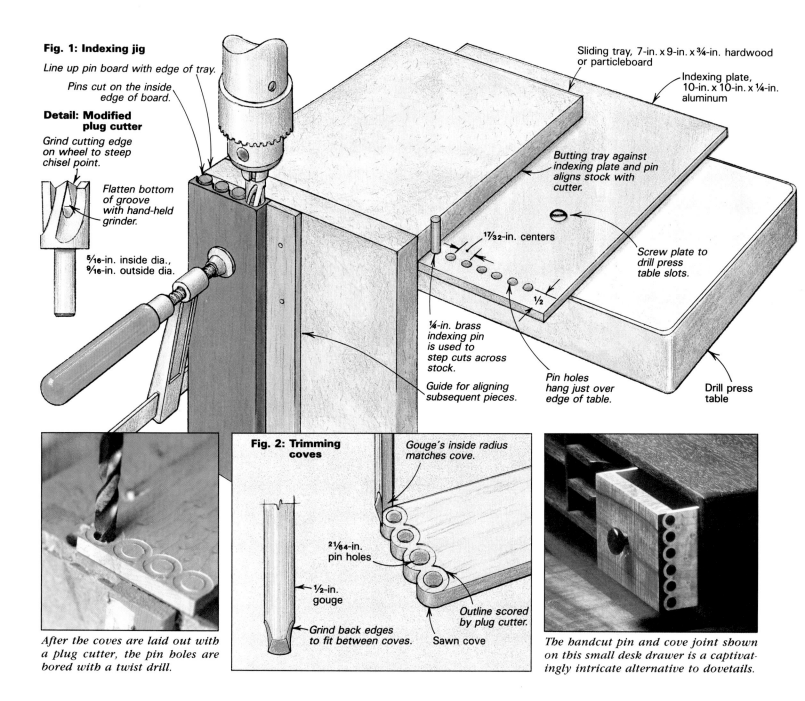

Fig. 1: Indexing jig

Line up pin board with edge of tray.

Pins cut on the inside edge of board.

Detail: Modified plug cutter

Grind cutting edge on wheel to steep chisel point.

Flatten bottom of groove with hand-held grinder.

5/16-in. inside dia., 9/16-in. outside dia.

Sliding tray, 7-in. x 9-in. x 3/4-in. hardwood or particleboard

Indexing plate, 10-in. x 10-in. x 1/4-in. aluminum

Butting tray against indexing plate and pin aligns stock with cutter.

17/32-in. centers

Screw plate to drill press table slots.

1/4-in. brass indexing pin is used to step cuts across stock.

1/2

Guide for aligning subsequent pieces.

Pin holes hang just over edge of table.

Drill press table

After the coves are laid out with a plug cutter, the pin holes are bored with a twist drill.

Fig. 2: Trimming coves

Gouge's inside radius matches cove.

21/64-in. pin holes

1/2-in. gouge

Grind back edges to fit between coves.

Outline scored by plug cutter.

Sawn cove

The handcut pin and cove joint shown on this small desk drawer is a captivatingly intricate alternative to dovetails.

line the coves, and once to bore the holes for the pins, above, left. Chuck the plug cutter in the press to do the alignment, but position the table low enough so you can install the 21/64-in. drill, and drill the pin holes without moving the table. Position the jig so the plug cutter will score the edge of the stock and leave a slight ridge on the outside edge. Then position the stock and/or the jig to create a symmetrical cut at each end position. Once this is established, again tack on a guide bar to help you line up subsequent pieces, and screw a hold-down clamp onto the sliding tray to lock the pieces on the jig as you make the plug cutter and drill pass over each edge to be joined. Finally, trim the scored cove pieces on a bandsaw or jigsaw. I cut as close to the score mark as possible, but leave the line as a guide for the chisel work.

Now—the handfitting. Choose a pair to be joined and mark them clearly. Chisel away the little triangles and the leftover ends of the pin sides flush with the bottom of the plug cutter's cut. To ease the fit, I also trim the sharp point where the adjacent curves meet. Fitting the joint is very repetitive, fussy work. I first pare straight down the ridge lines with the modified 1/2-in. gouge. Sharp tools are essential. Next, with a knife trim the corners

where the coves meet. Hold the joint together as it will ultimately fit, mark areas that don't fit, then trim the bottom edge of the non-fitting coves with a knife or chisel. Work from one edge of the piece to the other. This is a process of cutting, looking at the fit, cutting, looking, and so on, until the bottom fits. If you find the pins don't line up well enough to go into the holes, trim the pins with a small chisel until they do fit. When the joint goes together, flip the cove piece over and clean up the faces of the coves straight, but be careful not to overcut the joint. Leave the joint tight; you can drive it that last 1/16 in.

After fitting the joint, do any dadoing or rabbeting required for box bottoms or shelves. Apply glue to both the pin and cove sections, and tap the joint home with a mallet. If you have trimmed any areas too much, drive some glue-covered slivers into the gap. After the joints are dry, sand or handplane the score marks and apply the finish of your choice. □

Dave Gray designs and makes furniture at the Second Floor Woodworks, a cooperative he formed with six other woodworkers in Seattle, Wash.

Photos: David Gray, left; Geoff Manasse, right.

Twisted Dovetail Joint
Japanese puzzler explained

by Alan Peters

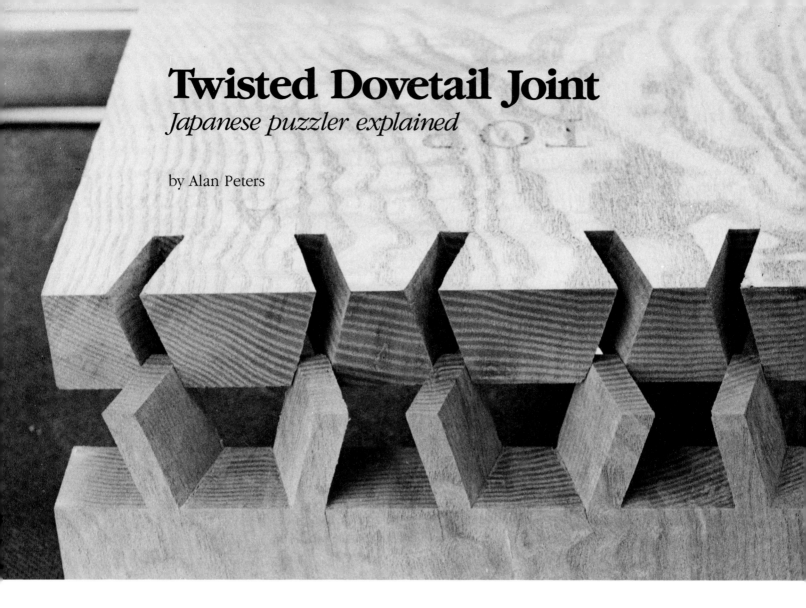

The Japanese twisted dovetail joint, *nejiri arigata*, was taught to me by a young Japanese furnituremaker, Kintaro Yazawa, who spent a week with me at my home in Devon, England, while on a pilgrimage to study the work of the British Arts and Crafts Movement. Structurally, the twisted dovetail joint is tremendously strong and it appears that it cannot be driven apart. However, in many ways it's not a difficult joint to cut. A glance at the photos will reveal most of the mysteries.

One difficulty I encountered was in assembling and gluing the 20-in.-wide table shown above—I would strongly recommend a shorter trial joint rather than what I arrogantly attempted in my first effort. Also, yew, which I selected for its decorative qualities, proved an unwise choice due to the wildness of the grain. Instead, I'd recommend you use a clear, mild-grained hardwood that saws and chisels cleanly. The timber should be machined or hand-finished to an accurate width and thickness, then accurately crosscut into three pieces, for the top and two ends.

The chief problem in making the joint is one of layout. The joints can't be scribed from one piece to the other as with normal dovetails and pins, so each piece has to be accurately marked out and cuts made directly to the line. All the endgrain shoulders are at a normal 90°, and whatever angle is chosen for the slope of the dovetails is constant both on the long grain and on the endgrain. This angle is best marked using a bevel gauge. Once the gauge is set, you simply flop it over to mark the reverse angle. I sloped the dovetails about 15°, but this angle isn't critical, as smaller or larger angles would also work.

In laying out the joints, I didn't allow for any joint projections

to be flushed off afterward, but gauged my shoulder lines exactly to the thickness of the material, which was 1¼ in. The gauge lines were heavily incised on the inside surfaces, but lightly cut on the outside, so they could be planed off after assembly.

It takes trial and error with dividers, plus some judgment, to arrive at well-proportioned, aesthetically pleasing dovetail spacing. Once that's decided, mark out each joint as shown on the facing page, top right, with identical measurements on both pieces. I used dividers to space the lines, then marked all the waste areas.

When cutting the top, aim for a series of identical parallel slots. I see no reason why, with a little ingenuity, this part could not be cut on a machine. I decided not to risk it on that lovely expanse of yew, and cut them by hand. I feel that the best joint comes when cut direct from the saw with no paring. I also consider it bad practice to adjust the workpiece in the vise so you're always sawing at 90° to the bench. It is far better to perfect the technique of sawing at any angle required.

To remove the waste, I used a coping saw, as shown on the facing page, then pared back to the shoulder lines with a chisel, the normal process with endgrain. Check the rows of slots carefully—if the sawcuts wandered, as sometimes happens, you will have to pare back to your pencil lines. Do this and any other tidying up *before* attempting to cut the two end pieces: It is possible that you may have to increase the width of one or another slot. If so, be sure that you alter the corresponding tenon on the matching end piece.

When cutting the ends, your aim is a series of parallel tenons all identical in angle (and also in thickness, unless they have

From *Fine Woodworking* magazine (November 1986) 61:84-85

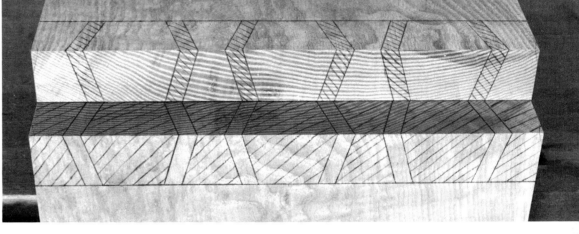

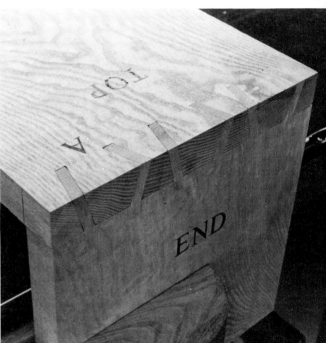

Top photo shows joint layout with top and end oriented as they will be in the finished table. Cut down the line with a backsaw and remove the waste with a coping saw. Next step is to chisel the shoulders square. Assembly (facing page) starts at the corners, then the joint closes at a 45° angle. The finished joint (assembled dry here) looks impossible, unless you know the secret.

been modified for previous errors). The problem is that they are all at a compound angle and, therefore, require extra care in sawing to the line. The waste is once again removed with a coping saw and pared back to the shoulder lines.

Dry-fitting the joint is tricky. The point of entry is right at the corners, and the joint then comes together at a 45° angle. I found it best to clamp the top down on the bench so that I could drive the ends on using a heavy hammer and large hardwood block. As this was only a dry run, I didn't seat the joint completely home, but drove it off again, eased the odd spot that was obviously too tight, then sanded the interior surfaces.

For final assembly I prepared leather-covered, stout hardwood blocks that would allow me to exert clamping pressure as shown in the drawing at right. By tightening top and side clamps alternately, the joint is brought together at a 45° angle. The leather on the blocks is obviously to avoid damage to the workpiece, but it also absorbs any discrepancy on the exposed surfaces of the joints, enabling pressure to be exerted on each individual portion of the joint.

I applied PVA adhesive sparingly on the side grain but not at all on the endgrain except on the four outside shoulders. In theory, clamps should not be necessary to draw up a well-fitted dovetail, whether standard or twisted. In fact, the first joint went together perfectly with mallet and block, but I did need the clamps on the second one. Once the shoulders were tight, the clamps were removed and the glue joint left to cure. □

Alan Peters is a furniture maker in Cullompton, Devon, England.

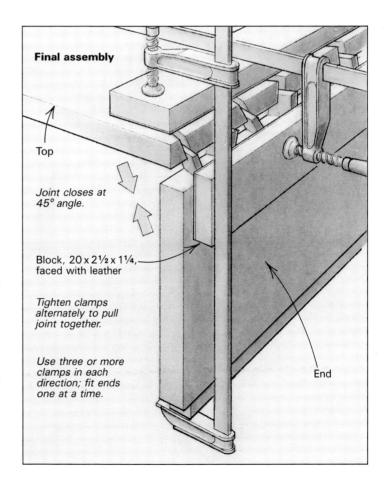

Final assembly

Top

Joint closes at 45° angle.

Block, 20 x 2½ x 1¼, faced with leather

Tighten clamps alternately to pull joint together.

Use three or more clamps in each direction; fit ends one at a time.

End

A sliding dovetail is very useful for joining boards cross-grain, and it can be cut entirely with hand tools. Above, Thomas notches the front edge of a shelf so the joint will be invisible when the two components slide together.

Cutting Sliding Dovetails
Guide blocks aid hand tool precision

by William Thomas

The housed dovetail or tapered sliding dovetail is one of the most underused joints in the cabinetmaker's repertoire. Typically it is dismissed as being too time-consuming and difficult to make. It is, however, the best way to join the end of one board cross-grain into the middle of another board without nails, screws or dowels.

The natural structure of wood causes problems with any cross-grain joint. In a typical dado joint between a shelf and a vertical case side, for example, the mating side-grain to end-grain surfaces make poor glue joints. Adding rabbets, or even tenons, does not change this basic relationship, unless you also add screws or nails. Dowels come loose as wood expands and contracts during the year. The sliding dovetail avoids these problems because it is an interlocking mechanical connection that doesn't require adhesives, so wood can move naturally without breaking the joint. And, all you need to cut the joint is a careful layout, a beveled guide block, a sharp chisel and a plane.

Joint Anatomy—Sliding dovetails are made in a variety of forms, but the most common one has the top surface of the joint dadoed straight in and the tapered dovetail cut into the bottom surface. The joint is typically stopped in the front and a shoulder is set back ¼ in. to ½ in. The most important feature of a true sliding dovetail is its taper, which is thinner at the front than at the back. This taper allows the joint to be assembled loosely for trial fitting, only becoming tight when driven home. It's always a surprise when the hand-tight trial fit needs to be driven apart with a mallet.

Tools for dovetailing—Cutting a sliding dovetail involves basic hand tools plus a couple of special items: a chisel guide block and a dovetail plane. The important feature of both of these tools is an angled edge. The chisel guide block is simply a board somewhat longer than the width of the stock to be joined; one long edge is square and the other long edge is beveled about 80°, or at about a 1:6 taper. The dovetail plane looks like a rabbet plane, but it has a sole

From *Fine Woodworking* magazine (December 1989) 79:54-56

with the same bevel as the guide block and a skewed iron. Dovetail planes are commercially available, but can easily be made by modifying an old skew rabbet plane, as explained in the sidebar below.

Laying out the joint—To avoid confusion, the joint should be carefully laid out in a systematic manner. Unlike dovetails commonly used for drawer or case work, one half of the joint cannot be scribed from the other, and the accuracy of the fit is entirely dependent on cutting the lines correctly. Start by locating the top line of the dado and scribing this line across the face of the socket board and down across the back edge.

Next, determine how deep the recess will be. A marking gauge should be set to this measurement and the bottom line scribed on

the back edge of the board parallel to the face. Along this line (not along the face), measure out the thickness of the pin board and mark the other bottom corner. Then, with a T-bevel set to the sole angle of the dovetail plane, scribe a line from this bottom corner up to the face. This establishes the shape of the joint at the back edge. Before going any further with the socket board, take the marking gauge and scribe a line across the bottom face of the end of the pin board and carry this line across the front edge.

To establish the front end of the socket, mark the shoulder set-back line on the face. I have never heard of a rule for how wide the front end should be, so I finally made up my own rule as follows: The narrowest width (the root or front inside corner) of the dovetail should be equal to half the thickness of the pin board.

Building a dovetail plane

Dovetail planes can be made from old wooden skewed rabbet planes, which are commonly available at antique-tool shops, flea markets and yard sales. There are plenty of them around, so find one that is free of warp, checking and dry rot. Avoid rusty irons and irons that have been sharpened so much that they will have to be reground at a different angle. If you are especially lucky, you might find a plane with a spur for scoring cross-grain. You could also construct a dovetail plane entirely from scratch or buy one from Woodcraft Supply, 41 Atlantic Ave., Box 4000, Woburn, Mass. 01888.

When making a dovetail plane, I've found that the most important technical point is that the corner of the skewed iron that cuts the deepest must be the trailing corner. In other words, when you look down at the plane as it cuts, the leading corner of the iron will overhang the end of the board and the trailing corner will be against the shoulder. This orientation is critical because it allows the iron to shear the wood with the grain. If the inner corner is leading, the iron will tear out the wood.

To ensure this orientation, remove the iron and wedge and make sure the side that will ride against the shoulder of the joint is perfectly flat. Set a T-bevel to 80° and scribe the iron on the front and back ends, so that its trailing edge will be located as described. Then, set the plane in a vise, with the sole facing up, and carefully joint the surface down to the bevel lines.

Since the iron is already tempered, it must be shaped with a high-speed grinder. Polish the face of the iron, paint it with layout dye and wedge it back in the plane with the excess sticking out. Then, lay a scriber flat on the plane sole and score a line parallel to the bottom of the plane on the iron. Grind to the line, with the tool rest set at 90° to the face of the iron. Be sure to grind square when removing this

much stock because the thickness of the steel will absorb the heat. Once parallel to the line, reset the tool rest to grind in the bevel. Work slowly and have a cup of water close by to quench the metal frequently, so you don't ruin the temper. When the bevel is parallel and straight to the sole, hone it in the normal way. Since old plane irons are often laminated with hard steel, I suggest using waterstones for this operation. Set the iron in the plane and drive the wedge home. With the iron retracted enough to not take a cut and with the plane in one hand, strike the front of the plane with a mallet. Then, try a cut. If the shavings are too heavy, strike the back end with a mallet to retract the cutter slightly. Rub the sole with paraffin wax and you're all set.

Finally, add a spur cutter to your plane to score the wood fibers ahead of the main iron. Acquire a small piece of ⅛-in. untempered tool steel, which can be shaped with a file. Next, lay out and cut a sliding dovetail recess with both edges beveled on the side of the wood body, starting at the top of the inside face of the plane and tapering down toward the sole. Now you can shape your piece of steel so it can be wedged tightly in this recess with about 1⁄16 in. extending below the sole. A skewed bevel should be filed in the protruding end, as shown in the drawing below. Next, file a notch in the outside face of the spur; this will facilitate its removal when necessary. After tempering the spur, hone the bevel, and then wedge the spur into place.   —W.T.

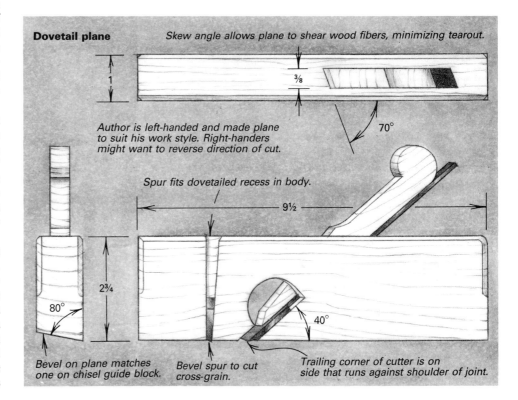

Dovetail plane Skew angle allows plane to shear wood fibers, minimizing tearout.

1

³⁄₈

70°

Author is left-handed and made plane to suit his work style. Right-handers might want to reverse direction of cut.

Spur fits dovetailed recess in body.

9½

80°

2¾

40°

Bevel on plane matches one on chisel guide block.

Bevel spur to cut cross-grain.

Trailing corner of cutter is on side that runs against shoulder of joint.

Drawing: Kathleen Rushton

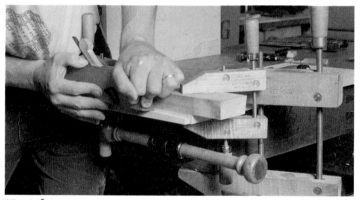

Thomas uses a guide block with an 80° bevel as accurate reference surface for paring the angled wall of the dovetail socket. Note how the socket tapers from the back of the joint to the front.

To prevent tearout when working with a plane that does not have a spur for cross-grain scoring, the author cuts a line with a chisel guided by the 90° side of the guide block.

The 80° bevel on the dovetail plane automatically cuts the proper bevel on the pin. The taper shown is created by planing more off the front of the pin than the back.

This means that the taper varies with the thickness of the stock, but it isn't necessary to know the actual amount of taper. This rule simply ensures that the joint will be as strong as possible given a particular board thickness. One of the most confusing relationships in this joint is that the root thickness lies along the inside shoulder of the male board, and therefore lies on the surface of the socket board. Starting at the top line, measure this root distance along the front shoulder line and mark the front corner. Then, using a straightedge and knife, connect the front and back corners on the face to establish the taper.

Cutting the socket—Traditionally, the socket would be sawn with a dovetail or other stiff-blade backsaw and then chiseled out. I'm not stuck on drudgery, so I rout the dado with a straight bit that is the same width or narrower than the root. This ensures the socket will have a clean bottom and a square top shoulder. After squaring the front shoulder with a chisel, I stand the board up vertically in a vise and clamp the chisel guide block on the taper line, as shown in the

top photo at left, so a chisel can be run down the beveled edge to cut the angled wall of the socket. Pare the shoulder in several passes using a 1-in.- to 1¼-in.-wide chisel. All surfaces must be flat and clean. Once everything is perfect, cut the pin board to match.

The pin board—The shoulder lines have already been scribed on the end of the pin board, so the first thing to do is notch the front corner to the setback line, as shown in the photo on p. 20. This is a necessary first step because the narrowest part of the root width must be marked on the shoulder. This root-width mark and the shoulder scribe line are the only layout marks necessary on the pin board. The dovetail plane will automatically establish the correct bevel angle.

Clamp the pin board down flat with the end overhanging the edge of the bench, and then clamp the square edge of the guide block along the shoulder line. Hanging the end off the bench allows the socket board to be slipped on for trial fitting without unclamping the pin board. If your plane has a spur to score a crisp line across the grain, you can start planing; otherwise, you must score the shoulder first by laying a chisel against the face of the guide block and dragging a corner along the line, as shown in the center photo at left.

Fitting the joint with a dovetail plane is mostly a matter of knowing when to stop, and you have two guideposts to help you gauge this. The first is the thickest corner (back, outside) of the dovetail. Remember, this corner is the same thickness as the board, so your aim is to just reach that point with the plane. The other guidepost is the diagonally opposite corner of the dovetail's cheek: The front inner corner marked on the front shoulder. Since the plane automatically establishes the correct bevel angle, all you need is to establish the taper and then remove stock until these two guideposts are reached. Start with short passes near the front edge until the plane appears to be parallel to the taper, and then take long passes until you're close to the marks, as shown in the bottom photo at left. Concentrate on keeping the correct taper and planing a flat surface. If your plane doesn't have a spur, stop every few passes and score the shoulder with a chisel. The correctness of the taper can be judged by sliding the joint together partway with the dovetail sides touching and observing whether the top face of the male board is parallel to the shoulder of the dado. When you reach the guideposts you previously laid out, the dovetail should fit perfectly.

Offhand, I can't think of many uses for one sliding dovetail. They are usually made in sets; for example, on each end of a shelf. This means that one is right-handed and one is left-handed. Both are made the same, using the same tools, and the only difference is that one male end is planed going up the taper and the other end going down the taper. Otherwise, they should be mirror images and must fit the same. It is wise to make the pin board extra wide at the back. This way if the joint is loose, you can cut the shoulder back slightly to allow the pin board to slide forward for a tighter fit. Then, the front edge of the board can be planed down flush afterward.

With practice, the sliding dovetail can be cut quickly and neatly. I know that many cabinetmakers use a router and jig for the whole job, but the beauty of doing it by hand is versatility. Routing dovetails involves constructing jigs that can handle each variation of stock width or thickness, and this jigging up pushes the mind to work further along toward repetition, uniformity and mass production. By acquiring two simple tools, the guide block and the dovetail plane, you can hand-cut joints of any size or taper. All it takes is some careful thought and work. Handwork exercises the mind as well as the muscles. □

William Thomas is a cabinetmaker in Hillsboro, N.H.

Routing sliding dovetails

by Pat Warner

Machine-cut sliding dovetails are easy to make; the setup is quick and the jigs are fairly simple. The dovetail pins are cut on a router table equipped with a sliding fence. The socket is more safely cut when the work is secured and the router is guided by a template.

Routing the socket: I rout the socket with a single pass of a dovetail bit of the desired width. You could cut the socket on the router table, but because the bit is trapped and the wide stock is difficult to handle, this may be inviting accidents and inaccuracies. I prefer to guide the hand-held router with a template, rather than a board clamped to the work, be-cause all too often the router base is not concentric to the cutter. Also, the router is raised above the crosscut tearout, which is produced when cutting or rout-ing across the grain and which can pre-vent the router from sliding across the board. Finally, the work site is more visi-ble, indexing is simplified and clamping down the template closer to the cut helps flatten any twist or cup in the workpiece.

The templates for routing the dovetail ways are simply modified bench hooks made of ½-in. birch plywood, 7 in. or more wide and at least as long as the slot. The long hook on the template makes the in-dex secure, and only one clamp is needed to hold it fast, as shown in the photo above, so there is nothing to get in the way of the router as it makes the cut. Only one edge of the template is used as a guide, so you will need both a left and a right template; both guide edges must be perpendicular. One problem with template routing is that only half of the router base rides on the template. To compensate for this relatively unstable arrangement, I have developed a modified router base with an offset-grip knob, as shown in the photo above, that in-creases stability and facilitates safe and pre-dictable handling. This one tactic has done more to upgrade my hand routing than any other routing accessory.

The template guide collar attached to the router base must be larger in diame-ter than the dovetail bit. The centerline of the socket can be located directly off the working edge of the template by add-ing one-half the collar diameter to the re-quired distance from the end of the stock. The socket can be cut from either the front or back of the panel by pulling the collar against the template with the grip knob. If you want a stopped socket, rout it from the back. For an easier job, I

Routing dovetailed sockets with a template and guide collar is more accurate than with an edge-guided router. The offset knob on the modified router base also makes controlling the router easier.

preplow the socket with a straight bit. Us-ing the same collar for both the dovetail and straight bits will ensure both cuts are on the same centerline.

Routing the tenons: Clamping the workpiece to a modified, bridled sliding carriage fitted to the router table fence, as shown in the photo below, allows for ex-tremely accurate adjustments when routing the pins. However, if the workpiece is not clamped to a sliding guide, dovetailing its

A sliding fence attachment holds the work while routing the pins. Adjust the fence so the workpiece is not trapped be-tween it and the router bit.

end can be dangerous because of the force generated by the design of the dovetail bit. Although this downward shear force is minimal, the workpiece can be difficult to handle. Installing a tight-fitting table insert around the bit can help.

Before routing, set the depth of cut to 0.005 in. less than the depth of the socket. A feeler gauge is handy for this type of measurement. Lay out the pin using either a sliding bevel gauge or the dovetailed socket itself as a guide. Now, set the fence on the router table to take slightly less than the scribed shoulder width per pass. The fence should be adjusted so the cutter is partly recessed into the fence; do not trap the workpiece between the fence and the cutter. Next, clamp the part to be cut to the sliding fence attachment, make the pass, and then rotate the piece before you make a second pass and rout the other shoulder. Check the fit, adjust the fence and make additional passes on each face until the pin fits the socket. Be sure to make all cuts in a single pass from right to left. If the tenon is to fit a blind socket, I turn the piece 90°, clamp it to the sliding fence attachment, and then rout a third shoulder with either a dovetail or straight bit. □

Patrick Warner sells routing equipment and teaches classes in router techniques and in making jigs and fixtures in Es-condido, Cal. For more information, contact the author at 1427 Kenora St., Escondido, Cal. 92027.

Secret Compartments

A furnituremaker's cache box

by Chris Becksvoort

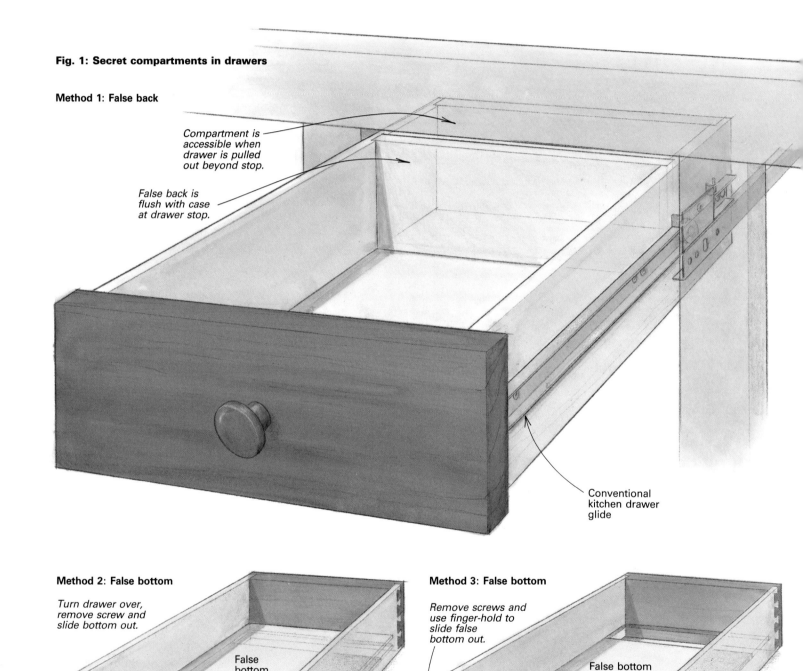

Fig. 1: Secret compartments in drawers

Method 1: False back

Compartment is accessible when drawer is pulled out beyond stop.

False back is flush with case at drawer stop.

Conventional kitchen drawer glide

Method 2: False bottom

Turn drawer over, remove screw and slide bottom out.

False bottom

Secret compartment for valuables

Method 3: False bottom

Remove screws and use finger-hold to slide false bottom out.

False bottom

Two-piece back and false bottom are screwed together.

Secret compartments were so common in the days before safety-deposit boxes that they could be considered a hallmark of custom-built furniture. And, because hidden compartments have been popular among the well-to-do since ancient times, craftsmen have had plenty of time to come up with all sorts of hiding places. They can be a simple drawer fit into otherwise wasted space inside a cabinet or complex and imaginative devices based on hollow members, springs, catches and sliding panels—anything to fool the eye. Secret compartments are often commissioned for a specific purpose, such as hiding coins, jewelry, precious documents or pictures; sometimes they are the furnituremaker's whimsical secret, unbeknownst to the customer until the piece is delivered.

These surprise compartments are my favorites. They allow me the most leeway in placement, size and construction; in addition, the customer feels like the recipient of a gift—an unexpected bonus. It also seems only right that a hidden compartment should be a secret shared only by the furnituremaker and the furniture's owner. Let's face it, a hidden compartment advertised in *The New Yorker* is no secret by anyone's standards, but merely a sales gimmick.

Some types of furniture lend themselves better to hidden compartments than others. The best are case pieces with drawers and desks with pigeonholes. But tables, beds, clocks and even lamps can be adapted to contain these intriguing tricks of the trade. I'll describe some of those I've used in my own work or seen in other pieces of furniture. These examples are only a few of the possibilities: There are many others, from the extremely simple to the clever and complicated. The next time you're designing a piece, take a little extra time to examine how you can utilize any wasted space in the furniture. You'll be amazed at how thrilled your customers will be.

Drawers—Years ago while working on a kitchen, it occurred to me that most drawer glides, except the full-extension models, leave the back 4 in. of the drawer essentially inaccessible. So I ran a cross-grain dado 3½ in. from the back end on each drawer side and inserted a side-to-side divider. When the drawer is pulled out to the stop, as shown in method 1 on the facing page, the false back is flush with the case. When the glide stops are released, the drawer can be pulled out to access the long narrow compartment beyond the false back. This area is good for storing seldom-used utensils or those that have always disappeared when you need them most.

One of the best methods for hiding photos, documents or other flat objects is a double-bottom drawer. If the compartment between the bottoms is kept as thin as possible, it is virtually undetectable, but the trick in this, as well as in other methods, is not to get greedy. If you pull out a 6-in. drawer and discover only 3 in. of

space inside, something appears amiss—you are not fooling anyone. On the other hand, you can probably get away with a 2-in. compartment in a 12-in.- or 14-in.-deep drawer.

The bottoms of my drawers are slid from the back into grooves in the drawer sides. To create a secret compartment, I run parallel grooves on the insides of the drawer sides and front, ½ in. to 1 in. apart. The back only gets the upper groove, because the actual bottom is slid underneath it and held in place with a screw. When the drawer is assembled, the false bottom is captured in the four upper grooves. The real bottom can be slid in and out to get to the hidden compartment (see method 2 on the facing page). An alternative method is shown in method 3. The two-piece back with a recessed finger-hold allows the false bottom to be slid out. Although the spaces created by these double bottoms are not easily detectable, they are bothersome to get to, because the contents of the drawer must be removed. In the first case, the drawer must be turned upside down to place anything into the compartment; in the second case, the false bottom, which is acting as the drawer bottom, must be removed. To avoid having to empty the drawer, you could use the two-piece back method, but attach the lower section of the back to the actual bottom of the drawer so they both slide out together, forming a tray, as shown in method 4 below. Taking this a step further, you could put sides all around this tray and create a minidrawer.

The traditional construction of a chest of drawers presents another opportunity for hidden compartments. Visualize for a moment the interior of an average case piece with drawers and a face frame. On such pieces, there is often unused space behind the face-frame members, both between the case side and the drawers and between the drawers themselves. This space can be utilized by simply building narrow wooden boxes to fit into these locations. These boxes are totally hidden unless someone removes the drawers to look inside the case. Even if the divider strip between the drawers is only 1 in. wide, a flat box with ⅛-in.-thick sides still yields about ¾ in. of usable interior space. Any number of methods can be employed to secure the box: magnets, dowels, ledger strips, inset spinners or sliding pins.

Some time ago, I was commissioned to build a chest of drawers that required a very well-hidden compartment for 10 gold coins. The usual false bottoms or boxes hidden in the case itself might be discovered. Security was the primary concern; access was secondary. I finally devised an "invisible" compartment, built the piece and delivered it. I told the owner it was up to him to find the compartment. He paid. I left. A few days later, he called to confess he still had not found the secret compartment. He had removed all the drawers and gone over the entire inside of the case with a mirror, a magnet and a fine-tooth comb to no avail. I told him to

Method 4: False bottom

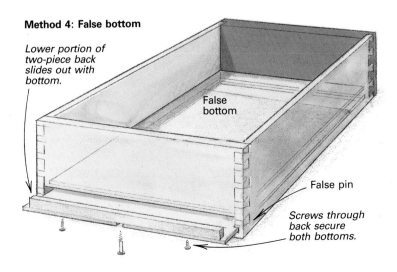

Lower portion of two-piece back slides out with bottom.

False bottom

False pin

Screws through back secure both bottoms.

Method 5: Mortised back

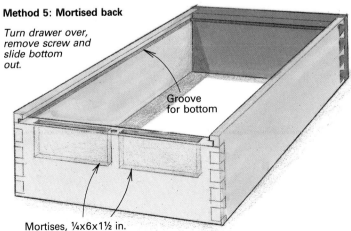

Turn drawer over, remove screw and slide bottom out.

Groove for bottom

Mortises, ¼x6x1½ in.

Drawings: Kathleen Creston

take out the middle drawer, turn it over, remove the screw holding the bottom, slide out the bottom and look. The drawer back was partially hollow. With a horizontal mortiser, I had made two 1/4x6x1 1/2-in. slots in the bottom edge of the drawer back, one on each side of the screw hole. The coins could then be wrapped in felt or tissue to keep them from rattling. With the bottom replaced, there is no reason to suspect the hiding place (see method 5 at the bottom of the previous page).

Desks—In addition to the drawer methods, desks lend themselves to a host of different hidden compartments. I've always suspected that pigeonholes in roll-top and slant-top desks were originally conceived by cabinetmakers to allow themselves room to play with these ideas. Everyone has seen a slant-top desk with two fluted half-columns that pull out and are actually narrow drawers. These are practically institutions, and not secret by any means (at least not now). Another common method often found in the pigeonholes of slant-top desks is a thin drawer behind the molding or scalloped facia above the pigeonholes. These parts either pull out like drawers or hang on hooks, clips or magnets. Roll-top desks sometimes have small corner brackets in the pigeonholes that pull out to reveal a tray just big enough to hide two, always elusive, pencils.

Pigeonholes, letter slots or compartments with doors are also ideal locations for false backs. A compartment behind a false back is not readily apparent if it is not too deep, especially if the surrounding areas are filled with books or papers. The created space can be reached either from the front, by reaching in and removing a part of the back panel, or through a removable panel near the back of one of the vertical dividers, as shown in figure 2A below. Either way, the access panel should be as unobtrusive as possible. I've used several methods with either hinged doors or loose panels. One of my favorite devices is the magnetic-touch latch, a boon for makers of secret compartments: Just push on the panel, and it pops right out. For a hinged door, one latch will suffice; for a

loose panel, two, with doorstops, should be used. Panels and doors should fit as tightly as possible without binding.

An alternative to the touch latch is illustrated in figure 2B below. In this method, the panel is made as wide as the opening, but 1/4 in. taller, with a discreet fingernail catch incised with a gouge on the front of the panel. The panel is lifted into the 5/16-in.-deep upper groove, pushed into place and dropped into the 1/8-in.-deep bottom groove. Because of the shallow bottom groove, the panel is still held in place above.

Whenever possible, access to the hidden area on desks or other large pieces should be from the front, sides or interior of the piece. Only once have I run across a compartment reached through a hinged door in the back. This entails moving the piece away from the wall to gain access, which is not only difficult, but in the case of a full bookcase or large wardrobe, almost impossible.

Hollow posts—Another traditional hiding place, somewhat reminiscent of Bat Masterson's cane, is the hollowed-out post. The hollows usually consist of drilled-out holes, which limit the amount and type of storage space available. On the other hand, you would be surprised at how many $20 bills can be rolled up and slid into a 1 1/2-in.-dia. hole. If coins are to be hidden, it's best to tailor the hole to accept a plastic vial, which is easier to remove than loose coins.

Turned posts are generally much easier to work with than square ones, because the cap for the compartment can join the post in an inconspicuous place. The underside of a ball or ring, or a scribe line is perfect for this. The bedpost in figure 3 below shows how convenient a finial is for capping a hollowed-out post. To make this sort of secret compartment, I turn the post as I normally would, but I allow 1/2 in. to 1 in. of extra length for the tenon, which I turn directly below the portion of the post that will become the removable cap. This tenon's diameter must match one of your drill bits so the cap will fit snugly into the hollowed-out compartment you will drill in the post. When I've turned the tenon

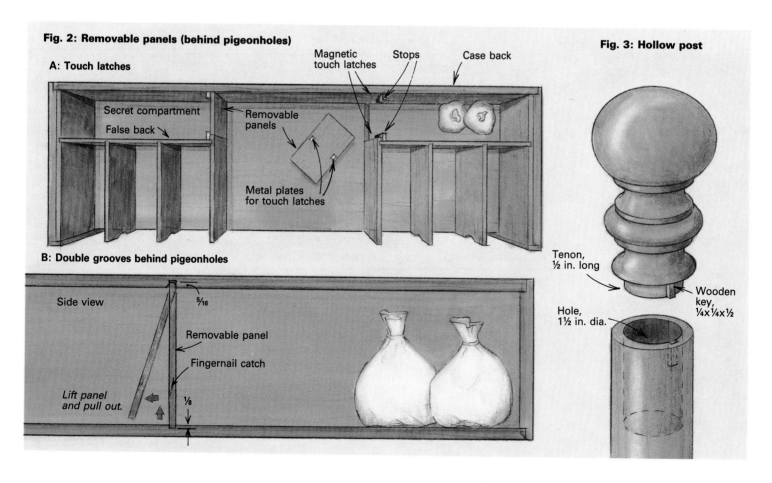

Fig. 2: Removable panels (behind pigeonholes)

A: Touch latches

Secret compartment
False back
Removable panels
Metal plates for touch latches
Magnetic touch latches
Stops
Case back

B: Double grooves behind pigeonholes

Side view
5/16
Removable panel
Fingernail catch
Lift panel and pull out.
1/8

Fig. 3: Hollow post

Tenon, 1/2 in. long
Wooden key, 1/4x1/4x1/2
Hole, 1 1/2 in. dia.

From *Fine Woodworking* magazine (January 1989) 74:42-46

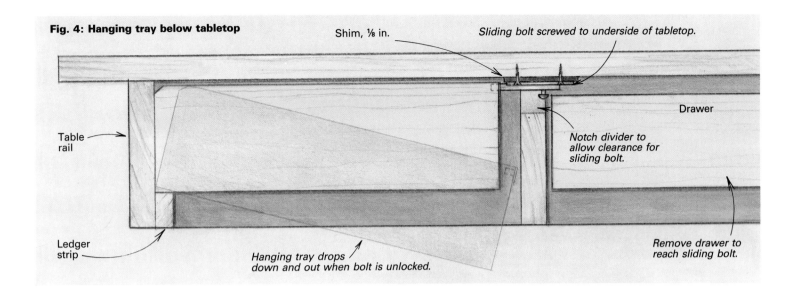

Fig. 4: Hanging tray below tabletop

Shim, ⅛ in.

Sliding bolt screwed to underside of tabletop.

Table rail

Drawer

Notch divider to allow clearance for sliding bolt.

Ledger strip

Hanging tray drops down and out when bolt is unlocked.

Remove drawer to reach sliding bolt.

to the proper diameter, I remove the post from the lathe and saw this top portion off just below the tenon. Using the bit that coincides with the tenon's diameter, I drill a hole in the sawed-off end of the post. The depth of this hole minus the tenon determines the size of the hollow storage area. The cap can also be drilled out for additional space.

Figure 3 also shows the small wooden "key" on the tenon, which not only aligns the grain, but keeps the finial from turning should some unsuspecting soul inadvertently place their hand on it. To locate this key, I place a thin wire in the hole, align the grain to its original position and force the tenon into the hole. The wire compresses the wood and thereby marks the location for a ⅛-in.-deep by ¼-in.-wide groove that I carve into each piece. The ¼x¼x½-in. key is then glued into the groove on the tenon. The drilled-out post can now be rechucked in the lathe and turned to suit, using either a wooden plug or a bullnose dead center to mount the drilled end.

Tables—There is a vast amount of space behind the rails or apron underneath the top of a table. Except for children parking their gum (or maybe because of this), very few people actually fondle the underside of a table, so this otherwise wasted space is ideal for concealing hanging trays. A hanging tray can be used even on small coffee or end tables and below the seats of chairs that have side rails. It can be hinged on one end or merely rest on a ledger strip, with the other end resting on a removable strip held in place with dowels or pins. In figure 4, above, I've shown an example of a table with a center drawer that has a hidden tray resting on a ledger strip on the left and held up with a sliding bolt on the right. With the drawer removed, and with one hand supporting the hanging tray, you reach in and unlock the sliding bolt. This unlocked end of the tray can now be lowered until it comes off the ledger strip on the other end.

If the table has a drawer, so much the better. Because most drawers don't extend the full width of the tabletop, you can place two drawers on the same track, one behind the other.

Tops and bottoms of cabinets—Other areas often overlooked and generally underutilized are the spaces between tops and the spaces inside boxed-in bases of cabinets. On many highboys, for example, the bonnet top is hollow, usually with no access. I recently built an armoire with a 3-in. molding around the top. In addition to the cabinet top, there is a false top ½ in. below the molding that acts as a doorstop. Two dividers were to be inserted

into dadoes in the false top and the first shelf. I couldn't bear to seal such a marvelous space without getting some use out of it. So, I made a trapdoor in the false top that I could push up from inside the cabinet to get at this space (see figure 5 below).

To build the trapdoor, I marked the locations of the two dadoes to be cut (front to back) in the false top, then ripped the top (side to side) into three sections, about one-fourth of the way from the front and one-fourth of the way from the back. I then crosscut the center section of the wide middle piece along the dado lines. The false top was now in five pieces. Next, I reglued the two long pieces and the two outside pieces of the center section together, creating a rectangular opening in the center where the remaining piece would fit snugly. I took one pass off the edge of this piece with a block plane, then screwed on two ribs perpendicular to the grain, extending ½ in. on each side. After sanding, the top was dadoed and installed, and the dividers

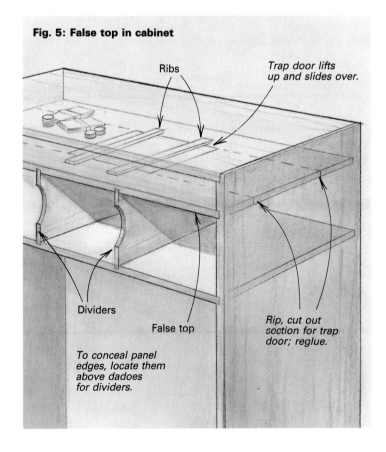

Fig. 5: False top in cabinet

Ribs

Trap door lifts up and slides over.

Dividers

False top

To conceal panel edges, locate them above dadoes for dividers.

Rip, cut out section for trap door; reglue.

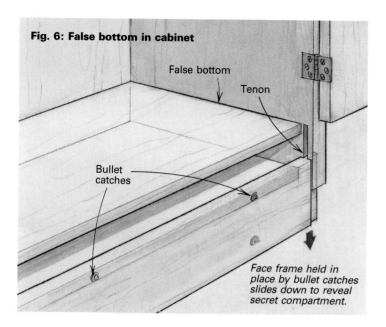

Fig. 6: False bottom in cabinet

False bottom

Tenon

Bullet catches

Face frame held in place by bullet catches slides down to reveal secret compartment.

slid into place. The loose center section could now be pushed up with the fingertips, yet it could not fall through, because it rested on the dividers and the two ribs (these also kept the trap-door from warping). The panel was virtually invisible, because the end-grain cuts were above the dividers. And, because the panel was only a shaving thickness narrower than the opening, the long-grain gaps were nearly impossible to see. This method could be used in false bottoms if the cross-grain cuts were angled to keep the panel from falling through and if the ribs, screwed to the underside of the loose portion to resist warping, were shorter than the width of the panel.

Figure 6, left, shows an example of a false bottom in a wall-hung cabinet. In this instance, I merely made the bottom portion of the face frame removable. It slides up and down with a tongue-and-groove arrangement at the ends and is held in place by bullet catches in the bottom. □

Christian Becksvoort is a contributing editor at Fine Woodworking *and a furnituremaker. He lives in New Gloucester, Maine.*

Secret compartments in built-ins

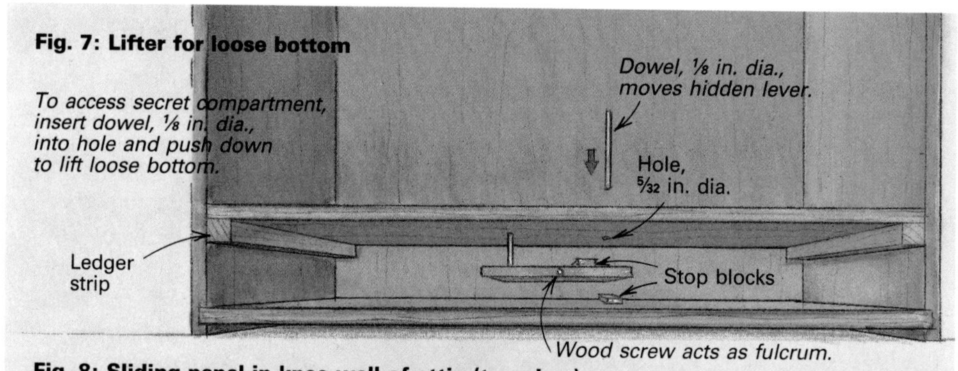

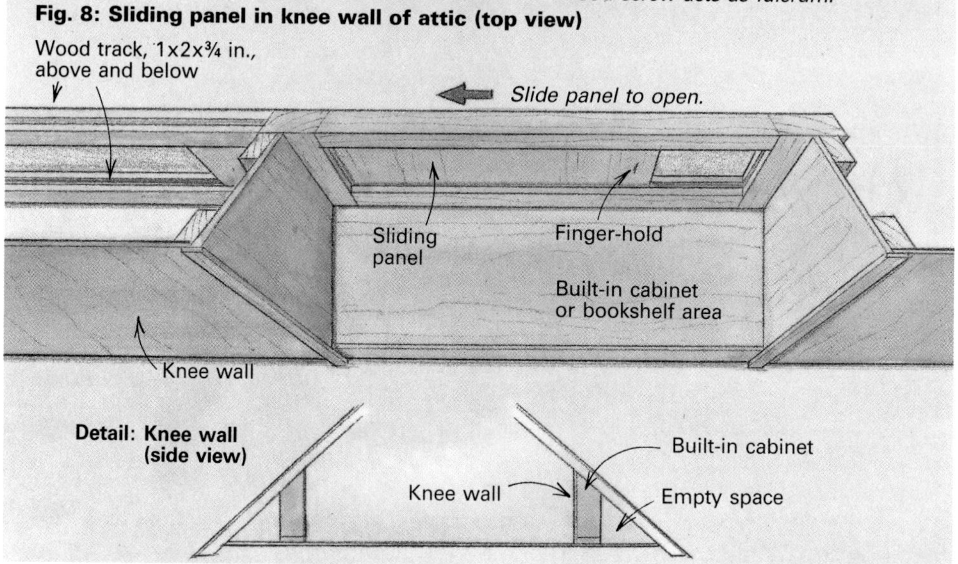

Built-in cabinets allow much greater opportunities for hidden compartments than any freestanding piece. Even something as small as a medicine cabinet in a 4-in.-deep partition can give access to as much or more space than the cabinet itself by using the space between the studs, above and below the cabinet. A full-size cabinet in a knee wall can yield a secret compartment large enough for a person to hide in.

Most built-in bookcases, and even kitchen cabinets, have toe spaces that create a large empty space about 4-in.-deep beneath the bottom of the cabinet. Many times, I've put in loose bottoms, either hinged in the back or merely set on ledger strips all the way around. Whether the cabinet sides are plywood or solid, the bottom must be the same material so wood movement between the sides and bottom is identical, or the loose bottom may be pinched, preventing its removal. The bottom must be as tight as possible to avoid suspicious gaps, yet loose enough to lift out. The trick is lifting this loose bottom with no obvious knobs or finger-holds. Several ways come to mind: a small piece of string, a sheet-metal lifter or even a knob that's screwed into place only when needed. I like to use the seesaw lifter illustrated in figure 7 at right. The only visible clue to this lifting device is a ⁵⁄₃₂-in.-dia. hole near the front of the bottom for inserting a ⅛-in.-dia. dowel to depress the lever and lift the bottom.

When remodeling older houses or adding a room in an attic, there are often large wasted spaces alongside closets and fire-

Fig. 7: Lifter for loose bottom

To access secret compartment, insert dowel, ⅛ in. dia., into hole and push down to lift loose bottom.

Dowel, ⅛ in. dia., moves hidden lever.

Hole, ⁵⁄₃₂ in. dia.

Ledger strip

Stop blocks

Wood screw acts as fulcrum.

Fig. 8: Sliding panel in knee wall of attic (top view)

Wood track, 1x2x¾ in., above and below

Slide panel to open.

Sliding panel

Finger-hold

Built-in cabinet or bookshelf area

Knee wall

Detail: Knee wall (side view)

Knee wall

Built-in cabinet

Empty space

places or behind attic knee walls where the roof meets the floor. This space can be partially used by installing built-in bookcases or chests of drawers, but these built-ins can also be perfect for concealing access to unused space behind and alongside them. Plywood backs can be hinged and held shut with magnets or with a turn latch attached to a slotted wood screw. I like to use a frame-and-panel back with a flat plywood panel that slides out of the way. The

panel is held in grooves in the frame pieces as usual on three sides, while the fourth side is made so the panel can slide by onto a simple wooden track inside the wall. A simple finger-hold is all that is required to slide the panel, but if you want to really impress, the panel can run on glides and be moved with pulleys and cable.

Be sure to think ahead though, because all this work needs to be done before the unit is ever installed. —*C.B.*

Panel-Raising by Hand
Ordinary hand tools can cut it

by Graham Blackburn

Blackburn uses commonly available planes like this Stanley No. 78 to raise panels.

S hapers are nice machines—fast and efficient. They're also noisy and dangerous. The same can be said for tablesaws. Both machines have far surpassed hand tools as the principal means of making useful items of wood on a commercial basis. Fortunately, hand tools still have a perfectly legitimate role in working wood, especially in small shops. They're readily portable, reasonably efficient and are easy to maintain. They're also safe and simple to use, and create hardly any mess. I still use hand tools on occasion to construct panel-and-frame assemblies for architectural woodwork and furniture.

Eighteenth-century joiners and cabinetmakers used a host of specialized panel-raising planes for this work, but, today, these planes are difficult to find, to use or to make. Fortunately, panels are just as easily made with the garden-variety planes available from most tool-supply houses. Granted, making raised panels with hand tools is time consuming. Occasionally, though, you may find this method easier than using machines. For example, I recently built a fireplace surround for an old house. It was constructed on site while the house was occupied. I didn't want to use circular saws and routers, which would have entailed a cleanup of greater magnitude than the job itself. By making room for a sawhorse and workbench, and by using only hand tools, the job proceeded efficiently—without totally disrupting the household routine.

With the design for the fireplace surround, overmantel and side panels worked out in advance, the job proceeded on a two-step basis. First, I made the frame for a particular section; then, I made the raised panels that were to fit in the frame. The application here is for architectural woodwork, but the same basic procedures apply to frame-and-panel furniture construction.

The framing members—stiles, rails and muntins—are first sawn to width and jointed true and square with a jointer plane before being surfaced with a smoothing plane. Mark the faces of each piece so that all future work can be referenced from the same surface. Next, I plow the grooves for the panels in the center of the stiles and rails. I chop the mortises in the stiles after the grooves are plowed using a chisel that's the same width as the groove. Proceeding in this order ensures that the mortises will be located in the center of the stiles and be properly aligned with the groove. I mark the rails for tenons, based on the mortises, then cut the tenons. Next, I get out my panel stock—I rip the stock to width, crosscut it and square up the panels.

An easy way to make panels that stand proud of their surrounding framework is to cut a ¼-in.-wide groove exactly in the center of ¾-in.-thick rails and stiles and use ¾-in.-thick panels that are beveled from the front only. This gives the work an

extra depth that I find appealing. It's certainly not the only legitimate way to proceed, however. More ornate examples of paneling involving applied moldings or molded edges demand a more complicated, less modular approach—as do panels that are visible and finished on both sides, or paneling that incorporates glazing or integral doors.

To ensure accuracy in building the frame, make and assemble the outside frame members first, then measure between the members to derive the length of intermediate framing. I find it easier to cut the framing's tenons first then mark the mortises directly from them.

When all the joinery is cut, knock the whole frame together dry, and check for winding (twist) and flushness, bringing all to truth with judicious paring and planing where necessary. Strictly speaking, this final true-up shouldn't be necessary, but one of the advantages of frame-and-panel construction is that it is somewhat forgiving of the occasional less-than-perfect joint, especially for wall-panel applications.

Now comes the fun part: making the raised panels. The first job is to prepare boards of sufficient width, either by ripping wide boards or by gluing up narrow ones. This is a design consideration that should be worked out beforehand.

Remember that the panel's area equals the opening in the framing plus the total depth of the grooves (sides, top and bottom), less just enough to allow for expansion of the panel. You don't want the panel to fit in the frame so loosely that it will pop out when it contracts. Equally disastrous is a panel fitted so tightly that expansion bursts the frame apart. The relationship of the panel to the framing is a function of four factors: the kind of wood used; how the wood is finished; the size of the panel; and the deepness of the grooves. For example, pine will expand and contract more than mahogany, and a painted panel is more stable than an unfinished panel. Thus, it's difficult to give hard-and-fast rules about the amount of space to leave at the bottom of the groove. When working with well-seasoned white pine (stock that's been allowed to air dry for several months after purchase), I use ¼-in.-deep grooves and allow a total of ³⁄₁₆ in. of excess width. In other words, there should be about a ³⁄₃₂-in. gap at the bottom of the groove beyond the panel. It helps to design a panel with bevels that slope very gently—15° is about right, with 25° being the steepest bevel allowable—since the wood fibers will crush slightly as the panel swells, and a shallow sloping bevel will exert less force on the frame.

After the panels are ripped to width and jointed, crosscut them to length and square them up on a shooting board. You need to mark each panel in two places: on the face to be raised (to estab-

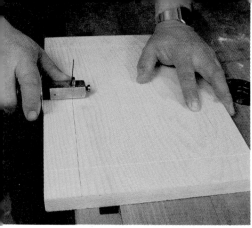 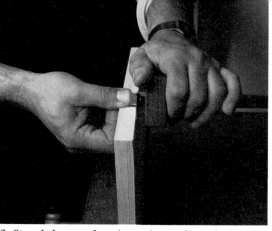 

1. The face of the panel is marked with a cutting gauge, both with and across the grain. The rectangle left by the marks is the area to be fielded.

2. Stand the panel up in a vise and mark the edge that fits in the groove with a marking gauge. Set a marking gauge to the width of the groove and slide the gauge along the panel's back.

3. A rabbet plane cuts the perimeter of the raised field. The scrap clamped to the edge of the piece prevents tearout when planing across the grain.

4. The final rabbet is cut with the grain. Note the lines left by the marking gauge, darkened with pencil, visible at the panel's edge.

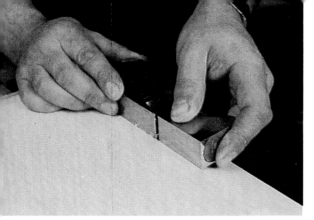

Panel-raising sequence

Cut A first with rabbet plane, then cut B with block plane.

Mark from cutting gauge

A

B

Frame, ¾ in. thick

Plow groove ¼ in. deep.

Panel, ¾ in. thick

Bevel angle 15° to 25°

Line from marking gauge

Leave ³⁄₃₂-in. air gap for well-dried white pine.

5. Clean up tearout at the field's shoulder with a shoulder plane laid on its side. The shoulder plane can also be used to trim the bevel, but a block plane works better.

lish the width of the bevel) and on the edge (to establish the thickness of the panel where it seats in the groove). Most panels—including the ones shown here—have bevels of equal width all around. The width of the bevel is a matter of personal choice and is often dictated by the width of the planes you're working with. To mark the panels, I set a cutting gauge to the width of the bevel and run the gauge along the perimeter of the panel. A cutting gauge is similar to a marking gauge, but it uses a small knife instead of a sharpened pin to score the wood. If you don't have a cutting gauge, substitute a marking knife and a T-square. The score marks created by the cutting gauge or marking knife form a rectangle in the center of the panel that will become the raised area. The tools also allow you to score the wood fibers both with and across the grain, ensuring a clean, crisp raised area.

Now, stand the panel edge-up in a vise and mark the edge of the panel that fits into the groove. Set the marking gauge to the width of the groove plowed in the frame and run the gauge along the *back* of the panel. (If you run the gauge along the front of the panel, the mark is relative to the wrong edge, and the panel will be too thick to fit in the groove.) Darken the scored line with a pencil. Marked in the proper manner—from the back—the panel will stand slightly proud of the surrounding framing. If you prefer the face of the panel to lie in the same plane as the framing, you'll have to make the panel out of thinner stock than the framing, or bevel the panel on both sides so the edge of the panel is centered relative to its thickness. If the back of the panel won't be visible, I'd go with panels made of thinner stock—beveling both sides of the panel would take an inordinate amount of time.

The panel is now ready to be raised, or "fielded." Position the panel on the bench so that you can raise the ends first, moving the plane across the grain. Clamp a piece of scrapwood the same thickness as the panel to one of the panel edges. This will prevent the plane from tearing out the edge as it cuts. It's important to plane the ends first, rather than the sides. This way, any tearout left from raising the ends of the panel will be cleaned up after raising the side bevels.

Set the fence on a steel rabbet plane so that the inside of the blade just touches the cut made by the cutting gauge, and turn the plane's spur out of the way. (The spur, meant to score the wood fibers when cutting across the grain, is unnecessary since the fibers have already been scored.) Set the plane's depth gauge to equal the height of the raised area—about ³⁄₁₆ in. on the example shown here. Now, plane a rabbet—not a bevel—on the end of the panel. If the plane doesn't reach from the edge to the fielded area, plane the edge first and continue the rabbet up to the raised section, guiding the cut with a wooden fence clamped to the panel. The Stanley No. 78 rabbet plane shown here or its modern

equivalent, the Record No. 778, are readily available. Other planes, such as the so-called universal and combination planes, work well, too.

After the rabbet is completed, work the sloping bevel from the corner of the rabbet to the marking gauge line on the panel's edge. The panel shown here has the bevel leading right to the edge of the panel. It's not impossible to plane a flat tongue on the edge of the bevel, but it's very difficult to clean up the juncture of the tongue and the bevel. The antique skew-angle block plane I use to work the bevel is well-suited for this job, but only one version of the plane—solid bronze and expensive—is still available (Woodcraft, 41 Atlantic Ave., Woburn, Mass. 01888; catalog no. 07021, $149.50). A regular well-sharpened block plane will work fine, but may require that you hold the plane slightly askew as you push it along, taking thin cuts and working with a little finesse. Work evenly, carefully extending each facet left by the plane until you have a continuous bevel to the marking-gauge line. When the bevel's completed, swap the panel end-for-end and work the other end in the same manner. When both ends have been cut, work the bevel on the sides. No scrap piece is necessary on the sides, since the plane shouldn't tear out wood when it's moving with the grain. The juncture of each bevel should be a straight line; this is a tell-tale sign that the bevels have been evenly raised.

After the panel has been completely raised, test the correctness of its edge thickness. To do so, slide a scrap of framing with the groove plowed in it around the panel's perimeter. Use a rabbet, shoulder or block plane to trim the edge of the panel where necessary, but be careful not to remove too much material. The shoulder plane is also good for cleaning up any irregularities or minor bits of tearout at the corners where the bevel meets the raised area.

All that remains is to actually fit the panel into the framing. When fitting very large panels, such as the central panel in an overmantel, it helps to pin the panel at the center of each end—to ensure equal expansion on both sides of the panel. Leave the rest of the panel free in its frame. Take care not to overtighten the clamps while gluing up the frame, lest you crush the joints and starve them of glue. Don't be too generous with the glue, either—it's liable to seep out of the joints and accidentally glue the panel in place. If you're really fussy, finish or paint both sides of the panels before gluing up the assembly. That way, no unfinished gaps will be left at the edges of the panel when it contracts during periods of low humidity. □

Graham Blackburn is a contributing editor to FWW, *and has written numerous books on woodworking and tools. His shop is in Santa Cruz, Calif.*

Cross-Grain Constructions

Four clever ways around problems

by Jim Cummins

Wood swells and shrinks in width and thickness as it absorbs and loses water according to the changing relative humidity of the air around it. But humidity hardly affects length at all. Therefore, any furniture construction that restricts wood movement by fastening one piece of wood cross-grain to another courts problems. Many old pieces built this way have cracked or warped because they couldn't withstand the drastic moisture changes caused by central heating. Contemporary builders can avoid cross-grain problems by using plywood and particleboard. Because of their balanced internal structure, both are very stable and may be glued "cross-grain" with impunity. Yet plywood and particleboard are not the most pleasant materials to work with, and they result in a contemporary look that's not always what a woodworker wants.

Modern solid-wood furniture usually leans toward the old designs and the old construction methods, making it prone to all the old problems. Yet ways have evolved to allow cross-grain movement while still using traditional design elements such as drawer runners and applied moldings. Typically, one piece is allowed to slip along the unmoving long-grain piece by means of sliding dovetails, screws fastened through slots rather than tight holes, or other devices (such as the buttons that hold tabletops to aprons) that allow movement without compromising strength.

Many of these solutions are very familiar because they have appeared in construction drawings for project after project. Here are a few less obvious ideas and embellishments that have recently come to our attention:

Tom Hagood of Birmingham, Ala., came up with a way to attach crown moldings, as shown in drawing A. The advantages are that it's relatively easy to make the joint using a router and dovetail bit, the applied dovetail piece replaces the screws-in-slots that would otherwise be visible inside the case and the molding may be easily removed if the piece has to be moved through doorways. Crown moldings typically leave a gap at the top between the molding and the case. This may be filled in with another strip of wood, but the usual treatment is to apply a solid top, with molded edges, that overhangs on front and sides, complementing the molding profile.

Walter Owens of Bloomington, Ind., routs full-width sliding dovetails to fasten drawer frames into carcases, as shown in drawing B. The inherent problem with sliding dovetails is that friction increases as the joint is assembled, often to the point where things jam. There's further risk of breakage when attempts are made to disassemble the parts so the joint can be adjusted. In the old days, sliding dovetail joints were usually tapered: Assembly was easy until the joint finally wedged itself tight, hopefully at just the right position. Skilled use of specialized hand tools is required to fit one of these joints correctly. Owens' method solves the problem neatly by adapting a router jig to make a

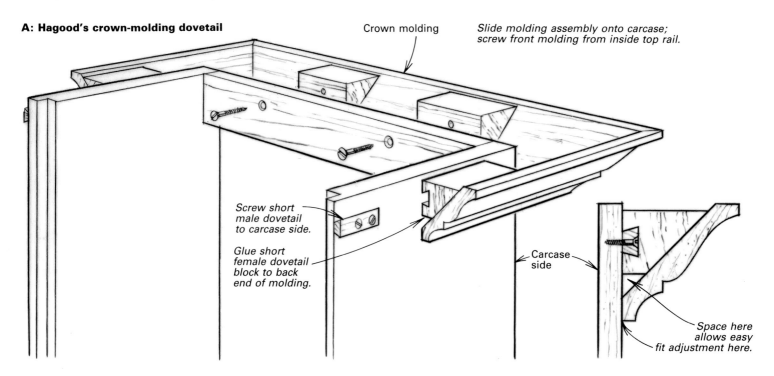

A: Hagood's crown-molding dovetail

Crown molding

Slide molding assembly onto carcase; screw front molding from inside top rail.

Screw short male dovetail to carcase side.

Glue short female dovetail block to back end of molding.

Carcase side

Space here allows easy fit adjustment here.

From *Fine Woodworking* magazine (September 1988) 72:80-81

B: Owens's sliding dovetail

For assembly, first glue back rail in carcase; glue side rails to front rail out of carcase. Next wax middle of groove and slide side pieces into carcase, applying glue to front-rail dovetails just before it slides into place.

Cut male dovetail on router table with front and back rails dry-fitted to side rails.

Dovetail jig

Space jig rails for desired dovetail width.

Plane or sand clearance at center of jig so ends of dovetail joint are tight and center free to move.

Rout dovetail across entire case side.

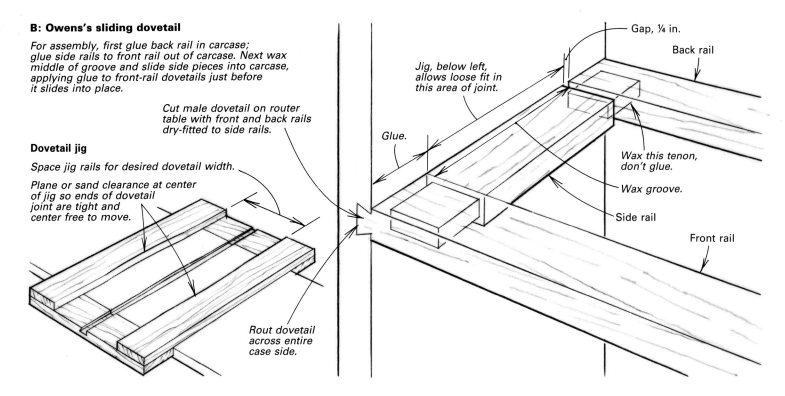

Gap, ¼ in.

Back rail

Jig, below left, allows loose fit in this area of joint.

Glue.

Wax this tenon, don't glue.

Wax groove.

Side rail

Front rail

---

dovetail that's tight at the ends, where the fit shows, and looser in the center, where movement is desired.

Norman Vandal of Roxbury, Vt., a contributing editor at *Fine Woodworking*, has come up with a trick of his own (drawing C). It requires a picture-frame-hanger bit (also known as a hang-slot bit) to rout a T-shape slot along the length of the drawer glide. This bit is normally used to plunge a hole in the back of a frame, and then to undercut it so that the frame may trap a nail head or screw head protruding the correct distance from the wall. (Hang-slot bits are available from most woodworking-supply companies.) Advantages are that the drawer guide rides in a simple dado rather than requiring a dovetail; the fit may be adjusted during assembly by adjusting the height of the screw heads, and after assembly, nothing shows.

Our final cross-grain tip, at least for now, comes from Warren May of Berea, Ky., who is partial to a casework style he calls

"Kentucky." He constructed a quilt cabinet in this style, in a two-board hutch design, using his router for straightforward methods of joinery and assembly. In addition, May has now devised a way to hold small applied moldings to case parts (drawing D). The miters at the front are glued tight, as is the front of the molding to the case. The back of the molding is secured with screws in slots from beneath or above, and these are hidden by other case members. May notes that this approach can work for attaching tiny transitional moldings as well.

These ideas prove that the visual appeal of traditional furniture designs doesn't have to be compromised simply because we choose to live in dry hotboxes all winter. No doubt more of these clever, slippery solutions are even now forming in the minds of creative woodworkers who want the best of both worlds. □

Jim Cummins is an associate editor at Fine Woodworking.

C: Vandal's T-slot

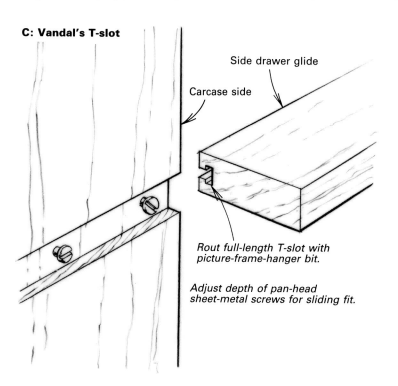

Side drawer glide

Carcase side

Rout full-length T-slot with picture-frame-hanger bit.

Adjust depth of pan-head sheet-metal screws for sliding fit.

D: May's molding trick

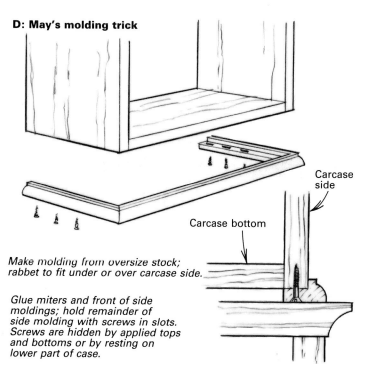

Carcase side

Carcase bottom

Make molding from oversize stock; rabbet to fit under or over carcase side.

Glue miters and front of side moldings; hold remainder of side molding with screws in slots. Screws are hidden by applied tops and bottoms or by resting on lower part of case.

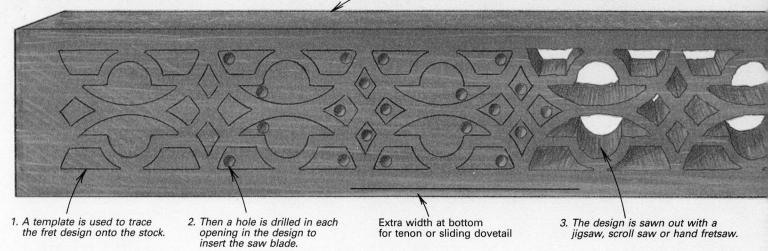

Fig. 1: Making a fretwork gallery

⅝ in. to ¾ in.

1. A template is used to trace the fret design onto the stock.

2. Then a hole is drilled in each opening in the design to insert the saw blade.

Extra width at bottom for tenon or sliding dovetail

3. The design is sawn out with a jigsaw, scroll saw or hand fretsaw.

Fretwork
Laying out and sawing intricate filigree

by David R. Pine

A fret is a thin piece of wood with a decorative pattern that is created by cutting away the entire background of a design with a fine-tooth saw. Well-designed and carefully sawn fretwork can add an extra dimension to an otherwise plain piece of furniture. In addition, the attraction to fretwork seems to be contagious; many potential customers who see examples of my fretwork are immediately convinced that it's just the finishing touch they are looking for.

Because of its delicacy and the expense associated with its production, pierced fretwork is generally found on furniture with some pretension of style. From the Chippendale period (mid-18th century) onward, fretwork was used for corner brackets, as a rim or gallery around tabletops or cabinet tops, and to decorate the frieze under a cornice or tabletop. It was also used to lighten the appearance of an otherwise bulky area on a piece of furniture, such as the pediment of a cabinet or the back splat of a chair. In some cases, intricate fretwork on an antique can double or triple the value of the piece.

The above drawing shows the steps in making pierced fretwork. The decorative pattern is traced onto a thin piece of wood from a template, based on a traditional pattern or original design. Because the background is sawn away, leaving the thin, continous lines of the pattern intact, a small hole for sawblade access must be drilled within each area of the design that is to be cut out. The design is then sawn out with a hand fretsaw or an electric jigsaw and cleaned up with files and chisels. The bracket, gallery or frieze is attached to the piece of furniture with tenons and/or nails and glue. A fretsaw is similar to a coping saw except the fretsaw's frame can adapt to various blade lengths (making it possible to use

broken blades). In addition, the blade is held in place with thumb-screws instead of the pin-in-slot method used on coping saws. The thumbscrews make it easier to disconnect and reconnect the blade for insertion through the holes in each successive cut-out area. Since the 18th century, much fretwork has been sawn out by hand, but I use my old Craftsman jigsaw that I modified to speed the work.

It's common to find antique furniture that has the geometric or foliate patterns characteristic of fretwork relief-carved directly into the surface of the furniture parts. Because this "blind fretwork" can't be split or knocked loose, as applied fretwork can, it is most often used on areas that will receive hard use or wear, such as chair or table legs. However, carving these ⅛-in.- to ¼-in.-deep patterns can be quite a tedious job on any wood and a nightmare on figured or cross-grained wood. Other than the similarity of the patterns, this is an entirely separate technique from the delicately pierced, applied fretwork I'll discuss in this article.

Laying out the design—All fretwork begins with a full-size drawing. Even if you use a traditional design from a source listed in the further reading section at the end of this article, you will probably need to adapt the proportions to suit the piece of furniture you're decorating. If the design is for a corner bracket, the basic shape is usually an isosceles triangle, for which the length of the two equal sides is some fraction (usually ⅕ or ⅙) of the height or length of the piece it embellishes. Brackets usually include tenons, as shown in the bottom drawing on the facing page. However, if the bracket is very delicate, inserting and adjusting snug-fitting tenons is liable to break the thin filigree, so it's safer to glue and nail the base of the bracket to the furniture.

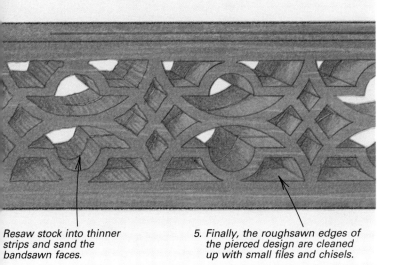

Resaw stock into thinner strips and sand the bandsawn faces.

5. Finally, the roughsawn edges of the pierced design are cleaned up with small files and chisels.

If the design is for a tabletop gallery or cabinet frieze, the basic pattern will be repeated end to end. The length of the basic pattern of a repeating fret is usually about ⅕ to ⅛ of the fretwork's total run before it stops or turns a corner. The design is laid out from the center of the run so the repeating pattern either ends at the corner or so the center of the pattern falls exactly at the corner. In the latter case, the fretwork continues uninterrupted a-round the corner. The height of a repeating fret is usually related to the vertical dimensions of adjacent moldings or some fraction of the total width of a frieze or pediment. In designs with circles or semicircles, such as the example in the above drawing, the radius of the circular or semicircular elements will affect the height and length of the pattern.

Frieze fretwork is usually glued to a pediment with the grain of both running in the same direction. Galleries on tabletops can be let into shallow dadoes as wide as the gallery's thickness. You'll need to allow for the depth of the dado when laying out the pattern. If the gallery is ⅜ in. or more thick, I dovetail the sections together where they turn corners and increase the height of the end pieces so they can be attached to the table with sliding dovetails, as shown in the drawing below. I glue the sliding dovetail into its slot only at the back corner, leaving the

remainder free so the cross-grain top can expand or contract. The fretwork that runs with the grain along the back can be nailed to the top.

Whether you're designing your own pattern or adapting a traditional one, play around with the arcs and angles within the defined area until you get a pleasing silhouette. Take into account the smallest arc your blade will cut without binding. Beware of long kerfs with no way out except by backing up the blade. Don't forget to include any tenons for attaching the fret to the furniture. The next step will be to transfer your design onto your template material.

Sawing out the design—It is important to note that the beauty of many fret patterns is in direct proportion to their delicacy, and it is imperative that this delicacy not be lost through repeated copying of one pattern onto another. Every time the pattern is traced around, the resulting fret is coarsened by the width of the lines. When jigsawing (or bandsawing), most woodworkers are accustomed to cutting close to the pattern lines and then working to the lines when cleaning up the roughsawn edges. However, fretwork is the exception to this rule. If the delicacy of the pattern is to be preserved, it is essential to remove the entire line and then some, as shown in the photo below. If part of the line is left when the original drawing is cut out, and again when the drawing is traced around for the template and then one more time when the template is traced around and the fret is sawn out, the resulting pattern will bear little resemblance to the first drawing.

The effect of this accumulated error was obvious on an Aaron Willard, tall-case clock that was brought to my shop. The piece had recently been restored by someone else and many missing parts had been replaced, including a band of fretwork above the hood. However, the owner was dissatisfied with the restored fretwork and directed me to "knock that clumsy stuff off there." He had taken a photo of a clock nearly identical to his, and had it enlarged until its fretwork exactly fit his clock's hood. I carefully cut the fret out of the photo and used it as a pattern for the replacement. The curving bands of the fret were barely ⅛ in. wide on the pattern, but after tracing around them with a pencil, they were nearly 3/16 in. (or 50% wider). It was obvious that the restorer who first tried to fix the piece had worked in his accustomed way, leaving some portion of the pencil lines showing so that he was sure of the shapes. Unfortunately, the width of those

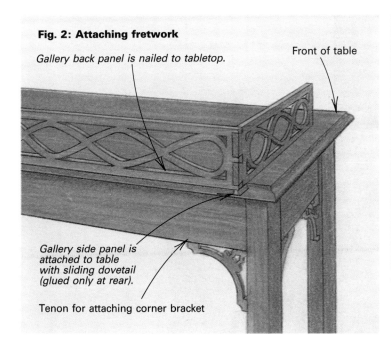

Fig. 2: Attaching fretwork

Gallery back panel is nailed to tabletop.

Front of table

Gallery side panel is attached to table with sliding dovetail (glued only at rear).

Tenon for attaching corner bracket

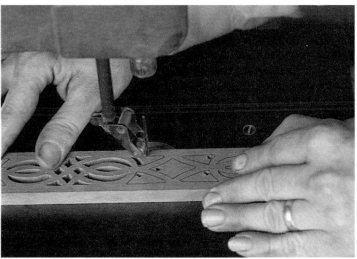

It's important to cut away the line completely to preserve the delicacy of the fret design. By replacing the saw's upper blade guide with a roller blade support from an old sabersaw, the blade need not be attached at the top. This makes it easy to raise the guide and insert the blade into the next opening to be sawn.

two pencil lines meant the difference between a lacy filigree and a coarse failure.

Keeping that lesson in mind, lately I've been using a fine-tip, ball-point pen instead of a pencil to trace around the template onto the stock. This results in a finer line that is more consistent and easier to see; it also eliminates the frustration of repeatedly breaking the pencil lead when it gets wedged in the small openings and sharp corners of the patterns.

When you're satisfied with your full-scale design, cut it out and trace around it, or transfer it with carbon paper onto some material suitable for repeated use as a template. If you use cardboard or heavy plastic, like that used for quilting-pattern templates, you can cut the template out with an X-Acto knife. For durability, I usually use 1/8-in.-thick hardwood or plywood, in which case the template is sawn out and cleaned up using the following process, which is exactly the same process you'll use for the finished fret.

First you'll need to drill through each opening in the design for blade access. Use a drill press and the smallest drill bit you can, without making it too difficult to thread the blade through the holes. The blades I use (the smallest I could find at my local hardware store) are slightly less than 1/8 in. wide. I drill 5/32-in.-dia. holes to accommodate these blades. Locate the holes near a corner of each opening, rather than in the center, to save time while sawing and to make it easier to saw into the corner from both directions.

When sawing out the fret design, it's important to keep the saw blade as vertical as possible. Any variation from the perpendicular will double when one cut meets another, and will add to the time it takes for cleanup. Be careful to make smooth cuts and saw the line away to save cleanup time. After the wood template is cut out, it's time to clean up ragged edges, smooth out curves and make intersections meet precisely.

For cleanup, I use various small files and chisels while supporting the work on a bird's-mouth fixture as shown in the photo at right. In particular, I have a small tri-corner file, one flat of which I ground smooth to make a "safe" side for filing into corners. A tiny (3/16 in. or so) corner chisel that I ground from the broken end of a mortising chisel and fitted with a handle is useful for paring corners true. Carving gouges can be used for smoothing bumps on larger curves, but don't wedge the chisel in a corner and split the fret.

If you're cutting out a lot of thin fretwork, it's usually more efficient to trace the design onto thicker stock, drill and saw out the pattern and then resaw on the bandsaw to yield the thin bands of fretwork. If you use this method, resaw the bands of fretwork and sand the bandsaw marks out of the surface with 80-grit paper wrapped on a block before cleaning up the filigree. After the cleanup on the pierced pattern is complete, the face of the finished fret is finish-sanded. Keep in mind that the thicker the stock the more important it is to maintain a perpendicular cut.

I mount the frets before staining the entire piece of furniture with water-base aniline dyes. After wet sanding with 240 grit, I dab the stain into the piercings with a brush and then lightly rub the fret's surface with 0000 steel wool to knock down any raised grain. Avoid brushing varnish onto fretwork; the drips will drive you crazy. Spraying light coats of lacquer doesn't present too many problems other than having to lightly sand between coats to eliminate the overspray that tends to collect in the small, cut-out corners. When applying an oil finish, excess oil should be blown out of the fretwork with compressed air and then blotted up before it dries.

Modifying a jigsaw for fretsawing—As I began work on my first commission for a band of fretwork, one thing soon became apparent about my old Craftsman jigsaw: If I had to disconnect the blade from the upper tensioning device and then reconnect it for every

The author supports the fret on a bird's-mouth fixture clamped to the workbench while smoothing out the roughsawn edges of the design with small files and chisels.

piercing, the job was going to take an extremely long time. It occurred to me that I might not need tension on the blade because the stock was so thin and the blades I was using were nearly 1/8 in. wide. But I knew I would still need a support that would backup the blade above the cut. To test my theory, I salvaged the roller blade support from a discarded sabersaw and had a local metal-shop worker weld it to a piece of mild steel rod. This item replaced the metal V-block and adjusting rod that came with my saw, providing more support with less drag (see photo on the previous page). I still had to raise this blade support for each insertion and then be careful to align the support to keep the cut vertical, but not having to refasten the top of the blade each time was really a time-saver. I was pleasantly surprised to find that this setup showed no increased tendency to break blades.

My new blade support saved time and let me efficiently saw fretwork for chair splats, corner brackets and even galleries that were shorter than the 22-in. throat distance between the blade and the blade-support arm on my jigsaw. When a job came along that required a gallery back more than 60 in. long, it was time to once again modify my saw. I remembered having read about a saw that was used for cutting marquetry, in which the blade support was suspended from the shop ceiling, which thereby created a limitless throat. Using a few 2x4s and lag bolts, I made a sturdy triangular frame and screwed it to the ceiling joists. I placed the jigsaw beneath the frame and screwed on a blade-support bracket at an appropriate height above the saw table. With the saw base

Each section of the fretwork gallery on this mahogany table, built by the author, was steamed in a pressure cooker and bent over a form after it was sawn out and cleaned up.

After steaming, a section of gallery is bent around this 4-in.-dia. form. The fret is forced tightly to the form with a clamp between the wooden block screwed to the metal band and the notch on the form.

The 22-in. throat of Pine's scroll saw limited the length of stock he could easily cut. To overcome this limitation, he attached a 2x4 frame to the ceiling to hold the roller blade support, removed the saw's arm and positioned the saw table directly below the upper guide.

positioned so the lower blade support was directly underneath the upper blade support (shown in the left photo above), I could saw fretwork of practically any length.

If you've recently replaced your old jigsaw with a new scroll saw, you might want to pull the old saw out of the corner and dust it off for fretwork. The scroll saw may allow you to cut tighter radii with smaller blades, but its design probably makes it impossible to run it without the blade attached at both ends. This eliminates the possibility of removing the upper arm, and it means you'll have to disconnect and reconnect the blade for each piercing.

Other applications for fretwork—Occasionally, thicker stock is fretsawn for use as a pediment top on a chest-on-chest or bookcase, or as a table apron or chair splat. It's possible to achieve a lighter effect on heavy stock by easing or chamfering the back side of these pieces around the openings. This is seen quite often on pierced chair splats.

Fretsawn wood, while naturally fragile due to the removal of most of its long grain continuity, does gain an advantage in another area: It is much more easily bent. Even so-called "unbendable" wood can be steamed or boiled and made to take curves not possible with solid stock. I discovered this when building the scalloped-top tea table shown in the top, right photo. My client wanted a fretted gallery to follow the shape of the mahogany top. Although I had read and been told that you can't bend mahogany, I still thought using it was worth a try, instead of using a bendable wood, like

hickory or birch, and then trying to color it to match the mahogany. The gallery was pretty uniformly pierced, and I used the blandest and straightest grain material I could find. The 1/8-in.-thick fretsawn pieces were cleaned up, then one at a time, each section was boiled for 20 minutes in a pressure cooker that had its saftey valve open. Each piece was then removed from the cooker and clamped around a curved wooden form with a metal band, as shown in the bottom, right photo. I was able to bend the fret into 2¼-in.-radius semicircles with about an 80% success rate. The more shallow curves of larger radius were no trouble. My guess is that the sawn interruptions of the long grain allowed the stress of the bend to dissipate somewhat, and all the exposed endgrain in the pierced pattern allowed free absorption of moisture and softening of the wood fibers. □

David Ray Pine makes period reproductions in Mt. Crawford, Va.

Further Reading

If you want to make some fretwork, but would like to see more designs, help is available from Dover Publications Inc., 31 E. Second St., Mineola, N.Y. 11501; (212) 255-3755. You can go right to the source with Thomas Chippendale's *The Gentleman & Cabinetmaker's Director.* Also, Franz Sales Meyer's *Handbook of Ornament* has a wealth of inspiration. Finally, Blackie and Son's *The Victorian Cabinetmaker's Assistant* has many examples of fretted panels and other marvels of the Victorian furnituremaker's imagination.

Hammer veneering is a technique for laying veneer without clamps or a press. Hot hide glue is applied to both sides of the veneer and a veneer hammer (shown above) is used to force the excess glue out from underneath. The veneer sticks as the glue cools.

Hammer Veneering
Laying the leaves without a press

by Christopher Faulkner

There are several ways to attach veneer, but the method I use in my own work is called hammer veneering. The technique is simple to describe: Hot animal glue is applied to the plywood ground and both sides of the veneer. The veneer is then laid on top of the plywood and most of the glue is forced out from underneath by bearing down with your weight on the head of a veneer hammer and moving the hammer over the glue-covered veneer. The glue is forced out at the edges and ends. As the hammer continues to move, the thin film of glue that remains underneath cools, fixing the veneer in place.

Hammer veneering has several advantages over other techniques: it doesn't require a press or clamps; it's relatively fast and, because there are no clamps or cauls in the way, you can see what you're doing as the veneer goes on. Hammer veneering is best suited for smaller veneering jobs or larger surfaces where many small pieces are laid one-at-a-time to make up a pattern. It's possible to hammer veneer large single sheets of veneer but

the glue cools faster than you can hammer and you'll need to re-melt it with a household electric iron.

To illustrate the technique, I'll explain how to lay a four-leaf match on a small tabletop. This project involves joining endgrain to endgrain and long grain to long grain. To make things more interesting, we'll add an inlaid line and crossbanding around the edge. To be honest, there's nothing basic about laying a four-way match, let alone adding inlaid lines and crossbanding. Before you try, I suggest that you read through this article, then take some hot glue, a veneer hammer, an old piece of plywood, an iron, ten 6-in. by 12-in. sheets of straight-grained veneer and practice. Lay a sheet then re-heat it with the iron, rip it off the plywood and lay another. When you've done all ten, read the article again. You will now have the basics.

If you've laid veneer with a press, you have probably trimmed the edges and ends of the veneer square, taped the joints together and pressed on the entire sheet at once. Hammer veneering

From *Fine Woodworking* magazine (November 1986) 61:86-91

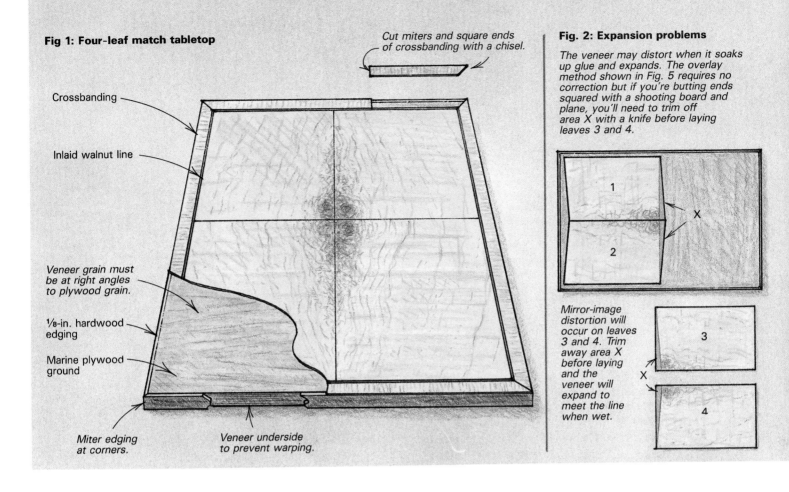

Fig 1: Four-leaf match tabletop

Crossbanding

Inlaid walnut line

Veneer grain must be at right angles to plywood grain.

1/8-in. hardwood edging

Marine plywood ground

Miter edging at corners.

Veneer underside to prevent warping.

Cut miters and square ends of crossbanding with a chisel.

Fig. 2: Expansion problems

The veneer may distort when it soaks up glue and expands. The overlay method shown in Fig. 5 requires no correction but if you're butting ends squared with a shooting board and plane, you'll need to trim off area X with a knife before laying leaves 3 and 4.

1

2

X

Mirror-image distortion will occur on leaves 3 and 4. Trim away area X before laying and the veneer will expand to meet the line when wet.

3

X

4

takes a different approach. Each leaf is applied separately. The joining and matching is done right on the groundwork as the leaves are fixed in place by gluing down the second leaf so its edge overlaps that of the first leaf, then knifing through both leaves at once. This is called the overlay method, and is the technique I'll use here to lay the four-way match. This method produces a very good joint. The disadvantage is that although the grain pattern created by the joined leaves will be an accurate match (since you're trimming the same amount from each sheet), you can't see the *exact* pattern until after you've made the cut. All this sounds complicated, but lay one leaf next to another with the edges overlapping and it will all make sense.

An alternative method is to joint the matching edges, before laying, with a shooting board and plane, as shown at right. With the edges squared in advance, you simply butt the edge of one leaf against the other as you lay them. If you shoot the edges, however, you may run into the expansion problems shown in figure 2, which must be corrected by trimming with a knife. Shooting is best suited for long lengths of reasonably straight-grained veneer, because the plane iron tends to tear out highly figured veneer. Sometimes, on 4-way matches, I'll shoot the cross-grain ends prior to laying, and overlay and knife through the long-grain edges.

My veneer hammer has a 2½-in.-wide iroko head with a ⅛-in.-thick strip of stainless steel (brass will do, but regular steel will stain the veneer) fitted into a groove and screwed from behind. The metal edge is rounded over with a file, then burnished with fine sandpaper. The edge should be flat or very slightly convex along its length. Some veneer hammers are 3½ in. wide, but I prefer the smaller size.

Hide glue is available in dried form from many sources. Remember that it must be soaked in water before it is heated. You can spend a lot of money for a thermostatically controlled glue pot, but any

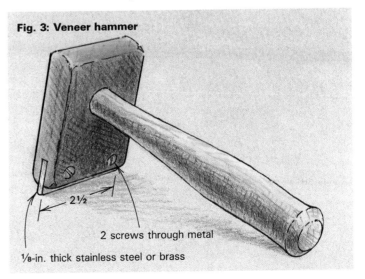

A shooting board is one way to produce an accurate straight edge on relatively straight-grained veneer. Highly figured veneer is best cut with a straightedge and knife.

Fig. 3: Veneer hammer

2½

2 screws through metal

⅛-in. thick stainless steel or brass

Hinged mirrors enable you to preview the pattern of a 4, 8 or 16-way match before you cut the veneer.

The first hammer stroke pushes from right to left, overlapping the edge. Glue on the surface lubricates the veneer hammer.

double boiler setup will work as long as the glue is not in contact with the source of heat. The glue must never boil. A glass jam jar in a saucepan of water has served me well for years.

I never veneer anything other than marine plywood of the best quality or solid wood that's hard and stable. On plywood, the veneer grain must run at right angles to the grain of the outer plies. On solid wood, the veneer grain must be parallel to the grain of the wood. Plywood has barely perceptible undulations on the surface as a result of the gluing process during its manufacture, and these have been known to ghost through the veneer. To remove them, plane the plywood lightly with a smoothing plane, with the grain. Then sand lightly with clean 80-grit sandpaper. A solid-wood ground gets the same treatment.

The veneer that I'm using in the photos is white ash—hard, rippled and very wild, with a distinctly un-flat surface. Typical stuff for matched work. I suggest that you avoid such wild-grained veneer for your first attempts at hammer veneering. Relatively straight-grained veneer is easier to handle.

To preview the 4-way match, I use a pair of mirrors fixed to a ply backing and hinged, as shown in the photo above. I can sit the mirrors on the bundle of veneer and, by changing their angle with one another, see what pattern a 4, 8, or 16-way match of any particular area will produce.

Once you've selected an area that makes an attractive pattern, remove the top four sheets from the bundle. With a razor knife and straightedge, cut the leaves 1 in. longer and wider than required for the finished top. Locate the cuts with respect to some grain feature—a knot or similar mark—so that each leaf ends up with the same grain pattern.

You'll also need veneer for the underside of the top in order to balance the shrinking and pulling caused as the top veneers dry. Two leaves will be sufficient, joined at the long-grain edges. The grain should run in the same direction as that of the leaves you'll be laying on the top, and 90° to the grain of the plywood.

You'll probably need to flatten the veneer before you can work with it. Spray the leaves lightly with water from an indoor houseplant sprayer. Not too much, just enough to raise the moisture content. Do the same to some unprinted newsprint (don't use a newspaper or the ink will stain the veneer) and place a sheet of the damp paper between each leaf. Now press the whole bundle of leaves together between two flat pieces of wood. After 24 hours, replace the damp paper with dry paper and leave for another 24 hours.

Before laying the veneer, the ground must first be sized on both faces. Size is diluted glue, one part glue to eight to ten parts

water. Put a bit of glue into a jam jar and dilute it with hot water. Mix well and apply with the glue brush. Stand the board up vertically to drain, and allow the size to dry for 24 hours.

As I mentioned earlier, for this particular top, I intend to overlay and knife through the edges. The directions given below apply to that method. If you elect to shoot the cross-grain ends instead, allow ½ in. extra length on the other end of each leaf so you have the option of switching to the overlay method if something goes wrong. I tend to allow myself options such as this because it's impossible to predict exactly what will happen.

Check your tools. The glue should be hot, the iron warm (just above the heat setting for nylon). The consistency of the glue is important. The best way to discover the right consistency is to raise the brush above the glue pot and watch the glue flow from the brush. If it's lumpy, it's too thick. The glue should flow in as thick a stream as possible. The stream shouldn't break up into drops. Glue that's too thin will thicken after a half-hour or so of evaporation in the pot.

Fix the plywood in position on the bench with bench stops, holdfast clamps or whatever system you prefer. Lay the balance veneers on the back, using the techniques explained below for the top veneers. The balance veneers should overhang the edges of the plywood by ⅛ in. When the glue is dry and the surface scraped, cut the ply to finished size. To cover the edges of the plywood I glue on a ⅛-in.-thick hardwood lipping with mitered corners before veneering the top. I never veneer the edges.

Re-clamp the plywood to the bench. There must be no obstruction on the lower right-hand quadrant of the board, where you'll lay the first leaf. With a marking knife, mark centerlines AB (horizontal) and CD (vertical) on the plywood. Don't use a pencil—the graphite will act as a barrier to the glue in a place where you need the glue the most.

Leaf 1 will be laid with its long-grain edge overlapping line AB ¼ in. and its cross-grain end overlapping line CD by ¼ in. (If you've shot the end square, lay the end right on line CD.)

Brush glue on the lower right quadrant of the ground. (This should take no more than 10 seconds.) Lay leaf 1 upside down on that glue and brush glue on the exposed side of the leaf with a less well-loaded brush (10 to 15 seconds). You can't rush or you'll break the veneer, but you must not pause or the glue will cool. Now turn the leaf over and slide the leaf into position so that it overlaps the centerlines, as mentioned above (5 seconds). The top side of the leaf will have picked up sufficient glue from the ground for the hammer to slide easily over the surface. About 35 seconds have now elapsed since you first picked up the glue brush.

During the next 30 seconds, while the glue is still hot, your

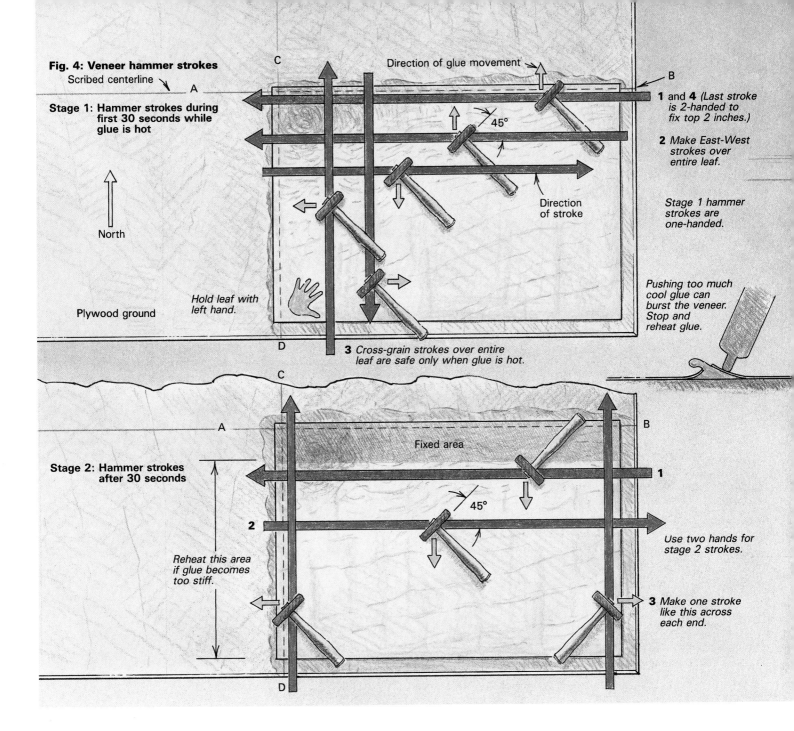

Fig. 4: Veneer hammer strokes

Scribed centerline

Stage 1: Hammer strokes during first 30 seconds while glue is hot

North

Plywood ground

Hold leaf with left hand.

Direction of glue movement

45°

Direction of stroke

1 and **4** (Last stroke is 2-handed to fix top 2 inches.)

2 Make East-West strokes over entire leaf.

Stage 1 hammer strokes are one-handed.

Pushing too much cool glue can burst the veneer. Stop and reheat glue.

3 Cross-grain strokes over entire leaf are safe only when glue is hot.

Stage 2: Hammer strokes after 30 seconds

Fixed area

45°

Reheat this area if glue becomes too stiff.

Use two hands for stage 2 strokes.

3 Make one stroke like this across each end.

goal is to force out most of the glue before it cools. The hammer movements for this stage of the process are shown in figure 4, stage 1. The leaf is now saturated with glue and tends to slide around on the plywood so hold the leaf in place with your left hand. Pick up the hammer in your right hand and make the first stroke from right to left along the edge AB, overhanging the edge a little. Turn the hammer head 45° to the direction of the stroke, forcing the glue out at the North edge, as shown in the drawing (5 seconds). Follow this with one-handed strokes along the grain, over the entire leaf, forcing glue out at the North, West and East edges. After this, make one-handed cross-grain strokes, forcing the glue out at all edges. Never pull or push the hammer across the grain except when the glue is very hot or for single strokes across the end of the leaf to get the last bit of cool glue out. Cross-grain strokes may tear the veneer or stretch it, which will result in small cracks when the veneer shrinks. This is called blanching.

As you hammer, a layer of soft, cold glue will build up around the working edge of the hammer. Let the glue stay there, it facilitates the hammer strokes.

Once you've forced out most of the glue, wait about a minute for the glue to cool. Make sure the leaf is still correctly positioned and then, with two hands on the hammer and a bit of weight from the shoulders, repeat the first stage 1 stroke parallel to line AB. Your goal is to fix a 2-in.-wide area along line AB. If the glue is still hot enough, you'll be able to turn the hammer 90° clockwise and continue the stroke in the opposite direction. The glue will come out from the edge with a crackling sound, now that it's cooler. Suddenly you'll find that the leaf is fixed. If it has become fixed in the wrong position, a bit of heaving with both palms flat on the leaf will shift it. If not, use the iron to re-warm the glue.

Stage 1 of the process is now complete. The leaf should now be fixed for a hammer width along line AB. Enough glue should have been forced out from under the rest of the sheet to allow the veneer to lie flat on the ground, with only a few undulations. Your goal during stage 2 of the process is to force out the remaining glue and fix the rest of the leaf.

If you are quick and the room temperature is over 65°F, the glue will probably not have hardened or cooled too much, and with good weight on the hammer you can keep the glue mov-

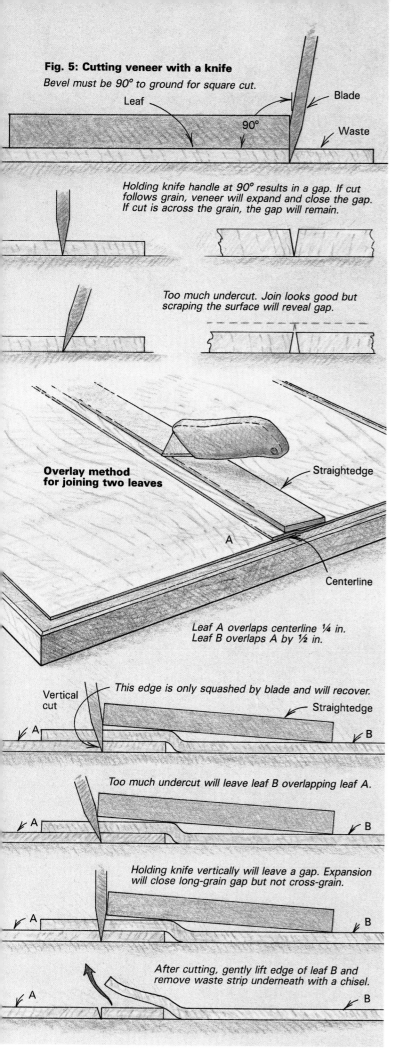

Fig. 5: Cutting veneer with a knife
Bevel must be 90° to ground for square cut.

Leaf

Blade

90°

Waste

Holding knife handle at 90° results in a gap. If cut follows grain, veneer will expand and close the gap. If cut is across the grain, the gap will remain.

Too much undercut. Join looks good but scraping the surface will reveal gap.

Overlay method for joining two leaves

Straightedge

A

Centerline

Leaf A overlaps centerline ¼ in.
Leaf B overlaps A by ½ in.

Vertical cut

This edge is only squashed by blade and will recover.

Straightedge

A · B

Too much undercut will leave leaf B overlapping leaf A.

A · B

Holding knife vertically will leave a gap. Expansion will close long-grain gap but not cross-grain.

A · B

After cutting, gently lift edge of leaf B and remove waste strip underneath with a chisel.

A · B

To join two leaves with the overlay method, knife through the center of the ½-in. overlap, then lift out the waste piece underneath with a chisel.

ing with long, slow, overlapping strokes along the grain. Glue must not be forced through the fixed area, so all glue must be forced South, East and West, using the hammer movements shown in figure 4, stage 2. Now the cool glue will really crackle out at the ends. You may need to make an occasional cross-grain stroke across each end towards the centerline AB, forcing glue out at East or West. The secret to good veneering is to time the hammer work so that you can move all the glue with a minimum of strokes. An overworked piece of veneer will become starved of glue, and won't stick.

It is frequently the case that the glue cools too quickly. You'll feel it. The glue will build up stiffly and threaten to burst the veneer ahead of the hammer. This is the time to pick up the iron and re-melt the glue with one slow stroke of the iron up and back along the leaf, taking care not to disturb the area that's already fixed. The excess glue on the surface of the veneer helps to spread the heat from the iron and prevents the iron from scorching the veneer, so if the veneer surface needs lubricating, put a little glue on top before using the iron. Remember, you're working with water so always unplug the iron before handling it to eliminate the danger of electrical shock. You can now hammer the work as before.

When the entire leaf is firmly fixed and you feel you have removed all the glue, lay the hammer down and use your fingertips and fingernails to feel or listen for bumps where there will be either glue or air. If there is glue which is too cool to move, re-heat it with the iron. If the glue is near the middle of the leaf, and you can't take it out to the edge, slit the veneer with the grain and work the glue out through the slit. If it's an air bubble, slit the veneer and put in a little glue with a brush. Allow it to cool somewhat, then work out the excess glue with the hammer. A clamp with a pad of wood and unprinted newsprint can be helpful if a lump refuses to flatten under the hammer.

After the first leaf is fixed, turn the board around so the fixed leaf is in the upper left corner and re-clamp it to the bench. Leaf 2 joins against the long-grain edge of leaf 1. Apply glue to the second quadrant and leaf just as you did the first, and position leaf 2 so it overlaps leaf 1 by ½ in. and the centerline AB by ¼ in. Hold it in place with the left hand and run the hammer once along the centerline next to the joint, but not over the double thickness of veneer. Still holding the veneer with the left hand, run the hammer over the double thickness. Use the stage 1 strokes to force the glue out, as you did with the first leaf.

When the 2-in. strip along line AB is fixed, clamp a straightedge along line AB and knife through both leaves with about three strokes. It is very important to hold the knife at such an angle that it produces a perfect 90° edge. Figure 5 shows what to

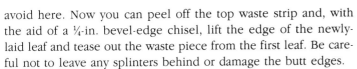

The inlaid walnut line around the border can be held in place with pins until the glue cools (top). To fix the crossband, begin with short strokes toward the center of the board then switch to strokes along the length of the crossband (right). Angle the head at 45° to the direction of the stroke. Allow the crossband sections time to expand, then square up the end with a chisel (above) before laying the next piece. The mitered corners are also cut with a chisel.

avoid here. Now you can peel off the top waste strip and, with the aid of a ¼-in. bevel-edge chisel, lift the edge of the newly-laid leaf and tease out the waste piece from the first leaf. Be careful not to leave any splinters behind or damage the butt edges.

There may be enough warm glue left underneath to simply lay the edge of leaf 2 down again and hammer. If not, apply a little glue and push most of it out with the hammer. Wait for the glue to cool then fix the leaf down with a well-weighted stroke from right to left along line AB. The hammer head should be angled toward leaf 2 to encourage the raised edge down alongside leaf 1.

Apply leaves 3 and 4 as you did the first two. After laying each leaf, knife through the end-grain overlay along line CD. Clean off all the surplus glue with a blunt cabinet scraper (a warm wet one is very satisfactory) and a damp rag before it hardens.

To prepare for the inlay line and crossband, trim the veneer with a cutting gauge to create a border 1 in. wide. Scrape excess glue from the ground on this border.

Cut some ¹⁄₁₆-in.-wide strips of contrasting veneer (I used walnut) for the inlaid line with a straightedge and knife. Apply some fairly cool glue along the edge of the veneer and gently smooth the strip of walnut against the edge of the veneer, standing the strip up on its edge. Wait a little for the glue to cool and hold the strip with pins if necessary. Holding a metal tool against the line acts as a heat sink to quickly cool the glue. Allow the glue to harden before attempting to lay the crossband.

With a knife and straightedge, cut the crossband strips. The grain should run across the width of the strip. Lay the corners first. Cut miters on the corner pieces with a chisel before laying them.

Apply cool glue to the ground (I don't bother to apply glue to the crossband itself), put a crossband strip in place and smooth it out with your fingertips, forcing some glue out. Spread that glue across the top of the strip. The first hammer strokes should be straight into the center of the board, up to the inlay line, with the head turned 90° to the direction of the stroke. When the strip becomes fixed, you can run the hammer along the band, with the head at 45°. Then let it cool, making sure the band stays tight against the inlay line. Don't clean off the cooling glue under the edge that overhangs the plywood—this glue helps to draw the crossband down tight onto the ground overnight. Square up the end with a chisel, before butting the next strip against it. I make the cut by eye, without bothering to use a square. Don't lay more than 15 in. of banding at once. Allow a few hours for the veneer to expand before continuing.

Next day, trim the top off the inlaid line with a chisel and a block plane. Scrape the surface with a sharp cabinet scraper, gradually decreasing the pressure on the scraper to finish up. This helps to remove the very small score marks that the burr on the scraper leaves. These will show up on dark wood only after you have applied a finish.

Because the glue is water soluble, veneered work must be well protected against liquid penetration. Usually a combination of synthetic, non-porous sealer and then natural wax is best, but everyone has his own finishing answer. □

Christopher Faulkner makes furniture and teaches woodworking at Ashridge Workshops, Tigley, Totnes, Devon TQ9 6EW, England. He offers one or two-year courses for full-time students.

The author created the radiating pattern on his tabletop by cutting wedge-shaped pieces from consecutive leaves of a walnut flitch and hammer veneering them to the plywood top. The underside is also veneered to prevent warping.

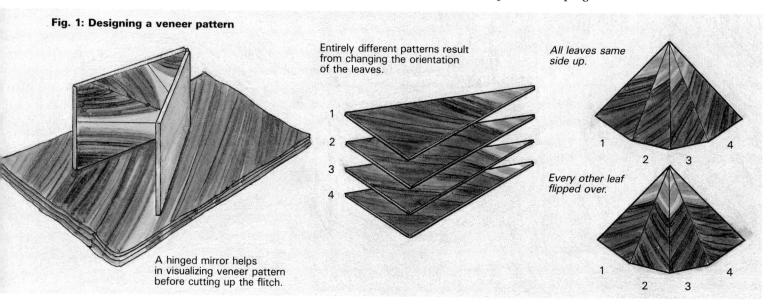

Fig. 1: Designing a veneer pattern

Entirely different patterns result from changing the orientation of the leaves.

1
2
3
4

All leaves same side up.

1
2   3
4

Every other leaf flipped over.

1
2   3
4

A hinged mirror helps in visualizing veneer pattern before cutting up the flitch.

Pattern Veneering
Fanned flitch decorates a tabletop

by Christopher Faulkner

Often the natural figure of wood can be enhanced by repetition of a pattern. Modern veneers are sliced thin enough so that the same figure traveling through the leaves of a flitch can be spread out and arranged to form a pleasing repetitive pattern. But veneer patterns can be difficult to arrange. Wild-grained veneers are hard to cut accurately and don't flatten easily. Also, positioning and gluing down lots of individual pieces in a press can be a nightmare, because you can't see the final fit until the glue is dry and then it's too late to fix misalignments.

In this article, I'll show you how I do pattern veneering and take you through the steps of applying a design to a round tabletop, using hammer veneering to glue the pattern pieces in place. Hammer veneering uses hot hide glue and a special hammer to press veneer pieces flat, one at a time. It's an excellent alternative to press veneering, because you can see what you're doing and fix problems as you proceed. I won't go into the details of hammer veneering here; I'll refer you instead to my article on pp. 38-43.

Controlling pattern—Most pattern veneer designs take advantage of the pattern created by repeating features, such as streaks, knots and areas of sapwood, in the consecutive leaves of a veneer flitch. Pattern pieces are cut with a knife and are mostly straight-edged, as opposed to marquetry designs where curved parts are sawn and fitted together like a jigsaw puzzle. Initially cut oversized, veneer pieces are first glued down and trimmed to size.

The pattern you choose should fit the shape and scale of the object, as well as the character of the veneer. Beginners have a tendency to design complex patterns and select flamboyant veneers that are hard to work with and visually overwhelming. I prefer patterns that reflect nature and the beauty of the veneer rather than elaborate geometry, so I chose a simple radial design for the central pattern on my round tabletop. It's made of 16 wedge-shaped pieces and surrounded by a line inlay and octagonal border. The wedges are laid around the top in the same order they were cut from the flitch, and every other leaf is flipped over, creating a book-match between adjacent leaves. The dark streaks on the walnut veneer I used form a series of lines that travel all the way around the top, resulting in an undulating, circular pattern, like an open flower.

After choosing the design and veneer, you must mark and cut out the wedge pieces and press them flat. I first make a cardboard template the exact size of a wedge, then I position it in various places on the veneer to locate the figure that works best with the design. I use a hinged mirror set to a narrow angle to preview what the pattern in adjacent leaves will look like (see figure 1). I orient the template so the grain of the veneer runs roughly perpendicular to the circumference of the table. If the grain is parallel, gaps will form at the seams of adjacent leaves as the wedges expand and shrink over time. Also, be wary of endgrain or flakiness in the veneer near the tips of the wedges, as the tips might crumble during gluing.

To sense how the pattern will finally look, flip through the flitch and observe how the grain pattern changes as it travels through the 16 separate leaves. Since I want prominent features, like dark streaks, to align in adjacent leaves all the way around the top, I cut the leaves oversized to allow the individual wedges to be shifted to precise positions before being trimmed to their exact size after gluing.

When I'm ready to cut the veneer, I place the wedge template on the top leaf of the flitch and mark a line about ½ in. oversize on the sides and 1 in. at the narrow end. I then number the leaves with chalk, taking care not to upset their order. Next, I take the entire flitch to the bandsaw and holding the bundle together tightly at the edges, I cut all the wedges out at the same time.

It's best to do the steps I've described sometime before you veneer the top to allow time for the leaves to be pressed. This is especially important with burled or curly-grained veneers that must be tamed before they'll lay flat. Alternate pieces of damp newsprint (not newspaper, as the ink will stain) with the leaves and press between plywood sheets for two days. Remove and repeat with dry paper, leaving it in the press for several days or weeks if possible.

Preparing a substrate—While the veneer is pressing, prepare the substrate. For a 25-in. round top, I start with a 24-in. square of AA grade ⅝-in. marine plywood. I glue a straight-grained balancing veneer to the underside to equalize the movement of the top veneer and prevent warping. It's best to lay this veneer perpendicular to the grain of the plywood, but you might choose a four-square pattern instead, especially if the table's underside will be seen. After I cut the square substrate into an equal-sided octagon, I apply eight solid-wood lipping pieces to the edges, using splines to join the lippings to the plywood as shown in figure 2. Next, I plane the lippings flush with the top of the plywood, then bandsaw the octagon into a circle. Finally, I scribe eight lines diagonally across the top to mark the position of the 16 pattern pieces. Don't use a pencil, because the lead will repel the glue where it needs it most at the edges.

Applying the veneer—I use basic hammer-veneering techniques and glue the veneer pattern to the top, but some exceptions are worth noting. Use the same hammer motions as you might on a larger piece of veneer, but take special care not to

The 16 wedges needed for the tabletop's pattern are cut at one time on the bandsaw from walnut crotch veneer.

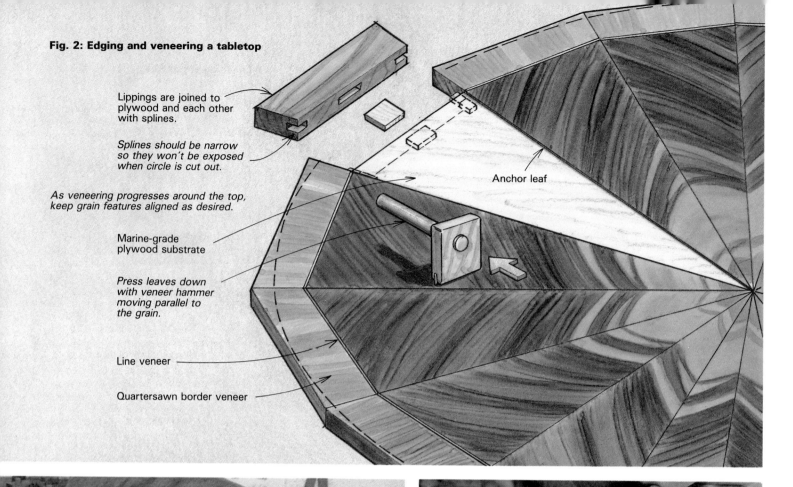

Fig. 2: Edging and veneering a tabletop

Lippings are joined to plywood and each other with splines.

Splines should be narrow so they won't be exposed when circle is cut out.

As veneering progresses around the top, keep grain features aligned as desired.

Marine-grade plywood substrate

Press leaves down with veneer hammer moving parallel to the grain.

Line veneer

Quartersawn border veneer

Anchor leaf

After laying the first or anchor leaf (above), trim the excess with a knife and straightedge, using the layout line scribed on the substrate as a guide. As the pattern progresses around the top (above, right), keep an eye on the position of prominent grain features. Position leaves as necessary so the pattern matches up with the anchor when the last leaf is pressed. After the pattern veneering's done and been allowed to dry for a few days, scrape off the excess glue (right) and level the veneer in preparation for sanding and final finishing.

draw the hammer across the grain (head parallel to the grain), which could easily break off the point or corners of the wedge. Remember that one hammer stroke in the wrong direction can spell disaster as there probably won't be any spare leaves with matching grain patterns. Also, try not to overwork the veneer by excessive hammering. This stretches it out, and can cause casting (small cracks) weeks or even years later.

The first leaf, called the anchor, is laid so its edges overhang the layout lines by equal amounts on both sides. Once the anchor leaf has set—preferably overnight—the excess must be trimmed off. For this I use a razor knife and straightedge, taking several light cuts instead of one heavy one to get through the veneer. To get a square cut, keep the bevel of the blade against the straightedge at 90°. Next, cut the edge of the next leaf that will butt up against the anchor. The new leaf will be glued as close as possible to the anchor, and whatever distortion is caused by the glue's moisture or the hammer action stretching the veneer will be trimmed off on the remaining overhanging edge. This is another difference between pattern and regular hammer veneering. If no delicate leaves are involved, you can overlap adjacent veneers, cut through both sheets at the same time, then carefully pry up the waste beneath the joint. Wedge-shaped patterns are too delicate to lift up, so adjacent leaves must be trimmed to butt together.

Glue and trim each leaf as described above, working your way around the top counterclockwise from the anchor if you're right-handed, as I am. Make sure to clean out the excess glue at the edge of each leaf after you've trimmed it—a scraper or sharp chisel works well for this. If you encounter any problems, like a burst or a split in the veneer, mark it with tape and repair it later. When you've completed half the pattern, stop and let the veneer dry overnight so the hammering will not disturb the delicate points of wedges opposite the ones you're gluing.

At this point, check how the pattern is moving around the top, keeping in mind that you'll want certain grain lines to come around and line up with the anchor at the end. Measure from the center of the pattern to the grain feature, and if it's slowly traveling outwards (they rarely seem to move inwards), reposition the following wedges slightly, distributing the error over several pieces so it won't show.

When I come to the final wedge, I trim the remaining side of the anchor leaf and measure the remaining space carefully. Trim both sides of the last leaf for a tight fit: If it shrinks even slightly as it dries, it will leave unsightly gaps at the seams.

With the central pattern done, I trim the outside edges of the wedges and apply the line veneer and octagonal border. I like to use a quartersawn veneer for the border pieces, because it's least likely to cause movement problems and its plainer grain doesn't compete visually with the central pattern. I alternate gluing border pieces to one side of the circle and then the other to allow the pieces to cool before adjacent ones are laid.

Once the entire top has had a chance to cure for several days, scrape off the glue and sand the veneers smooth and flat, feathering out the thickness of the border near the edge. Finally, I round over the solid-wood edge with a spokeshave and apply a durable, water-repellent varnish. I never use oil on a tabletop, as someone sooner or later is bound to leave a glass on it, and it's a shame to water-spot the top after so much hard work. □

Christopher Faulkner makes furniture and teaches woodworking at Ashridge Workshops, Tigley, Totnes, Devon TQ9 6EW, England. He offers one- or two-year courses for full-time students.

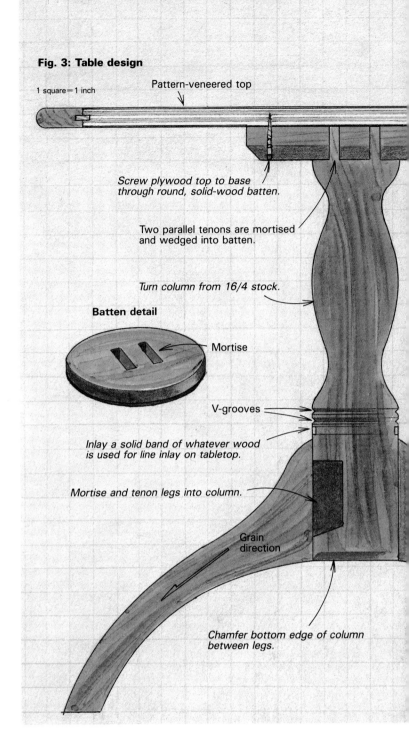

Fig. 3: Table design

1 square = 1 inch

Pattern-veneered top

Screw plywood top to base through round, solid-wood batten.

Two parallel tenons are mortised and wedged into batten.

Turn column from 16/4 stock.

Batten detail

Mortise

V-grooves

Inlay a solid band of whatever wood is used for line inlay on tabletop.

Mortise and tenon legs into column.

Grain direction

Chamfer bottom edge of column between legs.

Tripod table

The author mounts his veneered top to a small tripod he built from the same wood that's used for the pattern veneering—walnut in this case (see the photo at right). The tripod table consists of a single, central turned column with three curved legs mortised and tenoned to it (see the drawing above). A round batten is attached to the top of the turned column. The plywood top is then screwed to the round batten from underneath.

Fabric-Backed Tambours

It's not that difficult to roll your own

by Tim Daulton

There is something almost magical about a tambour, a seemingly solid row of slats that slides out of sight at the touch of a finger. Actually, a tambour is little more than a flexible sliding door, and not much harder to construct.

Like any sliding door, a tambour needs a pair of parallel tracks or grooves to guide its movement. It also needs some type of compartment, usually behind a false partition, into which the door can disappear. Both the sliding door and the tambour door open without swinging out in front of the cabinet. The tambour, however, can slip around corners to be stored out of the way, while a rigid sliding door must remain in the plane of the opening and can therefore limit the size of the compartment's opening. With tambours, you can transform curved surfaces or corners into doors, opening up numerous design possibilities.

Tambours can be designed to open either vertically or horizontally, and this versatility sometimes causes confusion when people describe tambours. A tambour that moves vertically, up and down, has horizontal slats; one that opens horizontally has vertical slats. In this article I'll describe a vertical-opening door, which has a natural counterbalance that makes it operate more smoothly than a horizontal one. In a horizontal-opening tambour, all the weight rests on the lower track, whereas the weight of a vertical-opening door is spread over two tracks. As the top slats move into the compartment, they help balance the weight of the lower slats.

The tambour slats can be connected with interlocked wood joints, wires or cords strung through holes, or a flexible backing of leather or fabric. Fabric backing is the simplest and most common method; I use it here to make a desk-top organizer (figure 1). I prefer plain cotton canvas—it's durable and available in a variety of weights for different-size doors. (To preclude later shrinking, wash and dry before use.) For this small door, I used 8-oz. artists' canvas. The natural color of canvas blends with light woods, and it can easily be dyed to match darker woods. For attaching the slats to the backing, I like contact cement, since it remains flexible and any squeeze-through can readily be cleaned off the slats. Hide glue or white glue can also be used.

Any carcase or cabinet can have a tambour door, but there are some practical limitations to consider. Before you assemble the carcase, remember that you must provide a way to install the completed tambour. There are two ways to do this. One is to trap the tambour between the carcase sides as the piece is assembled. Since this method precludes removal of the door for adjustments, it's suitable for only the simplest pieces. The second method, the one I recommend, is to leave one end of the track open, usually at the back or bottom, so that the tambour can be slid in place after assembly and then closed in. This allows more careful fitting, and the door can be removed for finishing or adjustment. When designing the track, it's a good idea to consider how you're going to insert the completed tambour. In the piece shown here, the back and bottom fit into rabbets cut in the carcase sides, so it was easy to leave them both off until I had installed the tambour (figure 2, p. 50).

You must construct the carcase carefully to ensure square, parallel sides, otherwise the tambour will neither fit well nor slide smoothly. Since a tambour often occupies one or more corners of a piece, thus replacing some structural framing, you may need to include interior partitions or shelves to help hold the case together. Measure carefully to ensure that the door will clear all interior elements, as well as the back and outside panels. Also make sure that no glue gets into inaccessible sections of the track during assembly.

Before you can begin to prepare slats for the tambour, you must consider the width of the opening, which affects slat thickness, and establish the curvature of the guide track, which determines the width of the slat. Slats should be ⅜ in. to ¾ in. thick, just substantial enough to keep from flexing too much between the sides. Thin slats make the door light enough to operate easily without slamming when opened or shut. I recommend laying out the proposed track on scrap material and test-fitting slats to determine optimum slat shape and track curvature for your design, but you could simply draw the track out carefully on paper instead. Just be sure that there's enough room for the tambour to open and close completely, without coming out of its pocket. Generally, the track extends into a pocket behind a false back or interior partition so that the door's workings aren't exposed and the contents of the case don't interfere with its operation. I suggest that you build the tambour with a couple of extra slats to ensure that the door won't be too short—the excess pieces can be trimmed off before assembly if they aren't needed.

The track can be really any shape that suits your piece, although I try to avoid extremely tight circles and to keep curves as gentle as possible to reduce friction. Tighter curves demand narrower slats; the larger the track's radius, the wider the slats can be. The front edges of the slats are often beveled, chamfered or rounded so that the joints appear uniform, even around corners, and so that they won't pinch fingers and things when closing. With reverse-curve or S-shaped tracks, which bend tambours in more than one direction, slats must be beveled enough to allow the bend. The back edges of canvas-backed slats

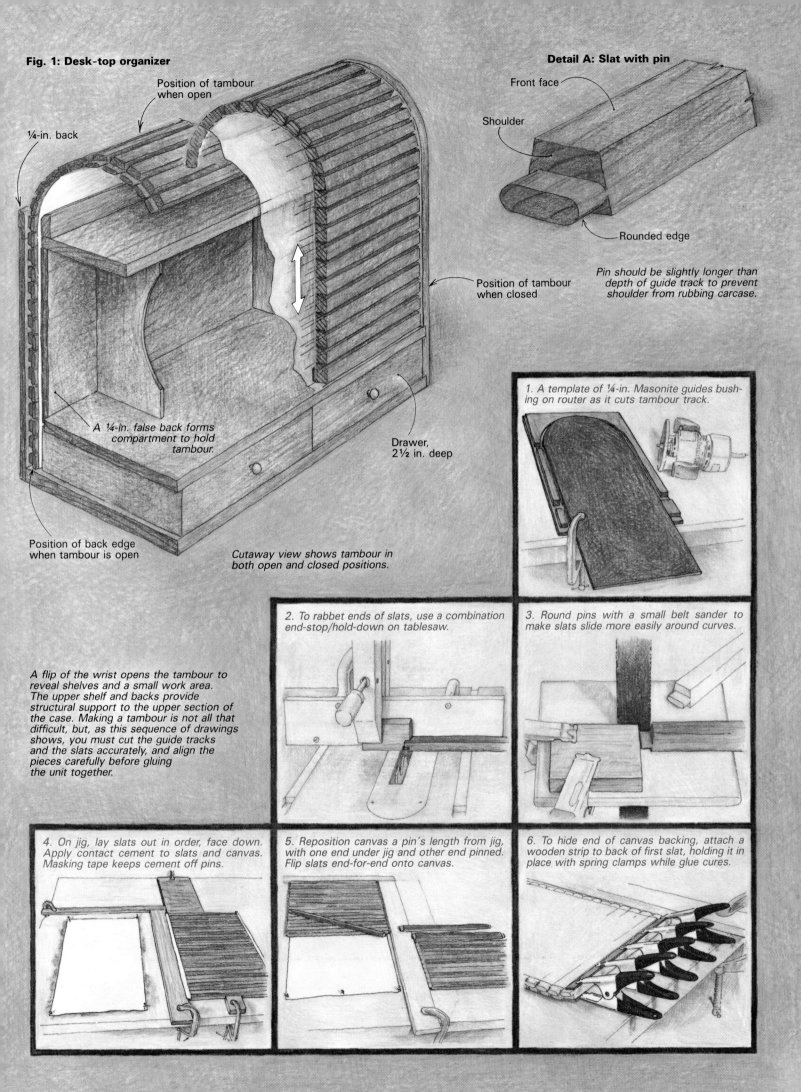

Fig. 1: Desk-top organizer

Position of tambour when open

¼-in. back

Position of tambour when closed

A ¼-in. false back forms compartment to hold tambour.

Drawer, 2½ in. deep

Position of back edge when tambour is open

Cutaway view shows tambour in both open and closed positions.

Detail A: Slat with pin

Front face

Shoulder

Rounded edge

Pin should be slightly longer than depth of guide track to prevent shoulder from rubbing carcase.

A flip of the wrist opens the tambour to reveal shelves and a small work area. The upper shelf and backs provide structural support to the upper section of the case. Making a tambour is not all that difficult, but, as this sequence of drawings shows, you must cut the guide tracks and the slats accurately, and align the pieces carefully before gluing the unit together.

1. A template of ¼-in. Masonite guides bushing on router as it cuts tambour track.

2. To rabbet ends of slats, use a combination end-stop/hold-down on tablesaw.

3. Round pins with a small belt sander to make slats slide more easily around curves.

4. On jig, lay slats out in order, face down. Apply contact cement to slats and canvas. Masking tape keeps cement off pins.

5. Reposition canvas a pin's length from jig, with one end under jig and other end pinned. Flip slats end-for-end onto canvas.

6. To hide end of canvas backing, attach a wooden strip to back of first slat, holding it in place with spring clamps while glue cures.

Drawings: Christopher Clapp

shouldn't be chamfered, as they must fit together closely at the fabric.

I cut the guide tracks using a router guided by a bushing against a shaped template (figure 1, step 1)—identical tracks can easily be cut by reversing the template on opposite sides of the carcase. To make the correct-size template, subtract the difference between the bit's radius and the bushing's outside radius from the full-size track layout. The track groove itself should be about half the thickness of the slats, usually $\frac{3}{16}$ in. to $\frac{3}{8}$ in., to accommodate the slat pins. Pick the closest size for which you own a router bit. A good template can be made from $\frac{1}{4}$-in. Masonite, which is smooth and dense and wears well. Cut it out carefully, and make it longer than the track will be to guide the router's entrance and exit. With a new template, I like to practice the cut a couple of times on scrap material to check the template's accuracy and to get a feel for moving the router around it smoothly. When you're satisfied with the template, attach it firmly to the top, side or bottom piece in the correct position. Tacks or screws in an inconspicuous place are more convenient than clamps. Check the alignment, and cut the first groove. Then flip the template over onto the mating piece, making sure the alignment is identical, and cut the matching track. Sand the grooves smooth with a small sanding block or folded sandpaper, and widen them slightly around any particularly tight curves to prevent binding.

Once I'm satisfied with the guide tracks, I cut the slat stock to length (I usually make extra slats to allow for defects), rip the pieces to size, and then rabbet the ends of each piece to form

pins, as in figure 1, detail A. The pins should be just slightly thinner than the track groove. Rabbeting pins allows the groove to be narrower than the slat thickness and remain hidden behind a neat joint at the front face. Rabbeting the front face of the slat, so the pin is on the back half of the slat, allows you to fit the tambour flush with the face of the piece. I cut the pins on each slat on a tablesaw, using a crosscutting guide and end stop (step 2), then round their corners with a rasp or a sander so that they'll slide smoothly around corners (step 3). The pins should be slightly longer than the track is deep so that they'll bottom out, preventing the slat shoulders from rubbing against the case. The slats themselves should have a little end clearance between tracks to allow for wood movement and inconsistencies in construction. Round or bevel the long edges of the slats with a sander, router or tablesaw.

After all the tambour slats have been prepared, sand them smooth and lay them out in order, matching grain and tossing out any pieces that are seriously warped. Fasten a couple of straight boards to your work surface at right angles to form a gluing jig (step 4). Cut a length of canvas slightly narrower than the shoulder-to-shoulder width of the slats and spread contact cement over it. Lay the slats out in order, face down, next to the gluing jig and spread cement on them. Let the glue set properly, and apply a second coat if necessary. Carefully align the canvas in the jig—I clamp one end under the jig itself and tack the free end down. Now flip each slat end-for-end and press it onto the canvas, making sure it's flush and square in the jig and tight to the next slat before the glue-covered surfaces make contact (step 5). Once all the slats are stuck down, flip the completed tambour over and press the canvas down firmly onto the slats. Rub off any excess glue, trim the canvas, and you're ready to roll. I like to face the back of the first slat with a thin strip of wood to finish off the canvas edge and to reinforce the bond there (step 6). Handles or knobs can be attached now if they won't interfere with the installation of the tambour, or they can be added after the tambour is assembled.

Regardless of whether the tambour is installed as the carcase is assembled or slid into place afterward, it will probably fit tightly at first. Slide it back and forth to locate the rough spots, and carefully sand the tracks or pins until the door runs without catching anywhere. Do as much sanding and finishing as possible with the tambour out of the case, where it's easier to get at, and be careful not to saturate the fabric with finish which may stiffen or weaken it. A bit of paraffin or paste wax rubbed into the tracks after final finishing will make the door operate more smoothly, but a little friction in heavier doors is desirable since it will keep them from rolling too rapidly at the end of the track and slamming when opened or closed.

After installing the tambour and making a final check for smooth operation, add stop blocks, if necessary, to keep the tambour from sliding down too far into the hidden compartment. Close up the end of the track, and the piece is ready for final finishing.

Building a tambour may be a little trickier than fitting a hinged door or cutting straight grooves for a sliding door, but it's not really all that difficult. And the results, in space efficiency, visual appeal and design variation, can be well worth the effort. □

Tim Daulton builds furniture in the woodcraft program at Arizona State University in Tempe. He recently returned from Osaka, Japan, where he studied old Japanese wood sculpture.

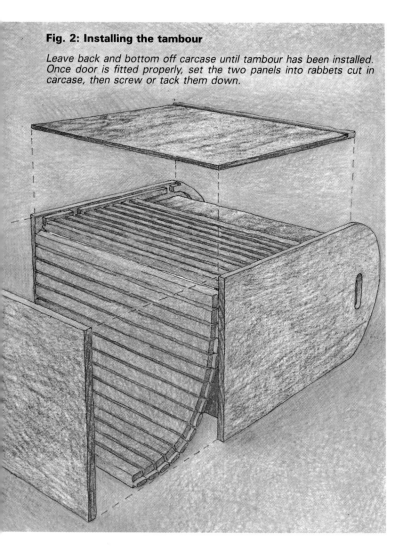

Fig. 2: Installing the tambour

Leave back and bottom off carcase until tambour has been installed. Once door is fitted properly, set the two panels into rabbets cut in carcase, then screw or tack them down.

Inlaid Tambours

Floral patterns on a flexible door

by David Convissor

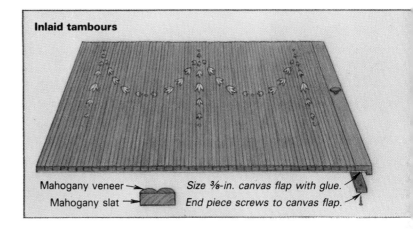

Inlaid tambours

Mahogany veneer →
Mahogany slat →

Size ⅜-in. canvas flap with glue.
End piece screws to canvas flap.

John Seymour and his son Thomas were among the finest of the Boston cabinetmakers at the turn of the 19th century. Although they produced an amazing variety of furniture, they are best known for their Federal tambour desks and secretaries. The tambour doors on some of their fancier pieces were decorated with a delicate, draped cornflower design inlaid into the tambour slats. I reproduced this design on the doors of my Seymour-style desk shown at right. Inlaid tambours certainly look impressive, but they aren't nearly as difficult as they appear.

Inlaid tambour doors are basically the same as conventional tambours: thin wooden slats glued to a flexible canvas backing. The inlays appear to have been worked into each slat individually, but this isn't the case. The flowers are inlaid into a sheet of veneer. Wood strips are then clamped edge-to-edge and glued to the back of this marquetry sheet. The veneer is then cut apart along the strip lines with a knife. This technique can be used to add parquetry patterns, marquetry designs or just some beautiful grain pattern to contemporary-style tambours. I molded each slat on my desk doors but, if you leave the slats flat, the surface will look solid when the tambours are closed.

The tambours on my desk are mahogany inlaid with holly. Both woods cut easily and are available in nice, straight grain. Instead of being sawn out with a scroll saw, the inlays and the corresponding holes in the veneer are punched out with gouges. Since the desk-door slats will be molded, to allow enough thickness, start with veneer that is at least ¹⁄₁₆ in. thick. Most veneer suppliers sell ¹⁄₁₆-in. mahogany. However, you might have to plane down the holly from a thicker piece or resort to gluing together two pieces of ¹⁄₂₈-in.-thick veneer.

Start by drawing the pattern full size on paper. As you can see from the photo of the desk, the flower pattern repeats and reverses itself four times across each door. You need to draw only one section, not the entire pattern. The pattern has only two shapes, a football-shaped flower petal and a round dot. To draw the flower petals accurately you'll need a template and to make the template you'll need three gouges—one for each size flower. I made the design shown with three #6 sweep straight gouges: 1 in., ¾ in. and ½ in. Make the template from 3- to 5-mil drafting film (available from any large art-supply store) by cutting out one petal shape with each chisel. Two chisel cuts punch out one petal, as shown in the drawing. Trace around the inside of the template cutouts to draw the flower petals on your full-scale drawing. Draw parallel lines ⅜ in. apart to represent the slats. Transfer the finished drawing to tracing paper and fasten the tracing with rubber cement to your mahogany veneer. Art stores also sell transparent pressure-sensitive vinyl which is more con-

Inlaid tambour doors decorate author's version of a Federal-style desk. Not a reproduction of any particular piece, it combines features of desks built by early Boston cabinetmakers John and Thomas Seymour.

Photo this page: Susan DeLong

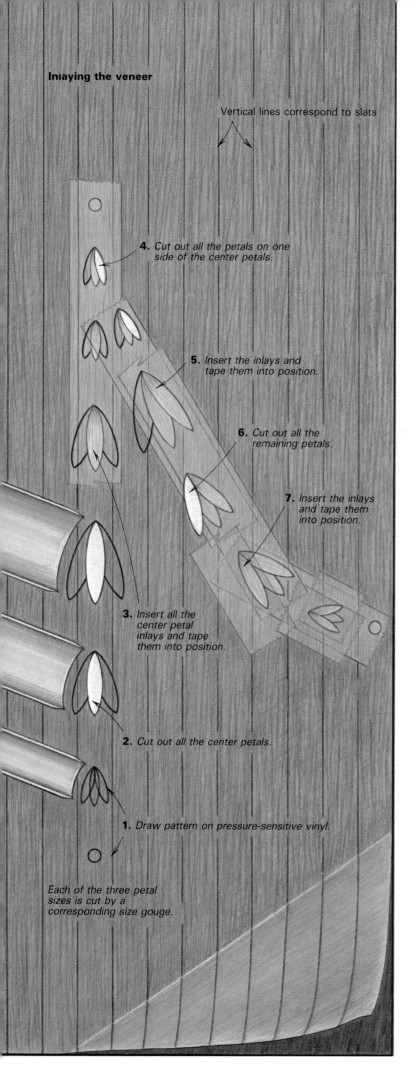

Inlaying the veneer

Vertical lines correspond to slats

4. Cut out all the petals on one side of the center petals.

5. Insert the inlays and tape them into position.

6. Cut out all the remaining petals.

7. Insert the inlays and tape them into position.

3. Insert all the center petal inlays and tape them into position.

2. Cut out all the center petals.

1. Draw pattern on pressure-sensitive vinyl.

Each of the three petal sizes is cut by a corresponding size gouge.

With full-size drawing on clear vinyl stuck to the veneer, Convissor punches out the center inlay recess with a #6 sweep straight gouge (top). The same gouge cuts the holly inlays. The hole for the side inlay cuts into center inlay piece to create a three-dimensional effect (bottom). The third side inlay hole cuts through the first two inlays. Cellophane tape holds inlays in place.

venient than tracing paper because it sticks without cement.

I suggest that you do the entire marquetry and veneering process with one section at a time. After you've finished four sections and cut apart the slats, you can glue canvas across the back of all four sections to complete one door. With the same gouges you used to make your template, cut out the center petal of each flower. Don't worry if the two cuts overlap at the ends of the opening because the overcuts won't show after the slats are molded. Cut the matching center petal inlays from the holly veneer with the same gouges. After working for a few minutes your eyes will become accustomed to the sizes and shapes and you'll be surprised how neatly the holly petals fit into the mahogany.

I shaded the inlays by charring one end slightly in hot sand. This shading adds depth to the flower design. Fill a cast-iron skillet with about 1-in. of fine builders' sand. Hold one end of each inlay in the hot sand for a few seconds so that the tip is shaded. Experiment to find the proper amount of time. Too long and you'll char the wood. With my electric hot plate on high, I find a 5-second count just right. After shading, insert the inlay into the veneer and hold it there with cellophane tape.

When all the center petals are installed, cut out all the petals on one side. To give the flower a three-dimensional appearance, cut right into the center petal so that the side petal appears to overlap it. Shade just the tip of the side petal in the sand and tape it in place. Now make the cuts for the third petal through both the center and side petals. Cut the dots at the end of the strings with a punch or a #9 gouge slowly twisted in a circle. Don't shade the inlays for the third petal or the dots.

When all the pieces are taped in place, turn the veneer over and brush a mixture of watered-down yellow glue and mahogany sawdust into the cracks. I force the mixture into the gaps with a

From *Fine Woodworking* magazine (September 1985) 54:71-73

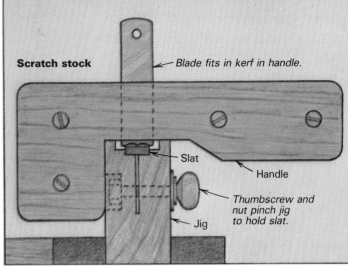

Scratch stock — Blade fits in kerf in handle.

— Slat

— Handle

Thumbscrew and nut pinch jig to hold slat.

Jig

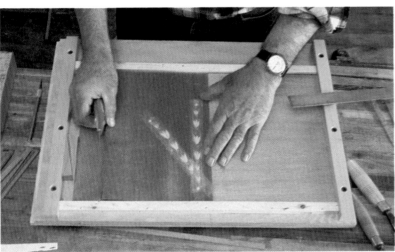

For veneering, the slats are locked up in a rigid frame. A wood strip tacked across the slat ends prevents movement when clamps are applied (top left). Edges of marquetry sheet must be trimmed so the lines on the drawing line up with the cracks between the slats underneath (left). The frame is large enough to hold the entire door for canvassing, but when working on one section of the pattern, plywood spacers take up the remaining space. After cutting the veneered slats apart, Convissor molds the slats with a scratch stock (right). A wooden fixture secures the strip.

flat scrap of metal. When the glue has dried, level the back side with a cabinet scraper.

To make the slats, I cut mahogany strips ³⁄₁₆ in. thick and ³⁄₈ in. wide and ½ in. longer than the finished door height. When the marquetry sheet is finished, it's ready to be glued to these slats. To keep the slats from moving around I've built a rectangular frame much like a printers' chase—the iron frame that holds hand-set metal type in place. Lock up the correct number of slats for one section of the pattern, as shown in the photo above. Tack a strip of wood over the bottom ends of the slats to secure them, and place the veneer face up over the clamped-up slats. Trim the ends and sides of the veneer so that the slat lines drawn on the tracing line up with the cracks between the strips underneath. Remember, the other sections of the pattern will later butt up against this one, so the end of the section must line up with a crack.

I cover the veneer with a heavy layer of newspaper or a piece of ¹⁄₁₆-in. sheet foam to take up any unevenness while clamping. A piece of ³⁄₄-in. plywood distributes pressure over the surface. When the alignment is right, clamp up a dry run to make sure that everything is ready and that no one has taken your clamps. Remove the veneer and brush a coat of white glue on the slats. Position the veneer and drive a few veneer pins or brads in the corners to keep the veneer from shifting when you apply the clamps. Cut the pins off ¹⁄₁₆ in. above the surface. Cover the veneer with the newspaper or foam, lay on the plywood and clamp it in place. A veneer press is nice if you have one.

Let the glue set for no more than 15 minutes. Remove the panel and flex it to be sure no glue has seeped between the slats. I flex the panel over a piece of half-round stock and run a razor knife blade between any slats that feel tacky. Now number the slats and draw some diagonal registration lines across the back

so that you can line up the slats and later reassemble them in the correct order. The slats are now ready to be cut apart. With a straightedge, score the veneer face along the slat lines with a sharp razor knife to prevent the cuts from following the grain, then turn the panel over. Rest it on a curved surface to spread the slats. Cut through the veneer with the razor knife using the edge of the slat as a guide.

When all the slats are cut apart they can be molded. I've made a simple fixture that holds one slat in place while I cut the molding with a scratch stock. A scratch stock, shown in the drawing above, is a simple, shop-made tool for making moldings, beadings and grooves for string inlays. A broken hacksaw blade makes a good cutter and you can grind or file any profile you want. To use the tool, set the blade to the depth you want to cut and pull the tool back and forth along the stock until the handle stops the cutting action. No, the inlays won't pop out. Sand the molded slats with 120-grit sandpaper, followed by 150-grit.

When you've completed the above process four times you'll have all the slats for one door and you'll be ready to glue on the canvas. Lock the slats for the entire door face down in the chase. Make sure that you have them in the correct order and that the diagonal lines are lined up. Apply white or yellow glue to the canvas and clamp it in place under a plywood batten for no more than 15 minutes. Remove the clamps and flex the tambour. Remove any glue from between the slats with a razor knife. I trim the door to width on the tablesaw with a hollow-ground planer blade after first scoring the back of the canvas with a knife. □

David Convissor is a professional furnituremaker in Littleton, Mass. For more on tambour doors and their installation, see the article on pp. 48-50.

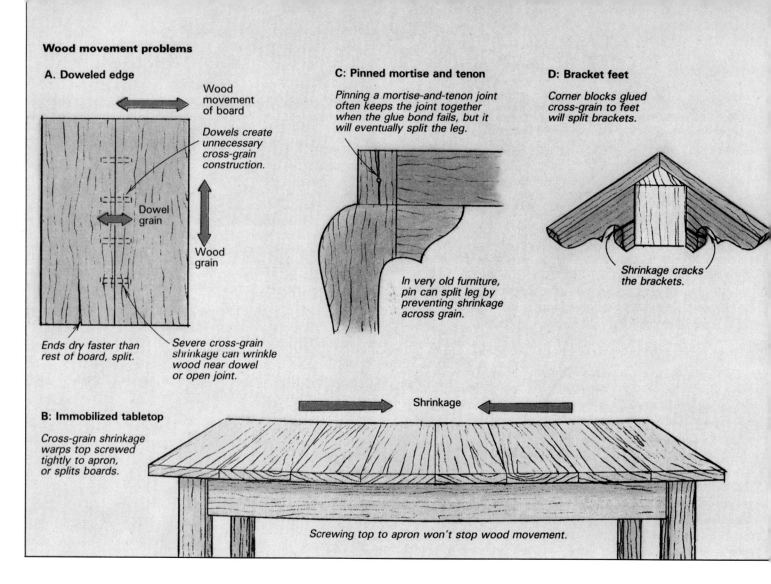

Wood movement problems

A. Doweled edge

Wood movement of board

Dowels create unnecessary cross-grain construction.

Dowel grain

Wood grain

Ends dry faster than rest of board, split.

Severe cross-grain shrinkage can wrinkle wood near dowel or open joint.

C: Pinned mortise and tenon

Pinning a mortise-and-tenon joint often keeps the joint together when the glue bond fails, but it will eventually split the leg.

In very old furniture, pin can split leg by preventing shrinkage across grain.

D: Bracket feet

Corner blocks glued cross-grain to feet will split brackets.

Shrinkage cracks the brackets.

B: Immobilized tabletop

Cross-grain shrinkage warps top screwed tightly to apron, or splits boards.

Shrinkage

Screwing top to apron won't stop wood movement.

Coping with Failing Joints

Wood movement is more destructive than abuse or neglect

by Bob Flexner

I hate to admit it, but when I began building furniture 12 years ago, I didn't fully understand the nature of wood. To make joints stronger and last longer, I used 4-in.-long, ½-in.-dia. dowels to join chair and table rails to thick legs. I routinely used dowels when edge-joining boards to make tabletops, and pinned every mortise and tenon. Friends of mine were gluing and bolting butcher-block tops together, assuming the long steel rods would help prevent the joints from separating. One friend was churning out oak dining tables, each with a 5-ft.-dia. solid top screwed tightly to a square frame "so it wouldn't move." After about a year, the tops bowed up like plywood left in the sun.

Waiting to see if your furniture will hold up over time is an unreliable way to learn—you might not live long enough to see

the failures. Old furniture, on the other hand, provides most of the information needed to predict where problems will arise. Except for breakage caused by rough treatment, neglect, bad design or just plain bad workmanship, the failures in old furniture occur almost universally in the joints, as shown above.

The common explanation for these joint failures is that the glue has given out. This is true, of course: The glue has aged, lost its flexibility and no longer holds as well. But that's not the whole story. The glue holds fine where wood was joined edge-to-edge. Look at all the glued-up tabletops and panels that have survived for hundreds of years.

Most of the failures occur where wood is joined at right angles, since this configuration stacks the force of wood's natural, mois-

Drawings: Lee Hov

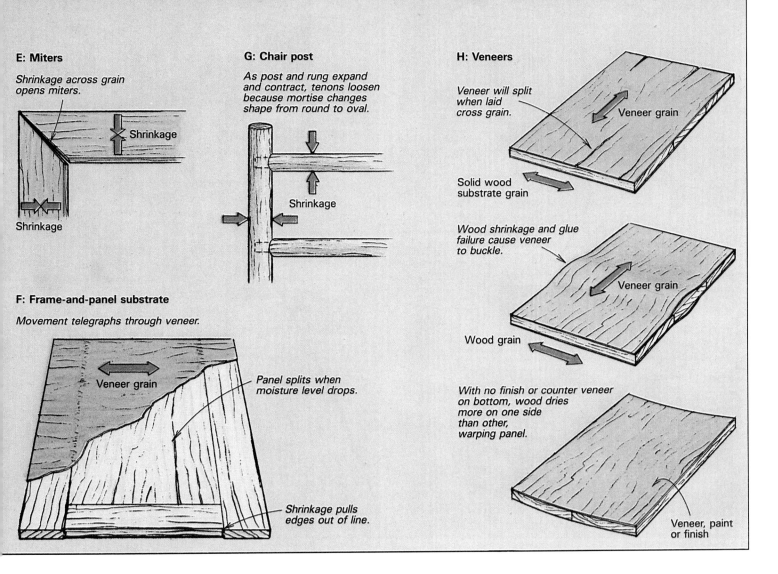

E: Miters

Shrinkage across grain opens miters.

Shrinkage

Shrinkage

F: Frame-and-panel substrate

Movement telegraphs through veneer.

Veneer grain

Panel splits when moisture level drops.

Shrinkage pulls edges out of line.

G: Chair post

As post and rung expand and contract, tenons loosen because mortise changes shape from round to oval.

Shrinkage

H: Veneers

Veneer will split when laid cross grain.

Veneer grain

Solid wood substrate grain

Wood shrinkage and glue failure cause veneer to buckle.

Veneer grain

Wood grain

With no finish or counter veneer on bottom, wood dries more on one side than other, warping panel.

Veneer, paint or finish

ture-related movements against the holding power of the glue. This wouldn't be such a problem if the shrinkage during dry periods and swelling during the damper months occurred uniformly in all directions. But, the movement is in one direction only: across the grain. There's virtually no movement along the grain. When boards are joined at right angles, the contrary shrinkage and expansion stresses the glue joint and causes it to eventually fail.

This failure will occur even quicker if the furniture is subjected to drastic humidity changes, such as when furniture is moved from a very damp to a very dry climate (or vice versa), or when old furniture is put into a building with central heat for the first time. Paint or finish won't eliminate this movement; they can only slow it down. You can see this in any building with painted wooden windows and jambs. In spite of the paint, they stick in the spring and summer when it's damp. And, in the drier winter months, they shrink and let the cold in.

There is, in short, no known way to bond wood together in cross-grain directions and expect it to survive in everyday use for more than 50 to 100 years. Everything we build or repair will come apart sooner or later. Realizing this is very critical. Furniture doesn't become antique because it's built so well that it never has problems. It becomes antique because it's built so that it can be easily repaired when the inevitable problems occur.

There's no reason to believe that any of the new synthetic glues now on the market will maintain their elasticity and bonding strength well enough to make failures less inevitable. In fact, the almost universal approach of choosing glue for strength misses the point of why furniture survives. Glue strength isn't critical if the glue is at least as strong as the wood, and almost all

the commercial wood glues are. A woodworker or restorer should pick a glue that can be removed easily and with little damage to the joints, so that the furniture can be reglued effectively in the future. It's wiser, therefore, to build or repair with future repair in mind than with hopes for permanency.

I'll illustrate the point by discussing repairs of some common furniture problems. When a joint comes apart without any of its parts breaking, the obvious solution is to glue everything back together. Unfortunately, these "reglued" joints often fail within a couple of years, usually because of the old glue left in the joint. Despite warnings on the glue bottle that the wood must be clean, many workers spread new synthetic glues over the old glue, and clamp the joint back together. For a good glue bond and a long-lasting repair, it's absolutely critical that you have clean wood and tight wood-to-wood contact in the joint.

When using synthetic glue, you must remove all the old glue, which will have sealed the wood surface enough to prevent the new glue from penetrating. The best method is to use a solvent. If you scrape or sand the glue off, you'll have to remove quite a bit of wood to eliminate all the glue-sealed pores, which will result in a weaker, looser joint. Most often, the proper solvent is hot water, vinegar or a vinegar/hot water mixture. These solvents will quickly melt hide glue, which is found on almost all pre-World War II furniture. And with the help of kitchen scrubbers such as Scotch-Brite pads, hot water and vinegar will remove white and yellow glue from tenons and mortises. Be sure to let the wood dry thoroughly, at least overnight, before regluing. Most other glues are more difficult to remove, but you can try lacquer thinner on contact cement and hot-melt glue. Acetone

A loose tenon can be built out to fit its mortise by gluing on a piece of veneer or a strip of wood. Clamp the piece down with a wooden block protected from glue squeeze-out by wax paper.

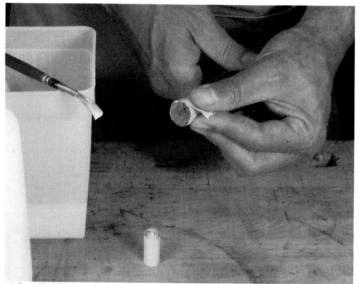

After being pulled tight to squeeze out excess glue, the curled plane shaving will hold its shape without clamps.

will sometimes dissolve epoxy or various super glues. No common solvent will remove plastic-resin glue. I chisel off the glue, then sand or scrape away any residue. Whenever glue is scraped off, the joint must be built out to give tight contact.

I use the above procedure to clean all mortise-and-tenon joints, whether they're rectangular, square or round. The biggest glue-removal problems occur with all synthetic glues. They're so much harder to remove than hide glue that I've stopped regluing with the synthetics out of concern for the person who will someday repair my work. Also, the great amount of water or other solvent needed to lift a synthetic glue can't help but damage the joint. In contrast, hide glue allows me to eliminate the cleaning step almost entirely, since new hide glue will bond well to old hide glue. The hot-water solvent for the new hide glue also dissolves the old hide glue, so the two glues melt together and become one. No other common glue that I know of has this characteristic. Clean out the old hide glue *only* when you find dirt, finish or deteriorated hide glue (which will be powdery) in the joint.

Most 20th-century furniture is made with dowels, however, and this requires a slightly different procedure, because dowels connect pieces of wood together with two separate bonds. Regluing one half of the joint doesn't guarantee a strong joint since the bond holding the other half of the dowel might fail in the near future. For this reason, unless the piece is old and valuable enough to warrant reusing the original dowels, I replace them.

Sometimes the dowels can be removed easily with pliers—tapping the end of the dowel with a hammer first will help break the glue bond. But, often, the bond won't give and the dowels

must be drilled out. In nine cases out of ten, the dowel will remain in the rail that has the same grain direction, and will separate from the leg where the grain direction runs at right angles to it—further evidence that contrary wood movement rather than weak or old glue causes failures. To drill out the dowel, first saw it off just above the surface of the wood. Take a brad-point drill bit 1/16-in. smaller than the dowel diameter and drill down the center of the dowel. Peel the last bit of dowel away from the sides of the hole with a 1/8-in. chisel, taking care not to damage the original hole. Then, clean out the hole with a drill bit matching the hole's original diameter. If there's still glue in the hole and you're regluing with a synthetic, you can wash out the old glue with solvent, or scrape it off with a needle-nose file. Scraping here doesn't damage the hole any more than the solvent.

Now and then, you'll find a tenon that doesn't fit tightly in a mortise. Filling these gaps with glue will lead to early failure. Thick glue becomes brittle and will crack under stress. You can prove this by pouring glue onto a piece of paper, letting it dry for a couple of days and bending the paper back and forth in the middle of the glue glob. If the glue is still fresh, it may bend a few times before cracking. When it's fully cured, however, it'll crack immediately. Similarly, thick glue won't withstand much wood movement or stress in a furniture joint. Tight wood-to-wood contact is critical for a strong bond—you can't glue air!

To build out a tenon, glue a thin piece of wood onto its side. For a rectangular or square tenon, use a piece of veneer of the same species of wood, or cut a thin piece from a thicker board. You want to fill the gap exactly, but if you can't get an exact fit, use a thicker-than-necessary patch and trim it down to fit the mortise. If the first patch is too thin and you have to add another, you risk weakening the joint because each additional piece makes air pockets and joint failures more likely. To ensure a good bond when attaching the veneer, clamp it tightly with a flat block of wood as shown at left, inserting wax paper between the patch and the block to prevent them from sticking together.

For a round tenon, plane a curl off a straight-grained piece of maple, cherry or other dense wood. You can control the thickness of the curl by adjusting the depth of your plane. Again, aim for too thick rather than too thin, and sand to fit. Coat the tenon with glue and wrap the curl once around, overlapping it just a little (see bottom photo, left) and tearing off the remainder. Pull the curl tight with your fingers and leave it—the curl will hold this shape without clamping. When the glue is dry, sand away any glue your fingers may have left on the surface.

Repairing loose veneer is a simpler process. Veneer comes loose because its movement is opposite to that of the surface to which it's glued, because it's been exposed to too much moisture or, most commonly, a combination of both factors. If you're using hot hide glue on an old piece that hasn't previously been repaired with synthetic glue, you need only slip a little fresh hide glue in under the veneer with something thin, like a scrap of veneer or a knife, and press it flat. Before clamping, squeeze out any excess glue so you won't have a ridge where the new glue meets the old, and use wax paper between the veneer and the flat block under the clamp.

If you're using white or yellow glue, or if the veneer has been previously glued with synthetic glue, you must remove the old glue first. The easiest way I've found is to fold a piece of 100-grit to 180-grit sandpaper in half or thirds and slide it back and forth between the veneer and the core wood while pressing on the veneer (see top photo, facing page). Continue until both sides are clean. Blow out the dust and insert the glue or inject it with a syringe. Finally, squeeze out any excess glue and clamp the veneer flat. On

curved surfaces, you'll need to shape a wood or Styrofoam caul to hold the veneer to the substrate while the glue dries.

You can use commercially available "liquid hide glue" (Franklin International, 2020 Bruck St., Columbus, Ohio 43207) to reattach veneers originally held with hot hide glue. This product is hide glue mixed with a gel depressant that enables it to be used straight from the bottle at room temperature. But liquid hide glue weakens when exposed to warm, humid weather, so it isn't a substitute for hot hide glue. It's usually strong enough, though, to hold veneer and—if it's heated first to around 140°—it'll melt together with old hide glue, making a bond with strength somewhere in between that of either type of hide glue used alone.

In my work as a restorer, I often see loose joints repaired with a nail, screw, iron bracket or other metal device. Often, these metal devices demonstrate a great deal of creativity, and many of them must have taken hours and hours to fashion. Seldom, however, have I seen one that has kept the furniture sturdy very long or failed to create additional problems. Metal doesn't respond to humidity changes the way wood does. The metal rods my friends were using, for instance, to hold the butcher block construction together ceased to have any effect after the first swelling crushed enough of the wood fibers so that the rod would never again be tight. Nails or screws through mortise-and-tenon or doweled joints do nothing to correct the failed glue bond and

To remove glue from under loose veneer, fold sandpaper in half and slide it back and forth while pressing lightly on the top surface of the veneer.

lead to the same type of damage that occurs with pinned joints.

In conclusion, furniture glue joints fail because of contrary moisture-related shrinkage and expansion of the wood in the joints. There's no way to prevent this when you have cross-grain construction. The long-term damage can be minimized, however, by considering wood movement when building or repairing furniture, and by using glue that will cause the least amount of damage when regluing inevitably becomes necessary. □

Bob Flexner repairs and refinishes furniture in Norman, Okla. His videotape, Repairing Furniture, *is available from The Taunton Press, Box 5506, Newtown, Conn. 06470-5506.*

Sacrificing strength for design

by Walter Raynes

In the last ten years, I've restored quite a few pieces of pre-1840 furniture built in Baltimore, Philadelphia and other major cabinetmaking centers of the United States. The designs of these pieces are often stunning, although the furniture itself is frequently badly damaged. It would be easy to attribute this broken condition to poor craftsmanship or normal wear and tear, but I think there's a more significant reason—the 18th-century cabinetmakers were striving for a visual effect, and they intentionally pushed wood to its structural limits. I can imagine the maker saying to himself, "I know it's weak, but it looks good and that's what I want."

This approach to furniture construction leads to what I call "acquired defects," to differentiate them from inherent defects like those Bob Flexner describes in his part of the article. The line between the two categories often blurs, but I think the division makes sense to those of us who look at furniture from primarily a cabinetmaker's point of view. I began to organize my thinking this way, largely through the influence of J. Michael Flanagan, curator of the Kaufman Collection of American Furniture exhibited recently at the National Gallery of Art in Washington, D.C.

For the 18th-century cabinetmaker, joinery was not an end in itself—it was a way to get a look. Thomas Chippendale was what we'd call today a trend-setting designer. He published catalogs of his designs and was influential in setting the style of the period. He liked chairs with ornate, delicately pierced backs and slender, curved crest rails. Because of the popularity of Chippen-

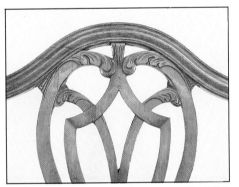

Weak cross grain on the crest rail of this old chair is prone to breakage, especially when it's mortised to accept the tenon of the chair back.

dale's designs, cabinetmakers resorted to sawn crest rails containing major sections of weak, short grain. The crest rails, not much bigger than a man's thumb, were further weakened when mortises were cut into them.

Despite the constraints of design, cabinetmakers still were using what appeared to be the best technology available to them. They used dovetails, for example, because they were the best means available for joining wood, not because they were artistic. Sometimes they cut exceptionally fine dovetails, which indicated their high level of skill, but the joints were only a means to achieve the design they wanted. For the most part, design considerations meant that there was little, if any, exposed joinery.

Considering the environment in which it was intended to be used, the furniture held

up well—despite structural weaknesses. Furniture was built in shops with basically the same environment as the homes in which it would eventually be housed, so it wasn't exposed to the drastic changes of humidity that came with the development of central heating. Many of the breaks we're repairing today have probably occurred since the introduction of central heat. The furniture that was just plain bad probably went into the fireplace not too long after it was built.

The late-18th-century Philadelphia chair shown at left is a good example of the problems created by design constraints. You can see two breaks in the short grain of the crest rail. I suspect the two breaks parallel the mortise that houses the splat tenon. The rail was already weak because of the short grain, and was weakened even more by cutting a mortise into it. It was the look the maker was after, so he had to live with the construction—potential weaknesses and all.

The splat and the crest rail also set up a cross-grain construction that may cause problems. The splat will expand and contract across the grain, but the long grain of the crest rail will restrain it. The delicate areas of the pierced splat are bound to break, as shown in the top left photo on p. 58. In addition to the possible effects of cross-grain construction, the pierced splat is also weak from a purely structural standpoint. The short-grain areas are subject to breakage, just from normal use. Once again, however, the maker created the look he wanted and allowed design to take precedence over construction.

Even when they weren't pushing the lim-

The long grain of the crest rail restrains the normal cross-grain movement of the pierced back, increasing the chances of breakage in thin, decorative elements.

Large splits shouldn't occur in floating-panel doors. But the back side of this door reveals that either glue used to attach the decorative veneer panels or shellac applied to the door locked the panels in place. Normal wood movement then split the panel.

its of a material, the 18th-century makers made mistakes. The chair leg shown in the photo at right is a good example. Instead of picking a straight-grained piece of wood, the maker chose one with grain running off at an angle. A short-grained section like this is highly subject to breakage under the stress normally found in a chair. This piece was inherently weak, and the maker should have known better. Perhaps he just ignored the problem because he didn't want to waste the wood or couldn't afford to spend the time to make another piece.

Economics had to be an issue. The early cabinetmakers in major urban centers had to be competitive, and they couldn't lavish their time on details for which people wouldn't pay. The break in the bottom photo is a good example. The problem could have been avoided by making two joints, just about where the breaks occurred, but the maker probably didn't feel he could afford to spend time cutting two joints; instead, he took a chance on the short grain. Economics probably contributed to broken bracket feet where the damage was attributed to wood movement being restrained by the cross-grain footblocks in the corner of the bracket. John Shaw, a cabinetmaker from Annapolis, Md., is known to have used parallel-grain, laminated footblocks to avoid cross-grain problems. While some makers were surely unaware of Shaw's problem-preventing construction, others undoubtedly avoided its use for economic reasons—it was faster and therefore cheaper to simply glue the footblocks.

Veneer introduced another technical problem that modern workers often fail to take into account. There was no plywood or medium-density fiberboard for substrates. Makers had to use a solid-wood substrate or build a frame-and-panel or board-and-batten substrate, leaving all sorts of joints to move

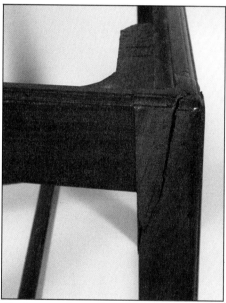

Grain running off the end of this chair post indicates a weak area that almost certainly will be pulled apart by stress on the mortise and tenon joining the rail to the post.

This delicate chair is a visual treat, but the narrow, short grain in its curved elements is prone to breakage.

and telegraph through the veneer. While veneers offered a way to avoid unpredictable moisture-related problems of highly figured woods, as well as an economical way to use the material to achieve a look, the substrate often moved enough over time to damage the overlying veneer.

The veneers themselves could contribute to a failure. The door in the photos above is a well-done frame-and-panel assembly. But it cracked—something that shouldn't happen with a floating panel. Look on the other side of the door, however, and you'll discover the problem is one of favoring design over structure. To get the look he wanted, the maker put two layers of veneer on one side of the frame and panel to form the oval decoration. Apparently, enough glue or finish seeped between the panels and the oval overlay to lock the panels in place. Shrinkage eventually caused the cracks.

The breaks and splits we see in period furniture today in no way detract from the skill, care and abilities of the original makers. And the designs continue to be a triumph. When you see a break in an old piece, it doesn't mean there's anything wrong with it, or that you shouldn't take the greatest care with its restoration. It's only logical that you'd find this type of damage—broken crest rails, cracked or shrunken slats and broken chair legs—especially on late-Federal pieces. In fact, if you didn't find evidence of this type of damage, you should feel uncomfortable about the claimed age of the piece. □

Walter Raynes builds and restores furniture in Baltimore, Md. Photos by author.

18th-century sash methods

by Eugene E. Landon

Rails and stiles meet with just a short cope; face of mortise is chiseled square.

I plane all my moldings by hand, being fortunate enough to have a good collection of old molding planes. Several profiles were used in the 18th century, and a few are shown in the drawing. You can make the coped lap joint shown here to fit any of these profiles, even ones made with a router. You don't need a matching set of planes or bits.

Really old windows and glazed doors usually had wider muntins than the narrower ones that became popular after the Revolution. I'm not sure why—perhaps because large panes of glass were difficult to make (at least in reasonably light weights), perhaps because of a carry over in methods and taste from the time when such work was done to hold wooden panels, rather than glass.

At any rate, I like the look. Hefty muntins, with their wide rabbets and substantial puttying, add a look of sculptural dignity to a door.

The 18th-century coped lap joint looks a lot more complicated to cut than it is. Cutting the squared notches is obvious—make two cuts with a dovetail saw, then break out the waste with a chisel. The drawings show the rest of the method clearer than I could explain it in words.

The main strength of this joint comes from the contact of the straight faces. You can undercut the cope itself so the miter lines will draw up airtight. In fact, when testing the fit, don't press the joint fully home until glue-up. Then, with a clamp from front to back of the joint, the sharp cope line will cut into its matching molding, and the joint will practically weld itself together. □

Gene Landon builds period reproductions in Montoursville, Penn.

You don't need matching cope-and-stick bits to make this overlapping scribed joint. More complicated shapes, such as those shown below, can be coped similarly, with just a few more straight chisel cuts to fit the outside edges.

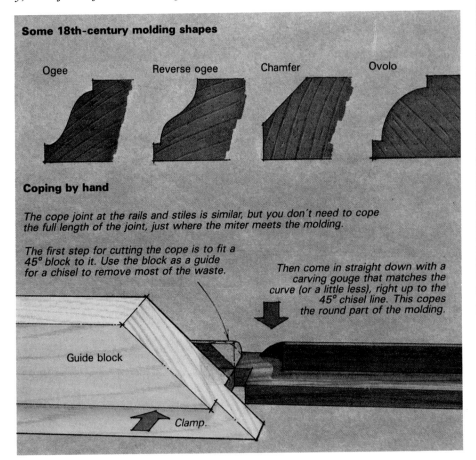

Some 18th-century molding shapes

Ogee   Reverse ogee   Chamfer   Ovolo

Coping by hand

The cope joint at the rails and stiles is similar, but you don't need to cope the full length of the joint, just where the miter meets the molding.

The first step for cutting the cope is to fit a 45° block to it. Use the block as a guide for a chisel to remove most of the waste.

Then come in straight down with a carving gouge that matches the curve (or a little less), right up to the 45° chisel line. This copes the round part of the molding.

Guide block

Clamp.

Coping with Sash

Glazed cabinet doors on shaper and tablesaw

by David R. Pine

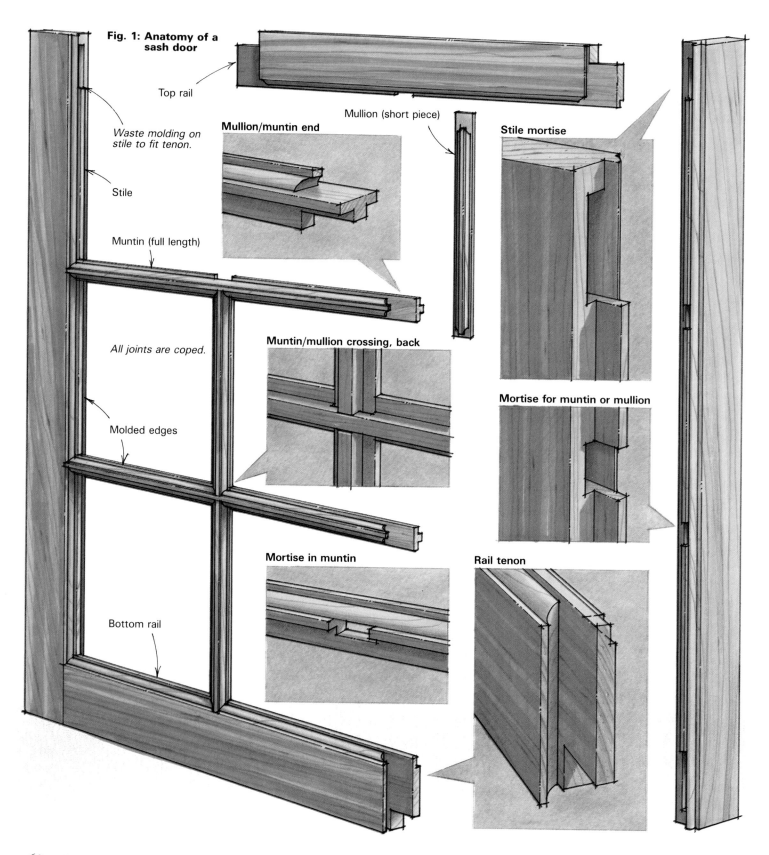

Fig. 1: Anatomy of a sash door

Top rail

Waste molding on stile to fit tenon.

Stile

Muntin (full length)

All joints are coped.

Molded edges

Bottom rail

Mullion/muntin end

Mullion (short piece)

Muntin/mullion crossing, back

Mortise in muntin

Stile mortise

Mortise for muntin or mullion

Rail tenon

From *Fine Woodworking* magazine (May 1987) 64:34-36, 38-40

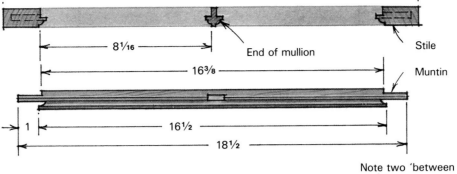

Fig. 2: Sash layout

Sash layout is made easy with just two scaled drawings: a side view through the stile and a top view through the rail.

20

8¹/₁₆

End of mullion

Stile

16³/₈

Muntin

1

16½

18½

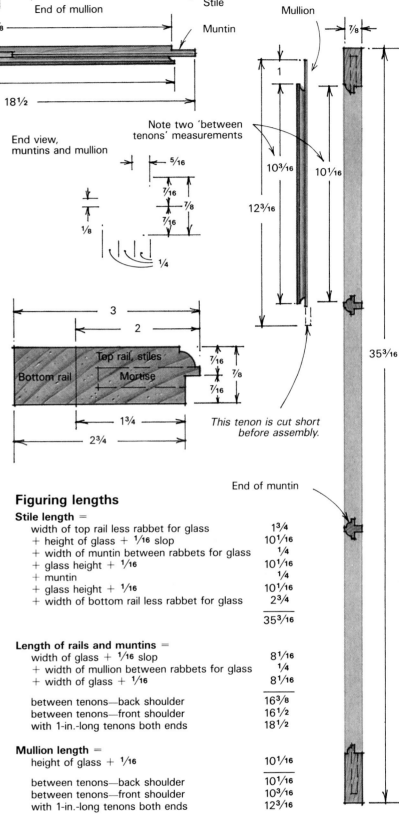

End view, muntins and mullion

Note two 'between tenons' measurements

Mullion

⁷/₈

1

10³/₁₆

10¹/₁₆

12³/₁₆

5/₁₆

7/₁₆

⁷/₈

7/₁₆

1/8

1/4

3

2

Top rail, stiles

Bottom rail

Mortise

7/₁₆

⁷/₈

7/₁₆

1³/₄

2³/₄

This tenon is cut short before assembly.

35³/₁₆

End of muntin

The ability to build a coped sash frame is a significant test of a cabinetmaker's skills. I remember the first time I set out to make a sash door. The fellow I worked for gave me the overall dimensions of the door and the specs for its design—two raised panels below the lock rail and nine "lights," or panes of glass, above it. My boss then left the shop to oversee another job. To compensate for my lack of experience, he left me a how-to book on millwork to answer all my questions.

With my mind agog with all I'd learned about stiles, rails, muntins, mullions, copes, stickers, rabbets, etc., I set out to make my door. Somehow, the book I had at hand considered the subject adequately covered when the terms were defined, leaving layout details to the reader's imagination. After much head scratching and a few sketches, I began cutting. Everything went well until after the final assembly. I decided to check to see how closely I had come to the specified 9-in. by 14-in. glass size. Lo and behold, of the three rows of three lights, one pane, the exact center one, was the right size. The corner lights were all ³/₈ in. too big. What had happened? The overall size was correct, thank goodness. More head scratching...finally it dawned on me that somehow I had neglected to allow for the rabbet on the door frame when I divided the opening into its nine equal spaces.

We went ahead and had glass cut to fit the various openings, and the discrepancy wasn't noticed by the client. I still think occasionally about the poor fellow who cuts glass to replace two or three broken panes in that door, but only checks one for size!

My second piece of sash had twenty 5-in. by 7-in. lights in it and actually came out the size I intended. Apparently, I learned from my experience. Maybe reading through the process will help you avoid some of the pitfalls when you make your first door or window. It's not so difficult, provided you're systematic and accurate. By adding a little imagination after the basics are understood, you could see your way clear to making a sash door with a router—cope-and-stick bits are readily available from many manufacturers of router bits. Prices range from around $30 at Sears to about $130 for top-of-the-line cutters from such sources as Trend-Lines and Garrett Wade.

In most applications, the uprights (stiles) are the full height of the door, and the top and bottom rails are tenoned into them. The sash bars that cross the frame opening are called muntins, or munts. Muntins usually run horizontally, which makes them the same length as the rails. Shorter pieces at right angles to the muntins are called mullions. I realize that this is not the standard terminology found in dictionaries, but these are the names everyone I know uses. The advantage is that each part has its own clear name, which helps avoid confusion, so I'd like to stick with the system throughout this article.

Traditionally, the mold worked on sash bars and frame edges was a small (about ¼ in.) quarter-round, worked directly onto the sash members—"stuck," not applied. In the days before

Figuring lengths

Stile length =

width of top rail less rabbet for glass	1³/₄
+ height of glass + ¹/₁₆ slop	10¹/₁₆
+ width of muntin between rabbets for glass	¹/₄
+ glass height + ¹/₁₆	10¹/₁₆
+ muntin	¹/₄
+ glass height + ¹/₁₆	10¹/₁₆
+ width of bottom rail less rabbet for glass	2³/₄
	35³/₁₆

Length of rails and muntins =

width of glass + ¹/₁₆ slop	8¹/₁₆
+ width of mullion between rabbets for glass	¹/₄
+ width of glass + ¹/₁₆	8¹/₁₆
between tenons—back shoulder	16³/₈
between tenons—front shoulder	16½
with 1-in.-long tenons both ends	18½

Mullion length =

height of glass + ¹/₁₆	10¹/₁₆
between tenons—back shoulder	10¹/₁₆
between tenons—front shoulder	10³/₁₆
with 1-in.-long tenons both ends	12³/₁₆

Cutting list

No.	Name	L x 2 x W x L	Comments
2	Stiles	35³/₁₆ x 2 x ⁷/₈	Mold, mortise, rabbet
1	Top rail	18½ x 2 x ⁷/₈	16½ between tenons at front, 16³/₈ at back.
1	Bottom rail	18½ x 3 x ⁷/₈	
1	Muntin	18½ x 4 x ⁷/₈	Muntin piece makes 4, need 2.
1	Mullion	12³/₁₆ x 4 x ⁷/₈	10³/₁₆ between tenons at front, 10¹/₁₆ at back. Makes 4, need 3.

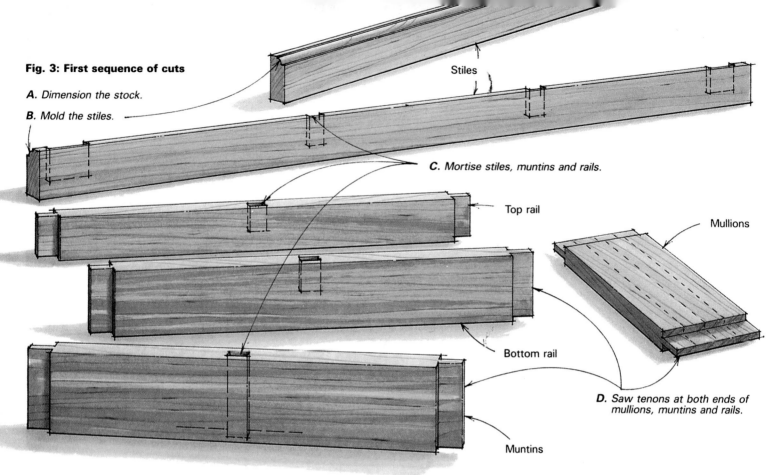

Fig. 3: First sequence of cuts

A. Dimension the stock.

B. Mold the stiles.

Stiles

C. Mortise stiles, muntins and rails.

Top rail

Mullions

Bottom rail

D. Saw tenons at both ends of mullions, muntins and rails.

Muntins

machines, muntins were sometimes full-length both ways, and crossed each other with coped lap joints (see facing page). When the machine age hit, however, it soon became clear that what I'm calling the mullions should be cut as separate pieces. This had several advantages. First, cutting the long and fragile muntins into pieces reduces the chance of breakage during machining and assembly. Second, short mullions could be made economically from scraps. Third, the hand-worked lap joint was avoided—all the undercut, or coped, joints in the door (including the rail joints) could be cut with the same machine setup.

The profile and measurements I prefer for sash bars are shown in figure 2. I think these proportions give a good sense of delicacy, yet still retain strength. My typical frame members for a cabinet door are 2 in. wide for stiles and top rails, 3 in. wide for bottom rails. Typical stock is ⅞ in. thick, or sometimes ¾ in.

To lay out sash, you need a plan drawing (with experience, you can get by with a rough sketch). Before you can begin to draw, you need to determine how much room the sash molding takes up. Sash can be made to accommodate a stock glass size (5x7, 8x10, 10x12, etc.), in which case the glass determines the sizes of the door's parts. Or, a given door size can be divided into any number of openings. This is not too difficult to work out on paper. The best approach is to make a scale drawing of the top and side edges of the sash, as shown in figure 2. Notice that I've allowed ¹⁄₁₆-in. play for the glass.

I've seen a number of drawings of windows that show the muntins running full-length from top to bottom, with the mullions horizontal. Everybody I know runs muntins from side to side—probably for the reason that many doors and windows are vertical, and you want to avoid making fragile pieces any longer than they have to be.

To successfully make sash, one must work, from start to finish, to very close tolerances. (It even helps to pass all the pieces through the planer on the same side of the bed.) Sash components must all add up to the same total if the door is to be the correct size, with all joints tight. Sometimes slight discrepancies find their

way in, but these can usually be accommodated later by making the next series of cuts to suit. The drawings and photos show a clear, logical cutting order that helps this process.

In getting out stock, choose clear, straight-grained material for sash members. It's best to dimension all the muntins as one piece. That is, they are ripped apart after being cut to length, mortised, tenoned and coped. The same is done with mullions. This means you'll be handling fewer pieces of stock through the operations, ensuring greater uniformity. Get out enough stock for two or three extra munts and mullions, however. These will be invaluable for test cuts and insurance.

After the stock is dimensioned, I mold the stiles (but not the rails yet), then lay out the positions of the mortises. With a hollow-chisel mortiser on my drill press, I mortise the stiles to accept the rails and muntins. Then, I mortise the rails and muntins to accept the mullions. Since the muntins are all together, punching a mortise clear through that one piece of stock is actually doing four or five mortises at the same time, and aligning them as well.

Next, I cut the tenons on the rails, muntins and mullions. Note that while only those mullions that enter the door frame itself need a long tenon on one end, I cut a long tenon on *both* ends of *all* the mullions. It's easier to bob them off later than it is to keep track of them throughout and make the extra cutting setups.

Notice in figure 2 that the rails, mullions and muntins all have two "between tenons" measurements—one on the top of the tenon, another on the bottom. This requires two setups, but I haven't found a good way around it. Neither of the two alternatives is satisfying—if you make the sash bars with a wider flat down the center, the sash looks clumsy; if you enlarge the rabbet for the glass, the sash is weakened excessively and may split when the glaziers' points are driven. So, cut both these "between tenons" distances exactly. Remember that a discrepancy of as little as ¹⁄₃₂ in. in the mullions can add up to ⅛ in. or ³⁄₁₆ in. over the length of a door pretty quickly. That's a big gap to fill.

The next step is to cope the top sides of the tenons. I use Delta's cope cutter #09137 (which matches their quarter-round

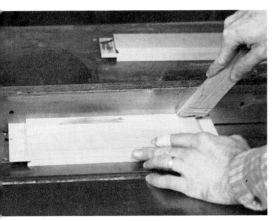

Above, stock for muntins and mullions is tenoned and undercut, or coped, to the reverse profile of the moldings before the strips are ripped to width. This, in effect, tenons and copes six mullions at once. The shaper jig, which rides in the table slot, consists of a plywood panel to support the work, and a backup rail that prevents tearout. After ripping (left), the molding profile is shaped onto the stock one edge at a time, using a featherboard to press the work to the shaper fence (right). Rabbeting is done on the tablesaw (below). The first passes cut the surfaces the glass will rest on. The second saw setting cuts the rabbet shoulders.

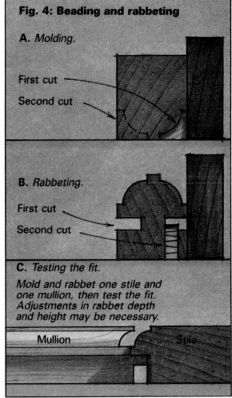

Fig. 4: Beading and rabbeting

A. *Molding.*

First cut

Second cut

B. *Rabbeting.*

First cut

Second cut

C. *Testing the fit.*

Mold and rabbet one stile and one mullion, then test the fit. Adjustments in rabbet depth and height may be necessary.

Mullion   Stile

#09136 cutter) fit on Delta's "stub" spindle, #43190. I made a small jig to slide in the shaper's table slot. This supports and backs up rails, etc., while coping tenons on their ends. Both the fence adjustment and the cutter-height adjustment are critical. Set the fence so that, with the tenons passing over the top of the spindle, the cutter just tips its flat against the shoulder you have already sawn. If the cut is too shallow, the joints won't pull up closed; if it's too deep, the distance between tenons will be altered. The other adjustment—the height of the cutter—is set to match the mold on the stiles; too high leaves a gap, too low splits the mold when the joint is closed. The flat top of the cutter should just brush the cheek of the tenon. The same setup copes rails, muntins and mullions, and you are coping the ends of a half-dozen munts and mullions at a time.

With this done, the mullions and muntins can be separated. I saw off both edges of the stock at $^{13}\!/_{16}$ in. wide, rejoint, saw off both edges and rejoint until I have enough, then pass the pieces through the planer, set at $^{3}\!/_{4}$ in., to remove the sawmarks.

Now all the remaining stock can be molded. Set up to match the stiles as closely as possible. You'll notice that the quarter-round mold will leave a feather edge around the cope if it's set up properly. Also, when the cutter crosses a mortise in rail or munt, it will leave a paper-thin slice of wood as it passes. The depth of cut should be set so that exactly $^{1}\!/_{8}$ in. is left after both sides of a muntin or mullion are cut. Keep in mind that the second pass in molding a muntin or mullion leaves only $^{1}\!/_{8}$ in. riding on the shaper table—the stock can easily tip if you aren't alert. Keep the stock held against the fence at the top where there's plenty of bearing surface, and keep your hands out of the line of the cutter. If a kickback occurs, you don't want to feed your fingertips across the cutter. You'll be glad there are no knots or snarly grained sections in your stock when doing this operation. Incidentally, it's not too hard to pass one of these pieces across the shaper on its side instead of its face, so be methodical.

The next operation is cutting the rabbet for the glass. I prefer to do this on the tablesaw. Each rabbet takes two passes. Of course, you could do it on the shaper in one, but it's a fairly deep cut ($^{1}\!/_{4}$-in. by $^{7}\!/_{16}$-in.) and likely to tear out or kick back. At this point, there isn't a whole lot of wood left on a mullion.

I use a wooden insert in the saw table that hugs the blade pretty closely. I prefer to use a smooth-cutting combination blade. Cut the face of the rabbet—the surface the glass will bear against—on all pieces first. Don't forget the stiles and rails.

Next, set up to cut the shoulders of the rabbets. This order of events leaves the widest bearing surface on the table after the second cut frees up the waste. Frankly, this is a scary operation; you won't want to be caught daydreaming should a kickback occur. The first two pieces cut will allow you to test the fit of the joints: cut one mullion, adjusting the fence setting so the center of the mullion is exactly $^{1}\!/_{4}$ in. Also, rabbet one rail or stile.

The most likely cause of an open joint is that the offset of the tenon shoulders isn't quite right. You can adjust this by making the rabbet deeper or shallower than $^{1}\!/_{4}$ in., but remember more than $^{1}\!/_{32}$-in. adjustment here will either eliminate—or double—your $^{1}\!/_{16}$-in. slop on the glass size. You may have to choose between tight joints or $7^{15}\!/_{16}$-in. by $9^{15}\!/_{16}$-in. lights. Shaving $^{1}\!/_{16}$ in. from glass isn't practical, so you'll end up paying for 9x12 lights.

To allow the joints to close, the mullion tenons must be trimmed back nearly to the cope where they abut one another in the muntins. This is a good time to cull out any pieces that are less than perfect. The other joinery work includes cutting a third shoulder on the tenons on the rails, and paring off the flat left

Coping by hand

If you don't have a shaper and want to make sash, the order of progression is a bit different. The muntins and mullions are still handled together during the mortising and tenoning operations. Then, they're ripped apart and molded and rabbeted *before* the copes are cut.

I've made a small 3-in.-long block to help lay out the copes for hand cutting. It's molded with a cove that's a reverse of the sash mold shape (this can be carved if you don't have a matching cutter). Both ends of this block are mitered off to the tip of the cove. This reveals the cope shape when the block is laid over the mold of the sash bar. Just trace it on, lay it on the other side (flipped end-for-end) and the cope is laid out.

The sash bars can be coped with—what else—a coping saw with a fine-toothed blade. Clean up with a small half-round file if necessary. Since it's not practical nor necessary to cope the whole end of a 3-in.-wide rail, common practice in hand work is to chop a cope pocket $^{1}\!/_{2}$ in. or so into the rails' ends with a gouge, leaving the rest of the tenon shoulder square, as shown in the small photo on p. 59. The stile molding has to be chopped off to accommodate the square shoulder, leaving the mold to run into the pocket, where it stops. This is also a good technique for paneled door frames.   —D.R.P.

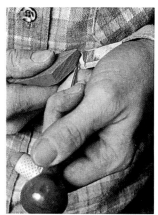 

The first step in hand coping a joint is to scribe the cope line with a 45° marking block (left). The second step is to saw to the line with a coping saw (right).

between the molding and the rabbet at the ends of the stiles.

Sand all the moldings and flats before final assembly. If you paint the tenons sparingly with glue, you'll minimize squeeze-out and save a world of cleanup time later on. Assuming good fits on your joints, you won't need to fill gaps with glue; there's already ample glue surface with all those mortises and tenons working together. Level the face and back sides of the joints with your favorite handplane, fit the door to the opening and hang. A sash door is heavy when glazed, so I allow room for the free side of a 28-in.-wide door to sag about $^{1}\!/_{16}$ in. from its own weight.

After you've applied your favorite finish (or primer to painted work), you can glaze—or put the glass in—the door. I've never seen old work that wasn't puttied, although I once used wooden strips to hold the glass instead. The project was a coffee table, and I thought the glass needed the extra support.

Putty looks much better, and isn't too difficult to learn to

A multi-paned glass door dresses up the author's walnut corner cabinet. Detail at left shows how crisp putty lines define inside surface of the glazing. The putty is tinted to match the wood.

install. Check the glass for defects or cracks, and drop each piece gently into place. Fix the glass with a glazing gun or by using glaziers' points. A piece of furniture requires that the glazing material get hard, while an exterior window or door will need glazing material that remains somewhat flexible—to allow for extremes of weather. DAP glazing compound is good for exterior work, and I use DAP Painters' Putty for furniture. The putty is white, and will need to be tinted (with earth colors ground in oil or painters' universal tinting colors) to agree with the wood of the piece. Use burnt umber and black for walnut, Venetian red and yellow ochre for cherry, raw sienna for maple, etc. The colors will make the putty too soft and gooey to use, so you'll need to stiffen it back up with ground whiting.

Getting the color right is a messy, often frustrating process, but it can be fun if you liked making mud pies as a child. Mixing is best done with a kneading action on a piece of scrap glass or Formica. Make up more than you need for a job—you'll never be able to match the color if you run out part way through. The consistency is right when a ball of the stuff will hold its shape without sagging and a putty knife pulled through it cuts cleanly

and doesn't drag. Make sure there aren't any lumps of hardened putty or areas of color variation.

To glaze a window, pull a hunk of putty off and work it into a rope shape between your palms. Use your fingers to work plenty of putty into the rabbet, then use a putty knife to force the putty into place. When you're sure it's in good and tight, wipe the knife clean on the leftover putty.

To bevel the putty, hold the putty knife diagonally, starting in one corner of the sash. In a smooth, firm motion, pull the knife toward you while holding the side of the blade against the corner of the rabbet, with the corner of the blade against the glass. Press hard. The putty should be squeezed into the space left between knife, glass and sash, with the excess pushed out and cut off by the corner of the knife and the edge of the rabbet. The angle of the blade is best determined by trial and error—you want the angle to be narrow enough so that no putty will be visible from the front of the door. Holding the handle of the knife too high above the sash tends to leave a rough surface behind the knife as it's pulled along. Finish each side by gently drawing the knife up out of the corner, then carefully remove the excess squeezed out by the knife. Go on to the next side of the light, beginning in the same corner you finished with last, and so on around the light. The corners may give you trouble at first, but they should finish up cleanly, looking as if the putty were mitered together, with a sharp crease right down the corner. You'll probably have to go over all of the corners several times to get them right.

It takes the putty several days to skin over. The sash should be left flat until then, at which point the glass can be carefully cleaned with a razor blade, and the wood with steel wool. You can wash the glass with window cleaner if you want; the spray doesn't hurt the fresh putty, only to the extent that the fresh skin will pucker and pull if you have to wipe it. It can take up to six months for putty to fully harden, but you can count on the glazing points to hold the glass in place until then. Leftover putty can be returned to the can and covered with a thin layer of raw linseed oil to prevent hardening. □

Ray Pine makes period reproductions in Mt. Crawford, Va.

Sash with matched planes

by Norman Vandal

The hardest part of making sash by hand is coping the molded pieces for a tight fit. Nineteenth-century joiners minimized this fussy cut-and-fit chore with matched planes, like the antique coping plane and mating stick-and-rabbet plane I bought years ago for $80. Since the key to tight sash is making the fillet, mortises and tenons the same thickness, the joiner would also buy chisels and gouges sized to match the plane iron. It's not so easy today; you'll probably have to make your own planes, and then grind your own chisels to match.

My basic method for sash is to make a layout stick—for rails and horizontal bars on one side, stiles and vertical bars on the other—locating mortises, fillets and any

Vandal's coping plane shapes groups of muntins to fit molded sash rails.

other pertinent features. Using a marking gauge, I transfer this information to cut-to-size clear pine or spruce stock. I chop all the mortises—whether through or blind—while the stock is square, then cut the tenons on the rails.

To cope the muntins, I clamp the pieces together on a piece of plywood, and plane them all at once. Sticking is done with the pieces supported between two rails in a long track-like jig. If you've worked carefully, the sash will lay up tight and square without glue. Just pin the joints and plane the faces before installation. □

Norm Vandal is a consulting editor for Fine Woodworking.

Barred-Glass Doors

Epoxied miters instead of tiny tenons

by Mac Campbell

There are few door treatments as decorative as barred glass. Traditionally found in large china cabinets and bookcases built in the 18th and 19th centuries, authentic barred-glass doors have been replaced in most modern furnishings by a pattern-cut plywood frame that's laid over a single pane of glass. This modern fakery is, no doubt, due to the tedious process of making the lattice for authentic barred-glass doors. Ernest Joyce, in *The Encyclopedia of Furniture Making*, details several traditional framing methods, including dovetails, veneer keys, and mortises and tenons. Since frame members are usually very thin, such joinery can quickly strain both the patience and the eyesight of the most skillful cabinetmaker.

Fortunately, modern adhesives offer an alternative to fakery and eyestrain: Quick-setting epoxy is strong enough to replace hundreds of tiny, elaborate joints at the lattice intersections with simple glued miters. This speeds up the building process tremendously. The two doors on the desk-bookcase I built, pictured on the facing page, contain 88 separate pieces of wood and 38 panes of glass, yet their construction wasn't tedious and required only reasonable care. To illustrate the improved process, I built a duplicate set of doors; the principles outlined here can be adapted to virtually any style or pattern of barred-glass door.

A barred-glass door consists of an outer door frame surrounding a lattice of straight or curved bars that meet at angles to form a decorative pattern. Each bar is made up of two layers: a rib, which divides the panes of glass, and the bar molding, which caps the rib, stiffens the lattice and acts as a stop for the glass. After the ribs are glued together with epoxy, the bar moldings are mitered and installed on top of them. The completed lattice is then set into the door frame, and the individual glass panes are fitted and held in place with glazier points and putty.

Designing the doors—You begin with a detailed drawing of the lattice pattern. The initial sketch need not be done full-scale; working out proportions is often more useful at this stage than determining exact measurements. To design the doors for the desk-bookcase, I divided the space inside the door frame into fourths widthwise, the outer fourth being split evenly on the left and right sides. Similarly, I divided the pattern in half the long way and made it symmetrical between the upper and lower halves. To simplify making the lattice, I designed the pattern so the ends of all bars need mitering at only two angles: 45° and 22½°.

Before you cut out any door parts, you must decide on the shape and size of the ribs, bars and door frame (see figure 1). Whatever molding profile is shaped on the inner edge of the door frame must also be used for the bars; otherwise, the miters will not match where the bars join the door frame. For my door, I chose ½-in.-wide bar moldings with a ¼-in. radius, half-round profile and a quarter-round with the same radius on the inside door frame. The width of the bars isn't critical, but they should be wide enough so that half the width less the thickness of the rib (joined to each bar in the middle) is adequate to conceal the glazier's points and putty that hold the glass. Since the back of the bars will be grooved to slip over the ribs for a stronger frame, I make the ribs as thick as the kerf of a carbide sawblade and groove the bars ⅛ in. deep on the tablesaw. The width of the ribs is not critical, as long as they provide enough room for the putty. I make my ribs ⅝ in. wide, which leaves ½ in. after the bars are fitted. The thickness of the assembled ribs and bars will partially determine the thickness of the door frame (see figure 1). Plan the depth of the rabbet in the door frame so the ribs will be even with the back surface of the door frame when the lattice is installed: It's not absolutely essential, but it looks better and the putty will be neater when the glass is set.

Construction—I build the door frame that will hold the lattice using standard joinery, usually mortise and tenon, though dowel or plate joinery would also work. I prefer to glue up the frame, then rout a rabbet for the glass on the back side and then rout the desired molding profile on the front. Since the router can't reach all the way into the corners, I must do some carving to square up the rabbets and face moldings, but this isn't much trouble. If you prefer, the door frame can be shaped with cope-and-stick cutters on a shaper first, then assembled—as long as you can duplicate the molding profile for the bars. Whatever your method, make each door frame true, square and flat.

After the frame is glued up, I trace the outline of the door opening at the edge of the rabbet onto a piece of plywood. This will serve as a full-size pattern of the door-frame opening and as a base for constructing the lattice. Lay out the pattern for the bars, marking their centerlines on the plywood with a pencil. The ribs will be laid out on these centerlines first, but because they're so thin, it's unnecessary to draw in their actual dimensions. Once you have the pattern drawn, darken the lines, then cover the plywood with waxed paper. This will keep the frame parts from sticking to the plywood as they're glued together.

Now you're ready to mill the rib and bar stock. This can be done with a tablesaw and a router or shaper, or with whatever combination of tools you have. It is important to mill all the lattice stock as accurately as possible, because small variations in width or thickness make getting clean joints difficult. Mill considerably more of both bar and rib stock than you think you'll need so you can discard any pieces that warp or are miscut.

A small miter box is handy for cutting the ribs and essential for

Drawings: Lee Hov

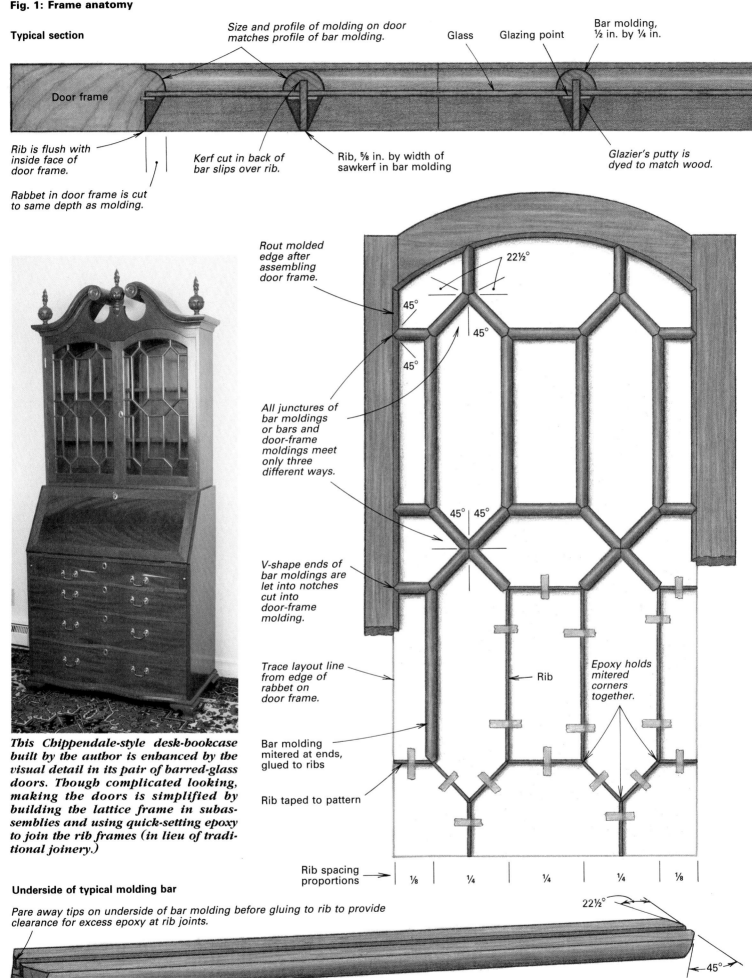

Fig. 1: Frame anatomy

Typical section

Size and profile of molding on door matches profile of bar molding.

Glass

Glazing point

Bar molding, ½ in. by ¼ in.

Door frame

Rib is flush with inside face of door frame.

Rabbet in door frame is cut to same depth as molding.

Kerf cut in back of bar slips over rib.

Rib, ⅝ in. by width of sawkerf in bar molding

Glazier's putty is dyed to match wood.

Rout molded edge after assembling door frame.

22½°

45°

45°

45°

45° 45°

All junctures of bar moldings or bars and door-frame moldings meet only three different ways.

V-shape ends of bar moldings are let into notches cut into door-frame molding.

Trace layout line from edge of rabbet on door frame.

Rib

Epoxy holds mitered corners together.

Bar molding mitered at ends, glued to ribs

Rib taped to pattern

Rib spacing proportions

⅛ | ¼ | ¼ | ¼ | ⅛

This Chippendale-style desk-bookcase built by the author is enhanced by the visual detail in its pair of barred-glass doors. Though complicated looking, making the doors is simplified by building the lattice frame in subassemblies and using quick-setting epoxy to join the rib frames (in lieu of traditional joinery.)

Underside of typical molding bar

Pare away tips on underside of bar molding before gluing to rib to provide clearance for excess epoxy at rib joints.

22½°

45°

The author made two special miter boxes to cut the angles on the ends of the ribs and bars. The box for the ribs, shown here, has a few stopped holes to provide a place for a finger to hold the thin rib steady while sawing. The other box is made the same way, with a wider groove to accept the bars.

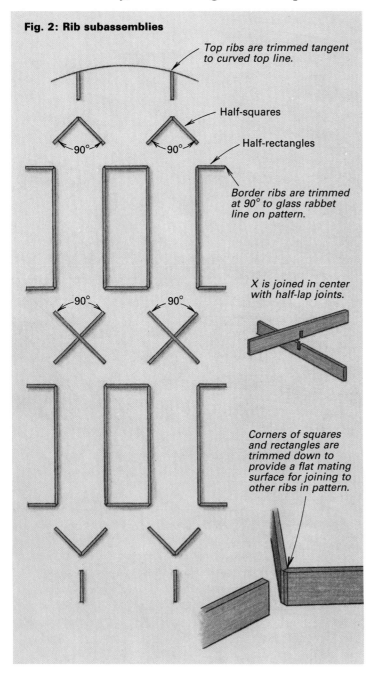

Fig. 2: Rib subassemblies

Top ribs are trimmed tangent to curved top line.

Half-squares

90°   90°

Half-rectangles

Border ribs are trimmed at 90° to glass rabbet line on pattern.

X is joined in center with half-lap joints.

90°   90°

Corners of squares and rectangles are trimmed down to provide a flat mating surface for joining to other ribs in pattern.

cutting the more complex miters on the ends of the bars. I made up two miter boxes just for the job: one for cutting ribs and one for the bars. Cut a channel in each miter box to hold each type of stock snugly and slot the boxes for cutting 90°, 45° and 22½° angles with the finest saw you have. (I use a 21-t.p.i. dovetail saw.) Drill several large stopped holes in the rib miter box so your fingers can hold the thin stock while it's being cut.

Rib subassemblies – Instead of cutting and gluing up the lattice of ribs as a series of separate pieces, it will simplify the joinery and speed up the construction if you consider the lattice pattern as a set of connecting geometric shapes: rectangles, squares and X's (see figure 2). In my pattern, the upper half of the door has a large rectangle in the center and two half-rectangles on each side. These are connected on top by half-squares that form the top points. The lower half of the window is designed the same way, with the top and bottom halves joined by two X's.

The rectangles and squares are constructed with simple glued-miter corner joinery. After the four pieces, say for a rectangle, have been cut to length and mitered, lay a strip of masking tape sticky-side-up on a sheet of waxed paper taped to the workbench. Place the four parts of each rectangle outer-face-down on the tape with their ends just meeting, and align each rectangle with a straightedge. Leave some extra tape at one end. Mix a small batch of five-minute epoxy, butter all the joints and fold the ribs together, as shown in the top, left photo on the facing page. Close the last joint with the tape that's left sticking out, and put a small weight on the glued assembly to keep it flat as it sets. If the miters are accurately cut, the rectangles will square themselves, but check by measuring the diagonals, just to be sure. Prepare all the rectangles and squares this way, and remove the tape when the glue has dried.

Cut two of the rectangles in half on their short sides, and cut the two squares apart at opposite corners. Lay these components on the pattern board. The corners of the rectangles will have a rib joining them at 45°, as will the corners of the half-squares. Chamfer these corners to create a flat for a butt joint with the rib. I use a disc sander for this, eyeballing the angle, but a sharp paring chisel will work just as well. Each of the two X's for each door are joined in the middle with half-lap joints. Cut these joints to fit snugly, then trim the ends of the X's to fit the pattern. After a section of the pattern is trimmed and fitted, mix up a batch of epoxy and glue the separate components together, then tape them down to the pattern board with masking tape to keep them in place.

After the entire rib frame is done, check to see that the ribs that meet the door frame are flush with the edge of the line that marks the glass rabbet. Trim and square these if necessary, and test-fit the door frame over the assembled ribs. The door frame should fit over the ribs securely, and it's better to have it a little tight than to end up with gaps between the ribs and frame. Wherever epoxy has squeezed up above the top edge of the ribs at the joints, sand it down flush, using a sanding block to keep things flat. Don't worry about squeeze-out around the rest of the joint; the putty will cover everything nicely when the glass is set.

Fitting the bars – The bars are fitted on top of the ribs next. As you can see in the drawing on p. 67, there are only three possible ways the bars meet in the lattice and only two possible end angles to cut: 45° or 22½°. Start with any rib in the pattern and mark and cut the two miter cuts on one end of a length of bar stock. Lay the bar on top of the rib and follow the centerline of the rib to mark the miter angle with a sharp pencil at the juncture of the ribs in the point of the miter. With the special miter box, cut the

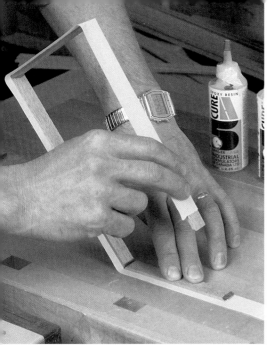

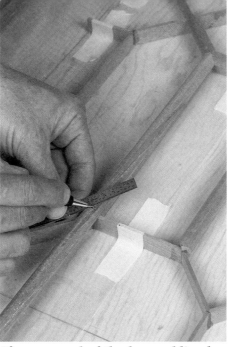

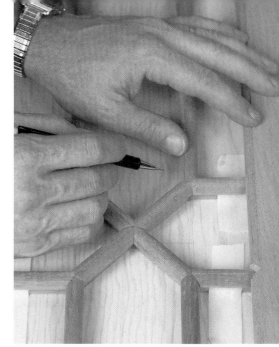

Gluing up the ribs in a series of subassemblies is more accurate and faster than gluing the ribs together individually. Once the parts are cut to length and mitered, they're stuck to tape, the joints are buttered with five-minute epoxy and the parts are rolled up to form the subframe – in this case, a rectangle.

After one end of the bar molding has been mitered and fitted into the pattern, the other end can be marked. Using a pencil and ruler, sight where the point of the miter will be (the final length of the bar), and indicate on each half of the mitered point whether it's to be cut at 45° or 22½°.

After the bars have been glued to the ribs, the molding on the door frames must be notched out to accept the mitered ends of the outer bars. Lay the door frame over the lattice and mark each bar's centerline. Saw or chisel out each notch, cutting it a little undersize at first and then trimming to fit.

two miters so they intersect where your pencil marks cross. Mark the other end the same way (see the middle photo above), making sure the already-trimmed end is butted tightly into its corner. Fit the bar in place and continue on with an adjoining piece. For the bars that will meet the door frame, cut two 45° miters on their outer ends. The points formed by these cuts should just reach the end of the underlying ribs. Remove the masking tape holding the ribs to the plywood as you go along, replacing it as necessary to keep everything lined up. It's likely that some bars won't fit all the way over the ribs because of glue squeeze-out in the corner. Rather than trying to remove the hardened epoxy, relieve the miter tip next to the dado groove on the bottom of the molding (putty will cover this later).

I don't glue any of the bars on until the entire pattern is done, but you can glue as you go along if you prefer. To glue the bars, I use regular aliphatic-resin (yellow) glue—it's more than strong enough and it makes removing squeeze-out easier. Once all of the bar moldings are glued down, take a few minutes and clean up any squeeze-out. Then, sand the faces of all joints flush and trim the edges of any moldings that don't line up.

To fit the assembled lattice into the door frame, first lay the frame on top of the lattice. The glass rabbet should be resting on the pointed ends of the bar moldings. Mark each bar's mitered end on the molded edge of the door frame (see top, right photo above). Remove the frame from the lattice and cut out the mitered notches in the door-frame molding with a dovetail saw, leaving them undersize for the time being. Untape the lattice from the base and place it into the door frame. Now, carefully saw down through the miters with a very thin saw (a razor saw is best), angling it slightly so the two pieces will fit together snugly. Repeat this process around the door and gradually work the bars into a good, snug fit. Alternatively, the notches in the door-frame molding can be trimmed with chisel and guide block ("18th-century sash methods," p. 59). Whatever method you choose, try to avoid having to fill the joint later, as this will spoil the clean look of the bars flowing smoothly into the door frame. When everything

is ready, glue the lattice into the door frame with yellow glue. Even though every joint is endgrain, I don't use epoxy for this final assembly, mainly because its open assembly time is so short and the strength of yellow glue is more than adequate for the job.

A barred-glass door with curved bars is made up in much the same way as the method described above. Because they are reinforced by the thicker bar moldings, the thin, curved ribs may be bandsawn instead of bent. The stock for the bars is bent-laminated around a form, then shaped with a router or shaper, as with straight stock. One difference from straight bars is that the dado on the back of a curved bar must be cut with a router, not a sawblade. It's easiest if the router is mounted in a table for this operation, and you'll want to match the thickness of the ribs to the bit you'll use. Also, cutting the miters is trickier than with straight stock, because you can't use a miter box. A sharp paring chisel or knife and some patience will do the trick.

Glass and putty – Once the door has been hung on the cabinet and is completely finished (lacquered, oiled, etc.), it is ready for the glass. Beveled glass is often seen on period pieces, but it's expensive, and I think the lattice gives the door more than enough visual interest. You can take the doors to a glass shop and have them cut plain glass panes to fit, or you can give the shop cardboard patterns to work from. If you make patterns, leave about 1/16-in. clearance to the frame on each side and make sure to mark which pattern fits which opening—in case there are variations in the frame. Unless you're an experienced glass cutter, let the pros handle this tedious job. The glass is held in place first with glazier's points, and then it's glazed with putty colored to match the frame wood. David Pine gives an excellent outline of this process on p. 65.

Once completed, barred-glass doors add a distinctive elegance to casework. They reward the effort required to build them generously, setting a piece well apart from the average run. □

Mac Campbell owns Custom Woodworking in Harvey Station, N.B.

A set of 1-2-3 blocks can serve as a means of setting up machine tools. For instance, it can be used to set a radial-arm saw's depth of cut, check a jointer's fence for squareness or set a tablesaw's rip fence, as shown here.

1-2-3 Blocks
Measuring less and enjoying it more

by David L. Wiseley

"I cut it twice and it's still too short. Where's the board stretcher?" Humor does little to blunt the sick feeling that strikes when you realize you've just measured wrong and cut a piece too short. I was all too familiar with this feeling until I learned how to reduce woodworking mistakes by reducing the amount of measuring I did in my shop. Reaching back to my early days as a die maker, I remembered a great way to cut back my dependence on a measuring tape: 1-2-3 blocks.

A standard tool used by tool-and-die makers, 1-2-3 blocks are a set of three hardened-steel, rectangular gauge blocks machined exactly 1 in. thick by 2 in. wide by 3 in. long. Individually or stacked together, the blocks serve as distance standards for marking out or checking dimensions with great accuracy. Also, by using 1-2-3 blocks instead of a tape or ruler, you eliminate the possibility of making errors by misreading the scale, and you can focus more mental energy on the project instead of worrying about measurements. You can buy a set of gauge blocks from a machinist supply house, but they are expensive, so I'd recommend making your own from wood. A set of wooden 1-2-3 blocks probably won't be as precise or durable as a steel set, but they should satisfy the demands of most woodworking projects.

Making a set—To make your own blocks, start with a 2-ft. length of any dense, stable hardwood, like kiln-dried maple or oak, and thickness plane a narrow ¾ board down until it's exactly 1 in. thick. Make sure the thickness is consistent on both edges of the board; if it isn't, your planer knives probably aren't parallel to the bed and need adjustment. Next, joint one edge of the board straight and square, and rip the board into a strip that's about 2¹⁄₁₆ in. wide. Then on the jointer or with a handplane, plane the rough edge until it's square and the strip is exactly 2 in. wide. Finally, using either a radial-arm saw or a miter gauge on the tablesaw, slice the strip into 3-in. lengths. Make a test cut on a scrap to ensure the blade is cutting the ends perfectly square.

Before using your new set of 1-2-3 blocks, you need to check them for accuracy. Check all the corners of each block for squareness with an accurate try square, then check all the block dimensions. A dial or vernier caliper is ideal for this, but you can get by with just a fine-line ruler or tape measure if that's all you have. If necessary, trim the blocks to final size using a fine-grit disc on a disc sander. Avoid using a disc with a foam-rubber backing pad, as this can distort the squareness of the blocks. You can also use a block plane for trimming if you prefer. Set the

1-2-3 blocks are a handy alternative to measuring with a ruler or tape measure. Here, a stack of blocks that's 4 in. high is held against a board, on edge on the workbench. The line is marked as the stack is slid along the board.

Used in conjunction with 1-2-3 blocks, plywood spacers allow fractional distances to be marked. Shown here, distances between spacer sizes can be marked by shimming the workpiece and subtracting that distance from the marking-block stack.

Another method for marking fractional distances uses square-steel tool bits—cutters commonly used on the metal lathe. By grinding the tip to a bevel and using it on top of 1-2-3 blocks, the tool bit serves as both a spacer and a marking knife.

plane for a fine cut: If you take too much off, you'll need to start over. Try to get the blocks within a few thousandths of an inch of the proper dimensions. When the individual blocks are done, stack the blocks, re-check their measurements for cumulative error and do any final trimming as necessary. Finally, chamfer all edges and corners of the blocks slightly, smoothing them with fine sandpaper. Finishing them isn't necessary, but you can apply a light oil finish or wax them if you wish.

Marking out—While it may take time and patience to make a set of 1-2-3 blocks accurately, they're not difficult to use. To mark a line on the face of a board 1 in. from the edge, say for laying out a line inlay, stand the board on edge on top of the workbench and butt a 1-in.-high block against it. Now lay the point of a marking knife or razor-sharp pencil on top of the block, as shown in the above, left photo, and slide the block along the board to mark the line. For marking distances greater than the length of a single block, blocks can be stacked in any combination to produce the required distance. For instance, you can locate a series of holes 6 in. from the edge of a carcase side, say for adjustable shelves, by laying two 1-2-3 blocks end to end. With a set of four or more 1-2-3 blocks, you can quickly locate mounting holes for hardware, lay out tenons or mortises, or mark guidelines for truing an edge with a handplane—all without a measuring tape.

If you want to check or lay out distances that are not whole numbers, fractional dimensions can be laid out using 1-2-3 blocks in combination with either plywood scraps or machinist's tool bits. For the plywood method, cut some 2-in. by 3-in. spacers from different thicknesses of plywood. Since standard plywoods don't come in all the thicknesses you may need and usually aren't precisely thicknessed, you'll have to do a little surface planing or sanding to make each spacer the exact thickness you desire.

I keep a set of plywood spacers handy in a drawer next to the bench where I do my lay-out work. To locate a line 2⅜ in. from an edge or other reference point, use the 2-in. side of a 1-2-3 block along with a ⅜-in. plywood spacer. Place the block on the spacer and scribe along the top. You can also use scraps of plywood to lay out distances less than 1 in. To mark lines at distances that don't correspond with your spacer set, shim up the workpiece, as shown in the above, middle photo. The thickness of the spacer under the workpiece is subtracted from the height of the 1-2-3 block and its spacer for the final marking distance. Admittedly, this is a little clumsy and you may prefer to use a marking gauge for such marking operations, but once you get the hang of using blocks

and spacers, my method is quick and accurate.

The second method, which I learned in a tool-and-die shop where I once apprenticed, uses tool bits: square-steel blanks normally used as cutters on a metal lathe. Tool bits are available from most machinist supply houses for about $1 to $3 per bit; you'll want at least one each in ¼-in., ⁵⁄₁₆-in., ⅜-in. and ½-in. sizes. Before using, grind a 45° bevel diagonally across one end of each tool bit, so a point is formed on the end. This point is used like the point on a marking gauge to scribe a very fine line that's in line with one surface of the tool bit (see the above, right photo). With a set of tool bits and four 1-2-3 blocks you can lay out any fractional size, from 0 in. to 12 in., in ¹⁄₁₆-in. increments. For instance, to lay out a line 2⁵⁄₁₆ in. from the edge of a board, stack a ⁵⁄₁₆-in. tool bit on top of a 2-in. block, then use the bit's sharp end to scribe the workpiece.

The tool bits also have several uses of their own. One that saves me lots of time and frustration is locating the center of the width of a board without measuring. On ¾ stock, simply lay the board flat on the bench and scribe a line along the edge with the ⅜-in. tool bit slid along the benchtop. Flip the board over and scribe a second line on the same edge. If the board is a little thicker or thinner than ¾ in., then there'll be two lines very close together. The center of the board is exactly half way between those two lines. If the lines are too far apart, a piece of thin cardboard under the tool bit makes a useful shim.

Other uses—Besides helping with marking jobs, 1-2-3 blocks can be used for positioning or spacing parts for assembly. The overhang of a tabletop and cabinet top can be a pain to measure accurately if the edges of the underside have been rounded over. With the table upside down, place four blocks, one on each side, against the apron and slide the top around until you can feel that the overhang is equal on all sides.

Machines can be set using the 1-2-3 blocks instead of a ruler. The homemade cut-off stop on the right side of my radial-arm saw fence is easier to set with 1-2-3 blocks than trying to see under the saw motor to read a scale. I use blocks for quickly setting the rip fence on my tablesaw, as shown in the photo on the facing page. Because the blocks' edges are square, I also use them to check the squareness of the sawblade relative to the table, as well as fence-to-table squareness on my jointer. □

David Wiseley runs House of Woodworking, which makes hardwood home and office accessories in Waters, Mich.

Wall Paneling
General application and design principles

by Graham Blackburn

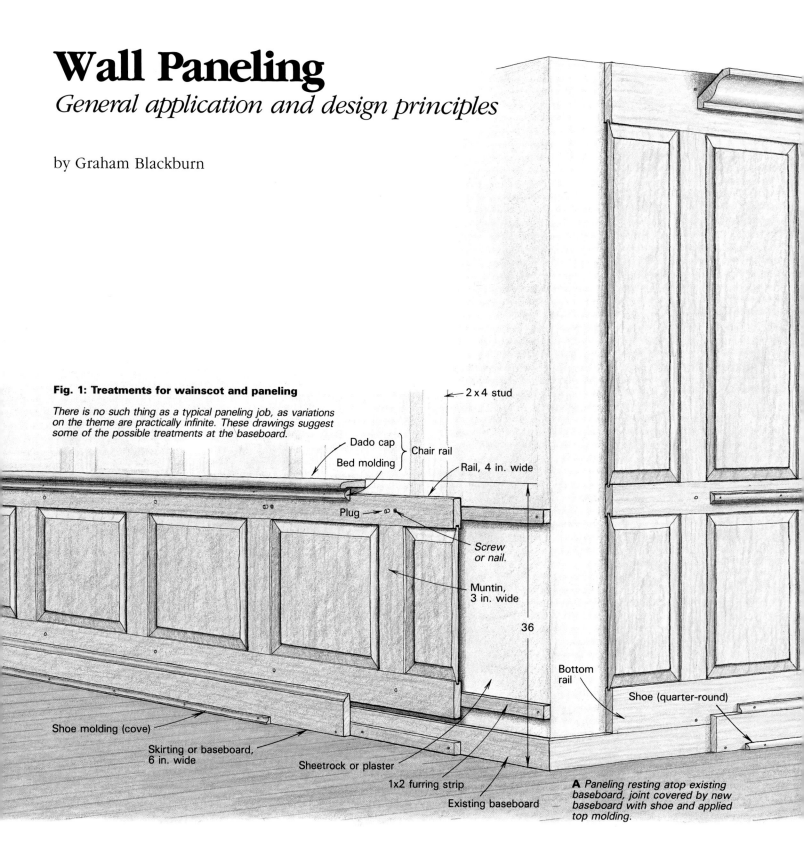

Fig. 1: Treatments for wainscot and paneling

There is no such thing as a typical paneling job, as variations on the theme are practically infinite. These drawings suggest some of the possible treatments at the baseboard.

2 x 4 stud

Dado cap / Bed molding } Chair rail

Rail, 4 in. wide

Plug

Screw or nail.

Muntin, 3 in. wide

36

Bottom rail

Shoe (quarter-round)

Shoe molding (cove)

Skirting or baseboard, 6 in. wide

Sheetrock or plaster

1x2 furring strip

Existing baseboard

A *Paneling resting atop existing baseboard, joint covered by new baseboard with shoe and applied top molding.*

Paneling came into general use as a form of interior decoration for walls during the latter part of the Middle Ages. Because of its infinite adaptability, paneling is a practical form of wall covering even today. Admittedly, one immediately thinks of older architectural styles—Colonial or Georgian, for example—but, used in the right way, paneling can be just as appropriate for the most modern setting, whether it be a boardroom needing tasteful dignity, or a small apartment looking for a way to disguise a Murphy bed.

The elements of a paneled wall—both half-paneling known as "wainscot" and full floor-to-ceiling paneling—are illustrated in drawings throughout this article. Essentially, paneling is a modular system in which solid-wood panels are held in grooves in a mortised-and-tenoned frame composed of rails (the horizontal members) and stiles (the full-length, vertical ones). The short framing members between rails are called "muntins." The grooves in the framing allow the panels to expand and contract with changes in relative humidity, and the frame also keeps the panels from warping.

The system is modular because it consists of a series of repeating elements that can be added or subtracted, depending on the space to be covered. These elements needn't be entirely regular—they can be modified in size and shape to conform to fireplaces, windows, beams, doors, etc. as required.

Turning corners

Although inside corners may simply be butted and covered with molding, a tongue-and-groove joint is more secure and makes assembly alignment easier.

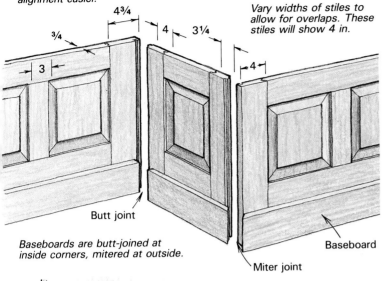

Vary widths of stiles to allow for overlaps. These stiles will show 4 in.

Butt joint

Baseboards are butt-joined at inside corners, mitered at outside.

Baseboard

Miter joint

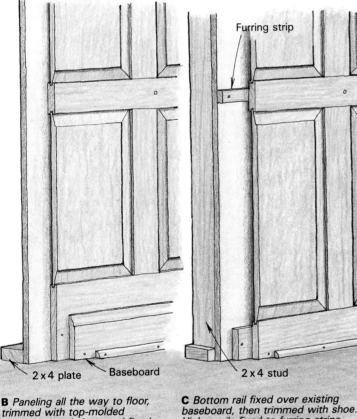

Furring strip

2 x 4 plate   Baseboard

2 x 4 stud

B *Paneling all the way to floor, trimmed with top-molded baseboard and shoe, and fixed through wall to plate.*

C *Bottom rail fixed over existing baseboard, then trimmed with shoe. Higher rails fixed to furring strips screwed or nailed to wall framing.*

Changes in architectural style and interior decoration have dictated the form of paneling in various eras. To mention just a few outstanding styles, there are the distinctive linenfold patterns of the late Gothic, the graduated rectangular panels of the Tudor period, the panels-within-panels of the Jacobean era and the pilastered and classically friezed panels of the 18th century. These characteristic forms may appear to be the dominant element in any particular type of paneling, but all are usually based on certain fundamental principles of design. When you know how to recognize them, these principles constitute the intrinsic "rightness" and success of a paneled wall in any style.

It would be a great pleasure to design a paneled wall of per-

fect proportion and symmetry, and then have a contractor stop by and build the house around it. Such, of course, is seldom the case. Whatever overall plan of design we decide upon, it must usually accommodate existing windows, doors, electrical outlets and switches, plus out-of-plumb and irregular surfaces. In the drawings, I've tried to suggest a number of ways of dealing with such things.

Before I go further, there are two points I must emphasize. First, it's the overall pattern of the paneling that must prevail if the wall is to be successful. If inconsistencies take over a major part of the job, the wall will look disjointed and inharmonious. Second, keep in mind that paneling a wall is a major project, deserving much forethought and preparation. Before beginning construction, produce as detailed a drawing as you can. This will help identify potential problems. If an unusual window presents a great disruption, for example, consider replacing it. The same is true for outlets and switches with inconvenient spacing or height—it may be less work to move them than to force the design around them, and the end result will look far better. This isn't to say that you must keep the design entirely regular. A wall that is too uniform can look "manufactured," while a wall with tasteful minor variations looks "tailored" and is all the better for it.

There are several ways to go about setting the proportions of the elements in a paneled wall. In the Middle Ages, craftsmen depended on mathematical theory and geometry to create design systems based on whole numbers and their relationships to straightforward forms, such as the square and the circle. As the guilds became more sophisticated, subtler ideas evolved, such as the ratio of the "golden mean" (or "golden section," as it's sometimes called), which I'll explain in more detail later. The Renaissance saw the reintroduction of classical Greek and Roman proportionalism, and this found its way into the design theory practiced by 18th-century joiners and cabinetmakers in the form of "the five orders of architecture." Such study can become extremely technical and is beyond the scope of this article, but those interested in pursuing the topic will find references in the books listed in the "Further reading" bibliography, p. 77. The most useful, pragmatic fact to remember about design is that, unless you have an "absolute eye" for what is aesthetically right (like certain musicians have absolute pitch), success will come only if you arrive at your design by way of some rational approach.

Look at the whole space, not just the area to be paneled. Try to imagine what will tie the whole thing together. If a room is broken up by a variety of windows and doors with varying heights and proportions, try designing the paneling so that part of it, such as a visually strong top rail and crown molding, stretches across the entire length of the wall. This molding can then be carried around the entire room, even if the paneling is not. If this isn't possible, try designing the paneling either with a strong regularity or with one particularly salient member—the wainscot shown in figure 1 is a good example. Its chair rail is a powerful enough feature visually to unify the design. Doors and windows will appear as relatively unimportant interruptions in a predominantly regular plan. Similarly, bookshelves adjacent to a paneled wall can have their shelves aligned with the rails, and may be able to carry unifying moldings.

Of course, if the basic space already possesses its own pleasing rhythm, such as a wall with a fireplace in the middle and two equally spaced windows on either side, then it makes sense to design the paneling around the existing pattern, for the space is already tied together.

The design should look balanced and stable, not as if it were

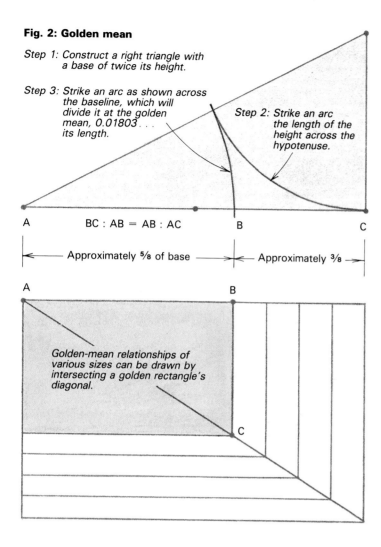

Fig. 2: Golden mean

Step 1: Construct a right triangle with a base of twice its height.

Step 3: Strike an arc as shown across the baseline, which will divide it at the golden mean, 0.01803... its length.

Step 2: Strike an arc the length of the height across the hypotenuse.

A   BC : AB = AB : AC   B   C

Approximately ⅝ of base ———— Approximately ⅜ ——

Golden-mean relationships of various sizes can be drawn by intersecting a golden rectangle's diagonal.

golden mean is simply the division of a line at such a point that the smaller part is to the larger part as the larger part is to the whole. This translates into dividing the line at roughly five-eighths of its length. By using one part as the width and the other as the height you will construct a "golden rectangle." There are several ways of arriving at the golden mean of any given line; one of the easiest is shown in figure 2.

Having decided on a general overview of how the area should be divided up (two of the countless possibilities include: a thin row of panels at the top, a wider one in the middle and, perhaps, the widest row at the bottom; or, two narrow columns of panels flanking windows, with a much wider column of panels in the center) it's now necessary to delve into greater detail and decide the relative dimensions of the various framing members. The variations are endless, and the best way to start getting an idea is to study all the examples you can find, both in real life and in pictures in books. Key points to look for are the width of the stiles in relation to the width of the various horizontal pieces; and the width of the horizontal *and* vertical members in relation to the size of the panels themselves.

After a while, you'll begin to notice a few trends, which can be expressed as generalities only (there are always justified exceptions). Stiles tend to be equal in width, while rails are often graduated in width, from the bottommost ones to the top ones. Furthermore, the upper rails are frequently the same width as the stiles, and the panels are usually no narrower than the combined width of two stiles. Outside stiles look best if they are somewhat wider than any inside stiles, and yet at corners—both inside and outside—the width of the stiles may be somewhat reduced, since the combined effect of two regular-width stiles would appear excessive.

I must stress that these proportions are generalizations only. There are also optical "tricks" that can change how things look. For example, the use of molded edges on the framing members creates extra lines of shadow and makes the framing members look narrower. Similarly, overlapping bolection moldings make both the frame members and the panels look narrower. Another extremely potent factor is the design of the panels themselves.

Panels can be simply flat, but it's more common to bevel the edges to produce a central "field." This field can also be "raised" by having a vertical shoulder, as shown in figure 3. Fielded panels can be made to look quite different by changing the width of the beveled areas. Try designing the same size panel with a very wide margin and then a very narrow margin, and observe the difference.

Internal proportions must relate to other features in the room, such as the size of any door panels or window trim. A framing system with very narrow framing members surrounding windows

about to topple over. This balance can be achieved by using heavier or bigger parts at or near the bottom. For wall paneling, this means making the skirting (or baseboard) the widest member or, perhaps, designing a chair rail to be visually strong by making it wider or more heavily molded. Chair rails are typically about 36 in. from the floor; their purpose is to protect the paneling from chair backs. Paneling doesn't always require a rail at this height, however, as can be seen in figure 6.

A more sophisticated plan, and one particularly well-suited to the problem of how to divide up an area into the typically smaller parts required by paneling, is to base the arrangement—even loosely—on the golden mean. This is a ratio discovered by the Greeks and used ever since by artists, sculptors and architects as a kind of pattern on which to base their designs. In its basic form, the

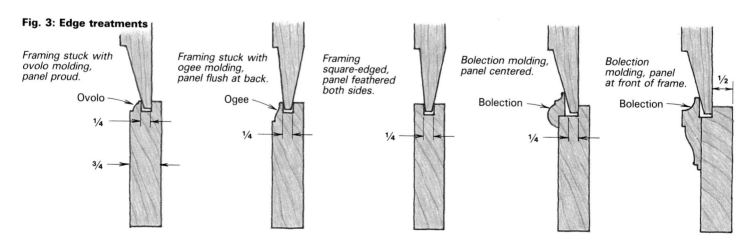

Fig. 3: Edge treatments

Framing stuck with ovolo molding, panel proud.

Ovolo

¼

¾

Framing stuck with ogee molding, panel flush at back.

Ogee

¼

Framing square-edged, panel feathered both sides.

¼

Bolection molding, panel centered.

Bolection

¼

Bolection molding, panel at front of frame.

Bolection

½

Laying out Georgian-style paneling

by Malcolm MacGregor

As it was two centuries ago, wall paneling should be considered the focal point of a treasured room, such as a formal parlor or a library. It's possible, of course, to panel an entire room floor to ceiling—and even panel the ceiling itself—but I advise my customers against it. Besides its huge expense, a fully paneled room is too much of a good thing. It's visually overwhelming and not very pleasant to be in. Instead, I prefer to panel only one wall of a room floor to ceiling, then tie it to the rest of the room visually by installing wainscot or a simple chair rail on the adjacent walls and running the cornice around the room.

In the mid-18th-century New England houses I often work in, the Georgian style—with its classically derived moldings and architectural elements—was quite popular, so most of my paneling follows Georgian design principles. As with any period, Georgian spans a stylistic range. At its most modest, a Georgian paneled room might be rather plain, with no architraves and only a simple crown molding topping off the paneled wall. More elaborate walls will include fluted pilasters flanking a formal fireplace, doorways with gabled pediments and the formal double-crown molding shown in the drawing. Typically, New England mid-Georgian design is strongly vertical, with two rectangular panels extending upward from the floor. Sometimes, a squarish median panel separates the two vertical panels. In either case, the baseboard is almost always rather plain.

Paneled walls traditionally have a visual focal point that anchors the design. In Georgian rooms, this is usually a fireplace around which the most complex elements (pilasters, bolection or multi-part moldings forming an elaborate architrave or a complex pediment, for example) are clustered. To either side of this center, the design is deliberately less busy, thus drawing the eye to the most interesting parts of the wall.

I begin a paneling job by very carefully measuring the floor-to-ceiling height at several points along the wall, as well as the side-to-side distance. With a 4-ft. level, I check the walls for plumb and floors for level, recording my findings in a notebook as I go. If the floor is relatively level, I chalk a level reference line on the wall that roughly represents the paneling's center rail. All vertical measurements can then be made from this line to establish the overall height of the panel section and the location of each rail. Similarly, one of the adjacent walls (or a plumb line drawn on it) can serve as a reference plane to lay out the position of various elements in the wall.

If the floor is way off—say 1½ in. in the run of the wall—I adjust my reference line to

Georgian cornice

3-in. to 4-in. crown

2 in. to 4 in.

Fascia

3-in. bed molding

Soffit

2 x 4s nailed to wall and ceiling

3½ in. to 4 in. showing

Top rail

Uppermost panel

Panel

Typical architrave detail

Molding

4

4

Wall

Door jamb

Door

split the difference. It's far more important that the wall be straight and square with the room—minor variations in plumb and level are easily masked by moldings or trim at the paneling's edges. By far the best way to account for structural inaccuracies is to install the paneling *before* the adjacent drywall and floor are installed. This is especially true in Georgian panel systems, because the bottom rail often doubles as the baseboard. It's much easier to lay the floor up to the rail than to scribe the rail to an uneven floor.

I draw my paneling design to scale on graph paper. Before figuring panel sizes and proportions, I decide upon the size and profile of the architraves surrounding the fireplace and/or doors, since the space between these fixed elements determines how much room I'll have for the panels themselves. The drawing shows one way to mate an architrave to the paneling. An architrave can be as simple or elaborate as you like, but in the interest of visual harmony, I try to make the combined width of molded sections closely match the width of the floor-to-ceiling stiles, which are usually about 4 in. to 4½ in. wide. I make the intermediate stiles (also called "muntins") 4 in. wide.

In Georgian walls, there's one critical horizontal alignment that's rarely violated: The paneling's center rail almost always aligns with—and is the same width as—the lock rail on the doors in the room. With this rail and the architraves drawn in as inflexible elements, I begin sketching in the paneling. I rely heavily on books for inspiration, but from the research I've done, I've settled on some favorite designs. Rooms with 7-ft. ceilings look best with two vertical panels, the top panel being about 1½ times the length of the bottom panel. In two-panel walls, I generally make the bottom rail 6 in. to 7 in. wide, the center rail 7½ in. to 8 in. wide (or to match the lock rails) and the top rail 3½ in. to 4 in. wide, exclusive of the crown molding.

Higher ceilings work well with three panels. In this case, what would normally be the center rail is split into two separate rails—the top one about 5 in. wide, the lower about 4 in. wide. A panel that's slightly wider than its length fits between the rails. Horizontal panels, such as the large ones above a fireplace, usually line up with the outer sides of the architrave, not the opening in the wall. Panel widths as narrow as 4½ in. are practical, but I never make them wider than 20 in.; seasonal shrinkage across that much wood can pop the panels out of their grooves.

The rails, stiles and panels are made in the shop, dry-assembled and carried into the room in sections. The sections are tacked to the wall to check for fit. The joints between sections should occur at floor-to-ceiling stiles. There's usually enough give in the paneling so that the tenons between sections can be slipped into their respective mortises as the panels are attached to the wall. Smaller sections of paneling can be assembled face-down on the floor and lifted into position. □

Mal MacGregor runs Piscataqua Architectural Woodwork in Durham, N.H.

that have totally different trim proportions and molding treatments will look very uncomfortable, and not at all tied together. One solution would be to remove the existing trim, and bring the edge of the paneling up to the window, as shown in figure 5.

One last but vital consideration in designing the overall plan together with the internal details has to do with how the paneling is secured to the wall. In practice, this usually isn't much of a problem. The overall structural integrity of the paneling makes it very easy to secure with screws—or even nails—at relatively few points. Applied moldings offer a choice of sites at which screws can be used, since they'll later be covered by molding. Screws can also simply be plugged, or—if the wall is to be painted—the paneling can be nailed to the wall and the nails can be set and filled. All

fixing, of course, must be done through the rails, stiles and muntins, because the panels themselves must be left free to expand and contract, unrestrained. The bottom of the paneling can be screwed into the floor, the plaster grounds or to wall-framing plates (see figure 1). Studs in wood-framed houses are spaced closely enough so that stiles or rails can be lined up with them and be screwed or nailed through. Masonry offers even more choices, although a little more work is entailed: holes are drilled wherever you want them, then filled with wood plugs to provide fixings for screws. In brick walls, occasional bricks can be removed and the resulting spaces filled with wood blocks called "noggins." Should you be working in a stone house constructed of super-hard granite, it's not hard to find a mortar joint that can be drilled out and filled with

Fig. 4: Top treatments

Flat ceiling

Crown molding — Crown molding

Crown molding works well to conceal attachment methods, provided ceiling is level.

Slightly out-of-level ceiling

Top edge of rail — Nail or screw — Cove molding — Plug

For small irregularities, it's easiest to cover gaps with quarter-round or cove that's narrow enough to bend.

Grossly irregular ceiling

Cap with cove

Otherwise, finish top with a cap molding, simple or ornate, and either leave existing wall to show or scribe Sheetrock to fit opening.

Fig. 5: Windows

Paneling — Simplified sash — Glass

The quickest and simplest treatment is to butt the paneling up to the existing window trim.

If paneling and trim are flush, molding can cover joint; if not, molding can butt against higher edge, covering minor gaps.

To cover gaps caused by problems with plumbness, squareness and surface height, a furring strip may be used to bring window trim forward to overlap paneling.

Fig. 6: Sample wall

The first design decision was to unify the wall with a visually strong dado rail beneath the windows, with a row of panels of the same height below it. The middle, frieze and top rails would also be kept in continuous horizontal lines as much as possible. Spacings of these higher rails approximate the golden mean (as shown at far right). The unequal spaces caused by the windows were made more uniform by dividing them into two vertical rows of panels each. With these major decisions established, minor difficulties were dealt with as described on the drawing.

Windows not same size: For small difference, widen rail as shown; if this space were much larger, it would be better to install two very narrow horizontal panels, as at top of window.

Old outlets in baseboard: Holes cut in new baseboard over existing outlets. If there had been many more outlets and/or switches, it would have been best to rewire the wall according to code, positioning the electrical boxes so that they would appear in frame members, not in panels.

A — Beam

a wood plug. Instead of these traditional wooden plugs, you can also substitute any type of modern wall anchor in a masonry wall.

By far the biggest difficulty you might encounter is with walls that aren't plumb and floors that aren't level. Occasionally, it may be a good idea to go with the flow, but usually the best rule is to true up the new work rather than attempting to accommodate any irregularities in the building. Nine times out of ten, this will look better and—despite what you may think—be easier to do. The first job is to establish an absolute level at the bottom of the wall (if the floor is uneven or sloping) and work upwards from the highest point of the floor. You have two choices: You can either make the bottom rail perfectly regular and level, covering any resulting gap with a baseboard that's scribed to the uneven floor line along its bottom edge, or you can scribe the bottom framing member itself. The first method is usually the best because it guarantees that at least a part of the bottom of the framing can be made to look consistently wide. By working from the floor's highest point, the baseboard or bottom framing member will never appear too narrow since you started at the point where it was narrowest. A bottom framing member that appears too wide here and there (from accommodating a dip or slope in the floor) looks far better than a bottom framing member that looks too narrow in spots.

An out-of-plumb wall is confronted similarly. Once again, work from the proudest part of the wall, and design the paneling so that gaps at doors and windows can be covered with scribed trim pieces in the same way as using a scribed baseboard at the floor line. If the wall is leaning badly one way or the other, this will entail blocking out some of the fixing points, so plan ahead to ensure that these will remain accessible. Sometimes it's best to plumb and level the wall with graduated furring strips, scribed to the wall and/or

blocked out where necessary before you begin paneling. If the wall undulates badly, say in an old house where settling has taken its toll, it may be wiser to allow a little out of plumbness in favor of a smooth, flat surface. Large humps in the wall's surface make it difficult to achieve tight joints between the framing members.

With this much covered in theory, I'd like to conclude with a concrete example of one way to panel an actual wall, dealing with the sort of peculiarities that theory never quite seems to anticipate. This wall is not imaginary, by the way, but is found in a country farmhouse built around 1840. Figure 6 shows the methods I'd use to get around each problem. More important than the individual solutions, however, is the general approach. First impose the design upon the whole wall and—only then—depart from it judiciously where needed. □

Graham Blackburn is a contributing editor to FWW, *and has written numerous books on woodworking and tools. His shop is in Santa Cruz, Calif.*

Further reading

Colonial Architecture of Cape Cod, Nantucket & Martha's Vineyard by Alfred Easton Poor. Dover Publications, Inc., 31 East 2nd St., Mineola, N.Y. 11501, 1970.

Early Domestic Architecture of Connecticut by J. Frederick Kelly. Dover Publications, Inc., 31 East 2nd St., Mineola, N.Y. 11501, 1963.

Period Details by Martin and Judith Miller. Crown Publishers, Inc., 34 Engelhard Ave., Avenel, N.J. 07001, 1987.

For general background on classical proportions: *FWW On Making Period Furniture.* The Taunton Press, Box 355, Newtown, Conn. 06470, 1985.

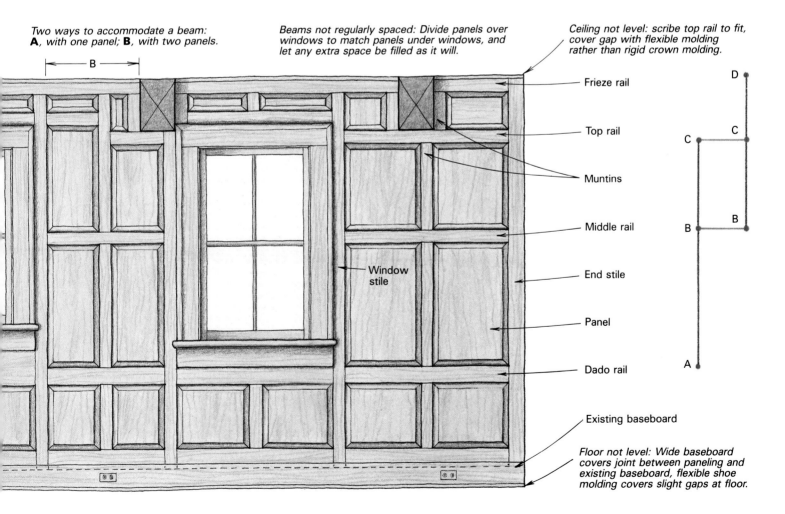

Two ways to accommodate a beam: **A**, *with one panel;* **B**, *with two panels.*

Beams not regularly spaced: Divide panels over windows to match panels under windows, and let any extra space be filled as it will.

Ceiling not level: scribe top rail to fit, cover gap with flexible molding rather than rigid crown molding.

Frieze rail

Top rail

Muntins

Middle rail

End stile

Window stile

Panel

Dado rail

Existing baseboard

Floor not level: Wide baseboard covers joint between paneling and existing baseboard, flexible shoe molding covers slight gaps at floor.

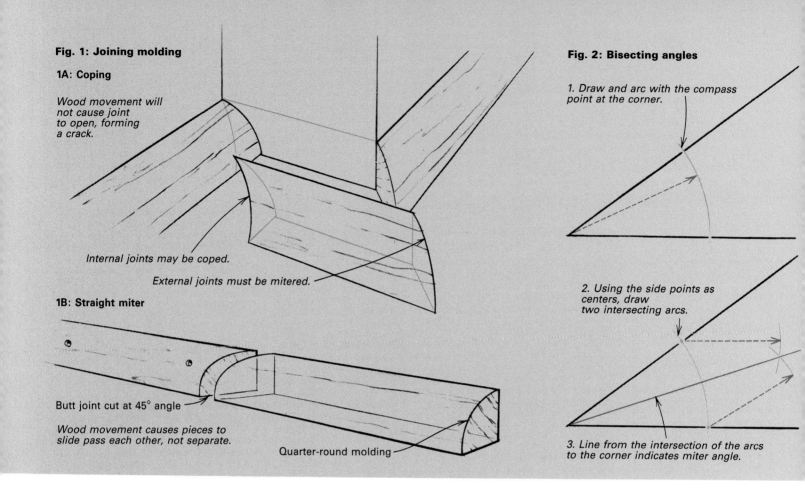

Fig. 1: Joining molding

1A: Coping

Wood movement will
not cause joint
to open, forming
a crack.

Internal joints may be coped.

External joints must be mitered.

1B: Straight miter

Butt joint cut at 45° angle

Wood movement causes pieces to
slide pass each other, not separate.

Quarter-round molding

Fig. 2: Bisecting angles

1. Draw and arc with the compass
point at the corner.

2. Using the side points as
centers, draw
two intersecting arcs.

3. Line from the intersection of the arcs
to the corner indicates miter angle.

Joining Molding
Coping with corners and complex miters

by Graham Blackburn

Making molding isn't as hard as it looks, but installing it in a room or on a piece of furniture can quickly turn into a nightmare of angled cuts, opened joints and mismatched profiles. And, if matching up all the coves, beads and rabbets as they run around and into corners isn't enough of a challenge, you have to deal with several wood-movement problems. Fortunately, with a little practice and foresight, you can handle the job with just a saw, compass, handplane and a variety of butt joints, miters and curved cove cuts.

As always in dealing with seasonal wood movement, you must bear in mind that all wood moves and that cross-grain fixed to long-grain invites trouble. Panel-holding molding is usually glued and nailed to the surrounding frame, and there is rarely any conflict with the frame's grain direction. In corners, the molding is usually mitered; you can keep this miter tight by cutting the pieces slightly long and springing them into place. Molding used as edging—around tabletops or at the junction of tops and skirts, for example—also is usually attached long-grain to long-grain. But

where you *must* fix a piece of long-grain molding across the grain of another piece, always allow for the inevitable movement differential between the two pieces. If it is of small dimension, nail and glue the molding at the ends and use only small nails at the center of its length. These nails must be pliable enough to give a little. For stouter pieces of molding, slot-screwing from the back side of the base into the molding might be better. Elongate the hole in the base and place a washer under the screw head so it can move as the base expands or contracts. Very large molding that must be affixed across the grain is sometimes made from cross-grain segments glued end to end. For more about cross-grain constructions, see the article on pp. 32-33.

Wherever possible, it's best to use continuous, unbroken lengths for long spans and locate any joints at corners and other places where the molding changes direction. If you can't avoid joining pieces, take advantage of any architectural feature that might visually distract from the joint. In any case, avoid joining the pieces near a corner, where any short piece will always look like a mistake.

From *Fine Woodworking* magazine (January 1989) 74:68-69

Fig. 3: Curved miter

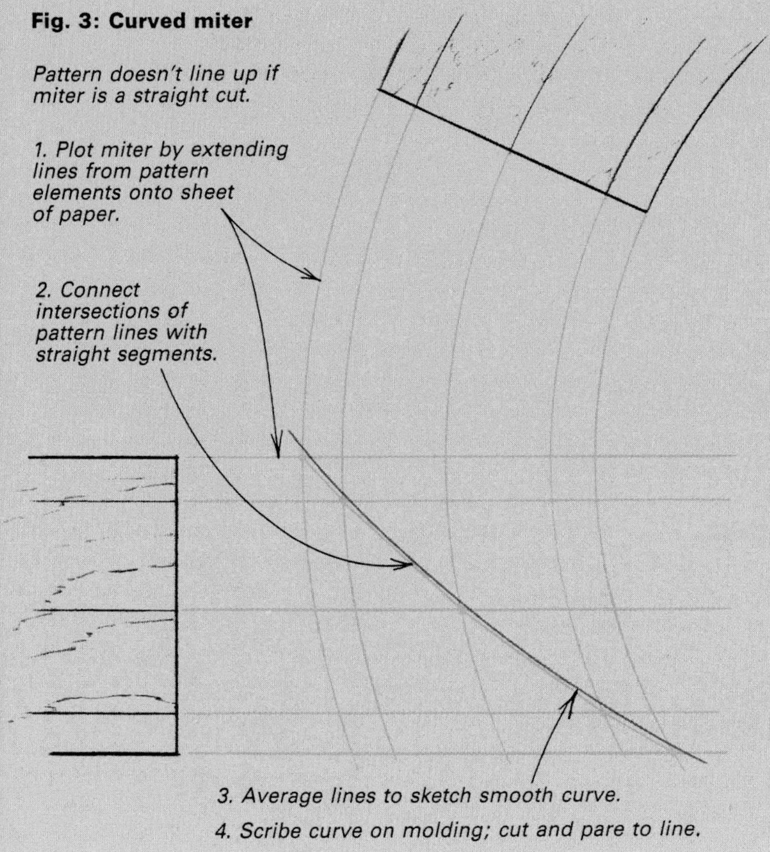

Pattern doesn't line up if miter is a straight cut.

1. Plot miter by extending lines from pattern elements onto sheet of paper.

2. Connect intersections of pattern lines with straight segments.

3. Average lines to sketch smooth curve.
4. Scribe curve on molding; cut and pare to line.

Fig. 4: Mitering crown molding

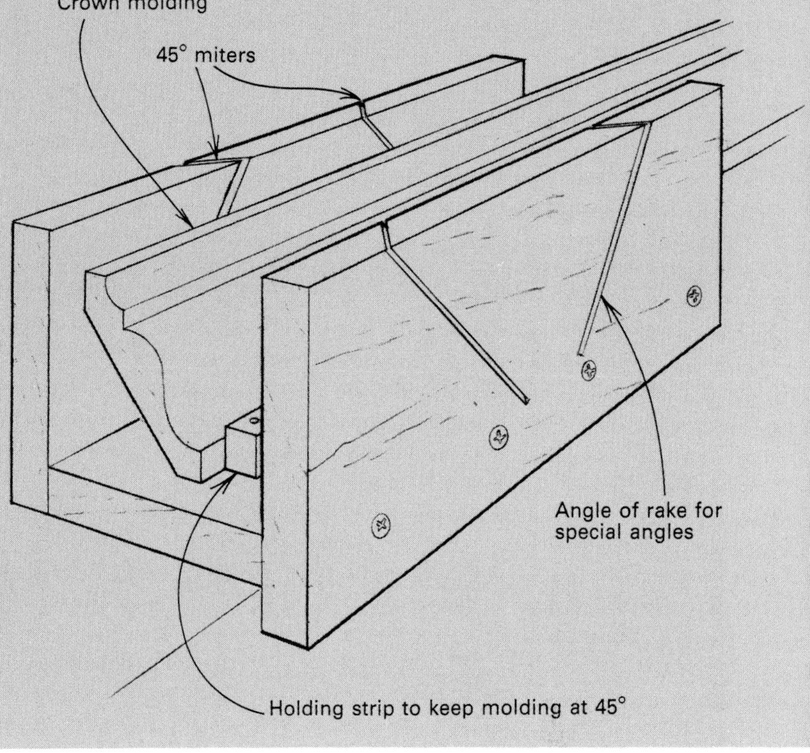

Crown molding

45° miters

Angle of rake for special angles

Holding strip to keep molding at 45°

If you can cut both pieces slightly long, make a simple butt joint by springing the two pieces together. While this will keep the joint closed, it can put a great deal of pressure on the ends of the molding, causing the joints there to fit poorly. Thus, it is better to cut the butt joint at an angle to create a straight miter, as shown in figure 1 on the facing page. If the pieces shrink, the mitered ends will slide over one another, rather than pull directly apart, exposing a gap.

Joining molding at inside corners requires either mitering or coping. Coping involves cutting one piece so it butts into the corner, then scribing the molding's profile onto the mating piece and sawing or paring the end to the exact reverse section of the piece, so it will butt into the profile. This allows the wood to move without breaking the joint and means you'll only need to make one special cut. If it's difficult to scribe the pattern directly from the intersecting piece, you can cut a 45° inside miter on the end of one piece and use a coping saw to cut along the curved pattern between the bevel and the face of the molding. Moldings with many tiny pattern elements are often very difficult to scribe and cope. Coping also cannot be used for external corners.

Mitering molding—On flat surfaces, mitering of simple profiles is a fairly straightforward matter of cutting 45° bevels. But, it can be difficult with complicated shapes, especially when the moldings intersect at angles other than 90°. The basic rule is that the angle of the miter must perfectly bisect the overall angle of the corner. With a 90° corner, this results in a 45° miter; if the corner of the panel isn't 90°, you can bisect the angle with a compass, as shown in figure 2 on the facing page, either working directly on the panel or on a sheet of paper. Using the corner as a center point, draw an arc that will intersect with both sides of the corner. Now, using these side points as centers, draw two intersecting arcs. A line between the intersection of the two circles and the corner will perfectly bisect the corner and indicate the miter angle. Use a bevel gauge to transfer the angle to the molding, saw proud of the line and trim for a perfect fit.

You have a slightly different problem when a curved section meets a straight section of an identical pattern. Here the miter *must* be curved. To plot the line, put a piece of paper under the moldings, as shown in figure 3 above, and extend the pattern lines as shown. Connect the intersections with straight lines, then sketch in a smooth curve, which can be scribed on the molding. Curved miters are best cut oversize, then trimmed to the line with a knife or chisel.

Straight miters may be sawn using a tablesaw or a miter box. Unless the molding will be painted, it is usually best to saw slightly oversize and then trim to produce a perfect joint. The best way to trim the joints is with a handplane and a miter shooting board, which is just a baseboard with a step at its edge and an angled fence to support the molding. Extend the mitered end over the step and trim it by "shooting" along the step with the plane running on its side on the baseboard.

Everything I've said about mitering so far refers to joining molding that fits flat against an interior surface. Crown molding, however, is often beveled on the back so the angled molding will butt between a wall and the ceiling or between other similar surfaces. If you want to miter crown molding, you must allow for the installation angle, which is usually 45°. You can produce the needed 45° compound miter by fixing holding strips in the miter box to hold the molding at the proper installation angle and by using regular 45° slots to guide your saw. If the miter is at an odd angle, as at the end of a raking gable or an arched pediment, knock up a special miter box or modify your regular box by adding a guide slot angled to produce the needed compound miter angle (see figure 4 above). Again, set holding strips to support the molding at the proper installation angle. □

Graham Blackburn is a writer and furnituremaker in Soquel, Calif., and is a contributing editor to Fine Woodworking.

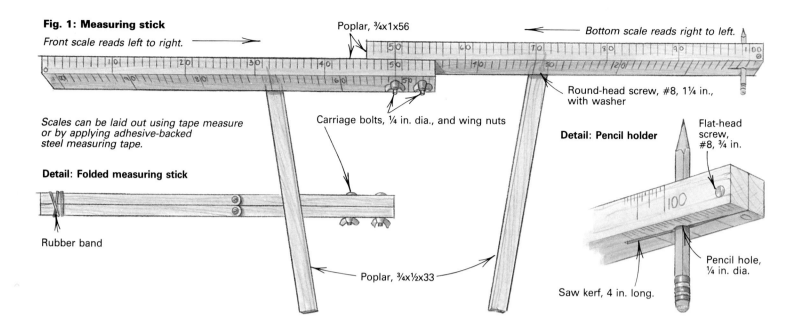

Fig. 1: Measuring stick

Front scale reads left to right.

Poplar, ¾x1x56

Bottom scale reads right to left.

Round-head screw, #8, 1¼ in., with washer

Scales can be laid out using tape measure or by applying adhesive-backed steel measuring tape.

Carriage bolts, ¼ in. dia., and wing nuts

Detail: Pencil holder

Flat-head screw, #8, ¾ in.

Detail: Folded measuring stick

Rubber band

Poplar, ¾x½x33

Pencil hole, ¼ in. dia.

Saw kerf, 4 in. long.

Installing Crown Molding

A measuring stick and some tricks

by William Lego

Hanging crown molding is 95% a one-person job, as Yogi Berra might say. With no helper, however, the procedure can be a bit hazardous to the homeowner's furnishings. And measuring a 16-ft. span by yourself while balancing on a ladder becomes a more significant problem with each passing birthday. In this article, I'll share a few proven techniques that have eliminated the need for a helper and saved me many measuring trips up the ladder.

First of all, I made a measuring stick so I could do most measuring solo while standing on the floor. The stick is in sections so it will fit in my car; it can be made in one piece, but would be more cumbersome. My two-piece model is 56 in. long in storage mode and 102 in. when assembled for use. Wing nuts hold the two halves together. To convert from one mode to the other, simply remove the wing nuts, turn one of the limbs end for end and retighten the wing nuts. A rubber band secures the handles to the two main sections when the device is not being used.

Making the stick—Rip two poplar strips for the main limbs and two strips for the handles, as shown in figure 1 above. Overlap the main limbs 10 in., clamp them in position and drill ¼-in. holes for the ¼-20 carriage bolts that hold the two limbs together. I laid out my scales using a tape measure as a guide while I copied the ⅛-in. calibrations and numbers on the limbs. However, you can also use two adhesive-backed steel measuring tapes, which read from both the left and right, from Woodworker's Supply of New Mexico, 5604 Alameda Pl. N.E., Albuquerque, N.M. 87113; (800) 645-9292. These tapes are available in 12-ft. lengths and produce a much more professional-looking device at a modest cost and considerable time savings. I located the right-to-left scale on the side of the stick that faces down in use and the left-to-right scale on the side opposite the handles, as shown above.

The handles are screwed loosely onto the main limbs with 1¼-in., #8 round-head screws with washers to allow movement. Drill a ¼-in. hole at the 100-in. mark on the right end of the stick to hold a pencil. Then, saw a kerf and drill a hole for a ¾-in., #8 recessed flat-head screw, as shown above, to clamp the pencil in position.

The stick in action—To measure from inside corner to outside corner, butt one end of the device against the inside corner and locate the outside corner on the pertinent scale. If the span is more than 102 in., mark the ceiling at 100 in. with the attached pencil. The line will be hidden once the molding is installed. Then, measure from the pencil mark to the outside corner and add 100 in.

For those inside corner to inside corner crown molding runs between 102 in. and 202 in., I butt the left end of the device to the left wall and make a pencil mark on the ceiling at the 100-in. mark (see figure 2 on the facing page). Then, I butt the right end of the device to the right wall and read the measurement at the pencil mark, using the scale beginning at the right wall. This dimension plus 100 in. gives me the width of the room. Because crown moldings generally run 16 ft. (192 in.), my measuring stick will handle most of my measuring needs.

From *Fine Woodworking* magazine (January 1990) 80:74-75

Fig. 2: Using the measuring stick

Step 1: Butt stick to left wall and make a pencil mark at 100 in.

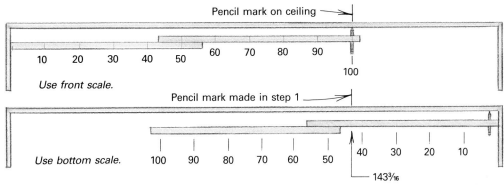

Pencil mark on ceiling

10 20 30 40 50 60 70 80 90

100

Use front scale.

Step 2: Butt stick to right wall and add 100 in. to the measurement that aligns with pencil mark on the right-to-left scale.

Pencil mark made in step 1

Use bottom scale. 100 90 80 70 60 50 40 30 20 10

143³⁄₁₆

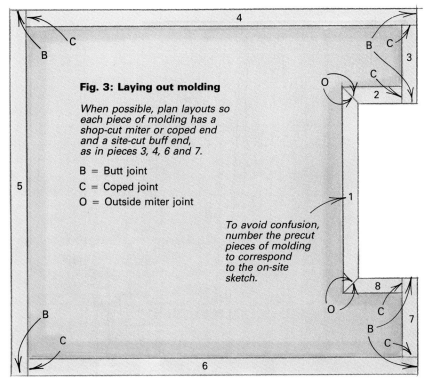

4

C
B

B C

3

C

O

2

Fig. 3: Laying out molding

When possible, plan layouts so each piece of molding has a shop-cut miter or coped end and a site-cut buff end, as in pieces 3, 4, 6 and 7.

B = Butt joint
C = Coped joint
O = Outside miter joint

5

1

To avoid confusion, number the precut pieces of molding to correspond to the on-site sketch.

8

O C

7

B
C

B C

6

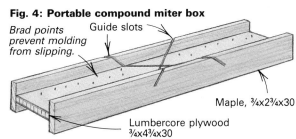

Fig. 4: Portable compound miter box

Brad points prevent molding from slipping.

Guide slots

Maple, ¾x2¾x30

Lumbercore plywood ¾x4¾x30

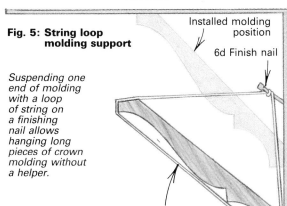

Installed molding position

Fig. 5: String loop molding support

6d Finish nail

Suspending one end of molding with a loop of string on a finishing nail allows hanging long pieces of crown molding without a helper.

String

Cutting molding—Coping moldings and attaching little returns to provide a finished appearance on moldings that dead-end in awkward places can be delicate business. I see so many finish carpenters squatting on the floor, squinting at their cut marks while operating their miter boxes for these jobs. But you don't see chefs stooping on floors for the most intricate aspects of preparing a soufflé. And dentists have elaborate chairs to position the patient so their work will be easier. For cutting molding, I've made an on-site table that puts the work at a more comfortable level and eliminates bending for tools.

Whenever possible, I cut joints ahead of time in my shop. By minimizing on-site joint cutting, I have more time to install the moldings before running out of daylight or interfering with the customer's supper hour. Precutting moldings does require some premeasuring, which I do when preparing a job estimate. I take rough measurements on the floor, coding all the pieces on my room layout, as shown in figure 3 above, and then add 6 in. for cutting the joints. If the pieces are laid out so each one has a coped or mitered end and a square butted end, I can cut the butted end on-site to the exact length. Pieces that require coped or mitered joints at both ends, shown in locations 1, 2 and 8 in figure 3, can be measured on the first visit and cut to length in the shop. Sometimes I cope one end in the shop and cut the miter on-site. In any case, I always take an extra 16-ft. length of crown molding for every two rooms on the job, in the event I need to recut a piece.

Going through the mental or physical gyrations to correctly po-

sition crown molding, upside down and backward, in the miter box is enough to daunt even the stoutest enthusiast. With the simple miter box shown in figure 4 above, I cut crown molding up to 4⅝ in. wide, face up and laid flat. First I cut two 18-in. pieces of molding to the desired compound angle in a standard hand- or electric-powered miter box and then test fit these pieces to be sure the angles are correct. After constructing the miter box, as shown in figure 4, stack the two pieces of molding and nail them together to form a broad guide face for handsawing the compound-angle slots. For less play in the sawkerf, cut the guide slots with the saw you will use with the box. Small brads, driven from the underside to just penetrate the top surface of the miter box, keep moldings from slipping during the cut.

Stringing up the molding—I have found that a nail and a loop of string can effectively replace a helper when installing crown moldings. Drive a 6d finishing nail into the wall at one end of the molding, as shown in figure 5 above. Be sure to put the nail high enough on the wall so that it will not prevent you from tacking the molding in place; you may need to bend the nail toward the ceiling to avoid the molding. Put one end of the molding through a loop of string hung over the nail. Then, nail from the other end of the molding, working back toward the loop, which can be detached and reused. The nail remains forever behind the molding. □

William Lego is a carpenter and woodworker in Rockford, Ill.

Making Split-Bark Seats
Weaving a durable bottom from hickory

by Jeff Shriver

From the last half of the 19th century until just after World War II, almost every Appalachian homestead had several simple, but well-constructed woven-bottom chairs. Most were variations on a theme: two bent back slats, with bent and splayed back posts, flattened on one side from the seat to the top of the post. Ash, hickory and hard maple made the posts, white oak was frequently used for the rungs.

Chair bottoms were woven of any number of materials, usually gotten from indigenous plant sources. Cattail leaves, corn husks and broom sage provided what's commonly referred to as "rush," but more often white oak splits or strips cut from the inner bark of the hickory tree were used. Hickory bark was the most durable, easily woven and inherently beautiful. Fresh from the living tree or after soaking in water, it's extremely soft and pliable. But when dried, it's nearly as hard as hickory wood itself and will withstand a lifetime of daily use.

Such old chairs are often available at flea markets, and renewing the bottoms of these worthy derelicts offers a rewarding and fascinating opportunity to learn a forgotten craft, increases the value of the chair, and most important, provides you with a place to "set a spell." Of course, the methods I'll describe in this article can also be used to outfit a new chair. Since seat weaving is a down-home green woodworking technique, you don't need much in the way of special tools, just a drawknife, a good pocket or utility knife and a bark spud. A shaving horse is optional.

To begin with, you'll need to familiarize yourself with the various hickories that provide the raw materials. Hickories are divided into two distinct groups: the pecan hickories and the true. The true hickories, shagbark *(Carya ovata)*, shellbark *(C. laciniosa)* and pignut *(C. glabra)*, indigenous to most of the United States and Canada, are eligible candidates for stripping. Shagbark and shellbark, as the names imply, have loose, shaggy gray scales or plates curling up at the loose end. Due to the variable degree of scaliness, it may be difficult to positively distinguish between the two without inspecting the leaves and comparing your observations to the hickory entries in a good tree identification book. In either case, they both work equally well. The pignut lacks the scales completely and is more similar in appearance to the bitternut *(C. cordiformis)* and the mockernut *(C. tomentosa)*, which are among the pecan hickories. Their deeply furrowed bark clings tightly to the tree and is light gray in color.

If you've access to a forest, you may want to locate and cut a live, standing tree. You'll know that the tree is healthy and freshly cut and there's a certain intangible pleasure of knowing from whence it came, and of being involved in every stage of the process. If you don't have access to any standing hickory and have no use for the wood inside the bark (in this instance it's a waste product), you may want to explore a more ecologically sound alternative; go to a sawmill and peel trees already cut. Due to its extreme hardness and difficulty in drying, hickory is accorded low status in the lumber industry. Tool-handle manufacturers buy most of it, almost always in the log form. It may take a month of calling or visiting sawmills to find any. Then, when you've succeeded, you may have to hasten to the mill and start working immediately, before the logs are sawn into small blocks.

One important factor to consider when looking for logs is the time of year when they were felled. This is crucial. Trees cut during the winter months, late summer or fall are virtually impossible to peel. Trees felled in late April, May and June will relinquish their bark with a minimum of effort. As the season advances, separation of the bark from the tree becomes increasingly difficult, and typically by late July, a pleasant occupation can become an arduous struggle resulting in cut and smashed fingers and shins, with little bark to show for your efforts.

After locating some usable logs, your next concern is handling these long, awkward timbers. At 64 lb. per cubic foot, hickory is one of the heaviest woods. To get strips long enough to wrap once around the chair bottom and a little excess, they'll need to be at least 4 ft. long. In other words, you've got some very heavy objects to wrestle around. The ideal tool is a peavey or cant hook, but in lieu of that, a spud bar will work, or any long, stout pole capable of offering some leverage. If you're at a sawmill and the logs are stacked in a pile, you'll have to roll them off to the ground where they can be rolled over a few times. You may want to seek the aid of whatever power log-handling equipment is available at the mill. The operators usually don't mind helping, just be certain to show your appreciation. In any case, the log needs to be lying on some reasonably flat surface, where it can be rolled over once completely.

An alternative to stripping whole logs is to peel the waste slabs left over after the cant has been initially squared. They're small,

1. To remove the inner bark of a hickory log, Shriver first kerfs the length of the bole with a chainsaw. A trenching shovel slipped between the wood and the bark loosens the slab enough to be peeled by hand.

manageable pieces, and they already have an edge you can get under to pry up the bark. You may have to make prior arrangements with the sawyer to leave the slabs whole, as most mills routinely cut this waste material into firewood.

Before you strip the bark, it's a good idea to calculate the amount you'll need. To estimate this, find the area of the seat (disregarding the splay) in square inches and multiply by five. Why five? The warp must cover the top and the bottom in one direction, that's twice the area. Then the woof, which runs at 90° to the warp, covers the top and bottom one time each. That's four times. The other 20% accounts for the splay and waste.

Estimating how much bark a given tree will yield, although fundamentally simple, is subject to a considerable degree of error. Using the formula for finding the surface area of a cylinder, π times diameter times length (in inches) and multiplying by two will give a ballpark figure. The actual yield will depend on log quality, incidence of knots, buckshot and fence-wire wounds, log taper and the thickness of the bark. You multiply by two because before you're through, you'll split all the material in half, doubling the amount (at least).

Just as there's more than one way to skin a cat, so, too, with skinning a log. For seat weaving purposes, you're interested in only the inner bark. To get it, you have to peel off both the rough, outer bark and the inner bark, separating the outer bark later. For a log 10 in. in diameter or larger, a particularly effective technique is to cut a longitudinal kerf through the bark down to the wood, in sections approximately 8 to 10 in. in width. A chainsaw is most effective at this task, but a hand axe will yield equivalent, if slower, results. If you're peeling a sapling, another method is to shave it off with a drawknife. Being thinner and more flexible, the inner and outer bark on these youths is much easier to peel. However, it's thin and can't be split as can the thick bark of old patriarchs.

At any rate, assuming you've chosen a large tree, start at the end of the log, slip a bark spud between the bark and the wood, and pry up. If you don't have a bark spud, a trenching shovel, spud bar, or anything that's thin enough to slip between the wood and

2. *After soaking the peeled slabs for a day, the author removes the rough outer bark with a drawknife.*

3. *The debarked slab is cut into strips with a stout knife or ripped on the tablesaw. The hold-down shown at right makes for safe tablesawing.*

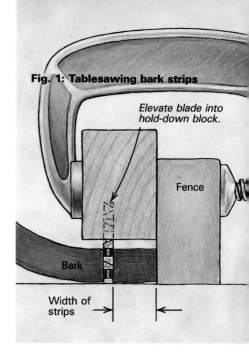

Fig. 1: Tablesawing bark strips

Elevate blade into hold-down block.

Fence

Bark

Width of strips

bark, and long enough to offer some leverage, will suffice. Keep prying up and moving forward. You can usually pull it off with your hands when there's enough pulled up to grip.

I've found that this process is eased somewhat by leaving the logs out in the sun for a week after they've been cut. The idea is, the wood looses moisture, shrinks and begins to separate from the bark. A word of caution though: after two weeks, the bark begins to dry out, starts adhering to the wood, and becomes as brittle as a corn chip.

After stripping the logs, immerse the bark slabs in water for at least 24 hours. This softens the hard, dry outer bark, the ends of the slabs that may have dried out, and removes any mud left clinging to the outer surface. The best technique is to tie all the slabs in a bundle and soak them in a pond or stream. Weight the bundle with rocks and secure it to the bank. A moving body of water is preferable to a still or stagnant pond. If left two or three days in a pond, the bark will develop an unsavory, acrid odor. However, if you choose a stream or river to soak the bundle in, you run the risk of it washing away. Just be certain the bundle is bound tightly and well-secured on shore. If no large body of water is available, anything large enough to submerge the material is adequate.

Next you're ready to shave off the outer bark. Two tools are required; a drawknife and a shaving horse. Inexperienced people often complain that drawknives aren't controllable, and can do little more than claw and scrape the wood. You may have to experiment with several kinds until you find one you like. Try turning the knife over, using it bevel side down (my favorite knife can be used only in this fashion). Be patient. It takes time to develop good control, but it will come.

The other tool, the shaving horse, provides a way to secure the bark while you shave. If you don't have access to one, you might consider constructing your own; it does not need to be fancy. For rendering material for only three or four chairs, you may not want to bother with building even a very simple shaving horse. Two C-clamps and a 2-ft.-long 2x6 clamped to a bench will suffice for a short run, although it's a little clumsy.

In either case, the idea is to place the bark on some support, secure it, and shave off the outer bark. If you're using shagbark or shellbark, the large plates will more or less break off, revealing a very thin, gray-green layer beneath. The external bark on the smooth-bark hickories is more tenacious and removed with more difficulty and care. What you're looking for is a greenish-

yellow, soft material with a highly visible, reticulose character. It's not hard to see. Keep shaving the outer bark, being careful to remove as little of the inner bark as possible. Keep working at it until all of the outer bark has been removed.

Finish shaving the rest of the slabs, then stack them in a weighted pile to keep them as flat as possible while they dry overnight. Cutting the slabs into strips can be accomplished in several ways. Using a sharp knife with a thin, stout blade and a straightedge as a guide, score a line in the center, the entire length of the slab. Then fold it in half along the score line and finish the cut, working from the inside of the fold. All the cuts are made using this cut-and-fold technique. It's best to keep the strips ⅝ in. to ¾ in. wide. Anything wider makes splitting the strips too difficult.

If you are preparing a large quantity of strips, using a tablesaw will expedite the process tremendously. Also, strips cut on the tablesaw have smooth, straight edges and are much easier to split than knife-cut strips. To get the initial straight edge to run along the fence, either cut the slab in half using the knife, or guide it freehand through the saw. This is not as dangerous as it sounds, just be certain to guide the slab through slowly and in a straight line (striking a chalkline is helpful). If it begins to catch on the back side of the blade, you're not guiding it straight. To minimize this problem, set the blade at a nominal projection above the table. To tablesaw the slabs into strips, use the method shown in figure 1.

By now, the strips are probably too dry and stiff to manipulate easily, so they'll need to be soaked in water for several hours until they are once again soft and pliable. When they can be wrapped tightly around your finger, they're ready for splitting.

Using a sharp knife, start the split at one end of each strip, being careful to start the cut as close to the center as possible. Now grab each strip between your thumb and index finger and pull them apart, being careful to keep the split running down the center. This is the key to the success of this splitting process; keeping the split in the center of the strip. If it starts to run to one side, pull on the opposite, thicker side until the split is again centered. Keep a close eye on both sides; it may be perfectly centered on one side and grossly off-center on the other. This can be corrected by carefully manipulating the strip in a twisting fashion, keeping in mind to pull on the thick side until the split is once again centered. If you find the split has gotten too thin on one side to effectively center it again, you

Drawings: Michael Janos

5. *Before splitting, Shriver soaks his strips until they're supple enough to bend easily around his fingers.*

4. *Bark from old trees is usually thick enough to be split three or four times, yielding weavable strips ⅝ in. to ¾ in. wide and about ⅛ in. thick. With a knife, start a split in the end of each strip then coax the bark apart by hand, maintaining uniform thickness as you go.*

6. *Shriver begins the warp by tacking a strip inside the front rung. The strip is carried under, around and over the side rungs.*

can cheat a little by using a knife to cut it back in. This may leave a "hangnail" that makes weaving more difficult, but it's better than wasting an entire strip.

Depending on the age and species you're working with, you may be able to split the strips more than once, possibly several times. The finished splits should be approximately ⅛ in. in thickness. After splitting, roll the splits in a coil and leave them to dry for later use. To prepare splits for weaving, soak them in water for at least 24 hours (less time is needed if the water is warm), until they can be folded without breaking or splitting out. I usually steep them for a few days, waiting for the water to darken to the color of strong tea. This effectively stains the splits to a uniform, rich dark brown.

Weaving a chair bottom is fundamentally a simple task learned in a few hours. The pattern described here is a traditional design found in most old, and many new split-bottomed chairs. The one key factor to keep in mind is uniformity of tension in the splits.

Individually the splits are thin, frail members. When woven as an integral unit, they can withstand enormous stress. If one or two splits are more taut than the rest, they'll bear more than their share of the weight, and, of course, will be the first to break. Aesthetically, the only important considerations are keeping the splits running straight and the weave tight.

A brief vocabulary will be helpful. The warp is the material that is initially wrapped around the seat in one direction. The woof, or weave, is that material which runs at 90° to the warp and is actually woven in, over and under. The cardinal points of left and right are expressed assuming the individual is looking at the chair from the front.

To begin the warp, nail a split to the lower inside of the front rung with a carpet tack. It's best to attach it to the right of center so there will be sufficient length to be woven into the pattern later on. Run the split first under the left rung then up and around on to the top, over to the right rung, around and under. Continue this process until the end of the split is reached, at

Fig. 2: The basic pattern weave

1. First weave goes over two warps then under two.

2. Second weave goes over one, then under two, over two.

3. Third weave goes under two, over two.

4. Fourth weave goes under one then over two, under two.

5. Fifth weave repeats No. 1.

Weave splay area with separate strips.

Returning beneath seat, first weave goes over three, under three...

...then over two, under three, over three...

...followed by over one, under three, over three...

...then under three, over three, etc.

7. *As more warp length is needed, bark strips are spliced on by tying them with thread let into notches cut about 4 in. from the end of each strip.*

which point you'll splice on another split to continue the warp.

The splice should always be done on the bottom, so some of the split may have to be cut off and discarded. This can be a painful procedure, considering the amount of effort put into making them, but alas, it must be done. Also, all the splices should be done as close to the center as possible. This ensures that both ends of the splits will, when the weaving is complete, become an integral part of the whole. The splice is simple; overlap the two splits (the fresh one and the ending one) about 4 or 5 in. With a sharp knife, cut two notches, one on each edge of the overlapped splits, then wrap several layers of heavy thread in the notches, and tie it off. The notches should be at least 4 in. from the ends of the splits, otherwise you may tear the notches out and pull a splice apart later on.

After splicing, proceed as before, keeping equal tension on all the splits. Also, don't pull them too tight or weaving in the woof will be a brutal task. To test for the proper tension, press down on the splits with the palm of your hand. The top layer should almost, but not quite, touch the bottom layer.

The transition from warp to woof goes like this: When you've reached the back of the seat, the last split on the top travels, as before, up and over the left rung, across the top of the seat, around the right rung to the bottom. But, instead of going across the bottom, the split is wrapped one-quarter of the way around the right rear post and around the back rung, up and over to the top of the seat. If you have made the transition properly, you should be at the right rear of the seat, and the split should be traveling at 90° to the warp. At this point weaving commences.

First, begin by going over two splits, then under two, then over two, and so forth until the front rung is reached. Then turn the

8. Warp to weave (woof) transition is made by wrapping up and over left rung, across the top of the seat, down and around the right rung to the rear rung.

9. The first weave moves toward the front of the chair, passing first over two strips, then under two strips, and so on.

10. As the seat progresses, a butter knife acts as a ramp to ease insertion of the weavers. The chair's splay forms an unwoven section that will be filled in with separate pieces.

chair over, wrap the split around the rung and this time go over three, under three, over three, and so forth to the rear rung. On the bottom, the three sequence is used to save time; the looser the weave the easier it is to weave, therefore, faster. Proceed around the rear rung, turn the chair back over, and instead of going over two, go over only one split initially, then follow the same sequence of under two, over two, etc. to the front rung. Turn the chair over and on the bottom go over only two this time, then, as before, resume under-three over-three weaving to the rear rung. On top again, the split will go under two this time but on the next run it will go under one, then you're back to the original over two and the sequence begins again. Underneath, from the beginning you start with over three, over two, over one, under three, under two and under one. At the end of this sequence, you start again with over three.

As in the warp, all splices are made on the bottom, however, tying is unnecessary. Simply weave the ending split as usual, until it ends, preferably near the center of the seat. Then begin weaving the fresh split from the front rung, being careful to maintain the pattern. This is most easily done by looking at the pattern, counting over to the front rung following the sequence of over three, under three, etc. Weave in the fresh split accordingly and overlap it 6 or 7 in., hiding the loose end under an ''under three'' portion. Proceed with weaving the top and the bottom, keeping the splits running straight and snug. At this point, don't worry about the unwoven portions formed by the chair's splay.

As completion nears, the weave tends to tighten and the weaving becomes increasingly difficult (particularly if you've wrapped the warp too tightly). At this point, an un-serrated butter knife will help in weaving the final stages. Use the knife to enlarge the gap where the weave is to enter and slip it in. Remove the knife and do the same thing where the split will exit, using the knife as a ramp to guide the weaver out.

The final weaver (i.e. the rear rung is filled with woof) is simply woven in as before and tucked in underneath an under three sequence on the bottom. To fill in the splay, cut several strips 12 to 14 in. long. Often the ends cut off during weaving can be used. Then weaving from the front, and on the top, continue the pattern as before. Since the side rungs run at an angle relative to the front, each successive split will be slightly shorter than the last. I usually fill in both sides on top, then flip the chair over and finish the bottom. The ends on top and bottom are again tucked under.

Completing your first seat may be a slow, exasperating experience, particularly if you don't pay close attention to the proper beginning sequence. If you make mistakes, pull the woof out and start over. Your fingers may cry out for relief after four or five hours. If you must temporarily abandon the task, douse the seat on both sides with water (preferably warm) and cover with a wet towel. Repeat the dousing when you return. If you are absent longer and the seat dries out completely, repeated drenching with hot water will renew the suppleness.

When dry, the seat should be tight and elastic. A quick pass with 100-grit sandpaper on an orbital sander, followed by a propane torch, will eliminate any wisps that remain. Lastly, I usually brush on a liberal coat of thin linseed oil, but this is optional. □

When he wrote this article, Jeffrey Shriver lived in West Virginia. He has since moved to Tucson, Ariz., where, in addition to chairmaking, he's exploring the architecture and furniture of the Southwest.

The author sights along the side-panel rungs of a stool to make sure they're aligned. By beginning with green wood and monitoring the moisture content of the parts, you can capitalize on wood movement as the pieces dry to make stronger post-and-rung joints.

Green-Wood Joinery
Dry tenons, wet mortises for long-lasting joints

by Drew Langsner

Most contemporary woodworkers depend on commercially sawn, kiln-dried lumber. Green wood, high in moisture content (MC), is generally avoided: We hear that it warps, twists and shrinks unpredictably. However, in past centuries, wood was commonly worked green, often with outstanding results. All successful joinery is dependent on attention to and control of the moisture content of the wood being used. Even with kiln-dried wood, it's necessary to take into account the potential for expansion or contraction of parts being joined. The techniques used in working green wood not only allow for wood movement, but actually use it to advantage to make post-and-rung mortises and tenons that are often superior to comparable joints in kiln-dried wood.

"Green woodworking" is a term coined by ladderback chairmaker John Alexander. The techniques begin with riving (splitting) your material directly from a log and rough-shaping the green (wet) wood with hand tools, such as drawknives and spokeshaves. Riven wood has very high tensile, shear and bending strength, because each rived "billet" follows the natural, long fiber direction of the wood. "Green-wood joinery" does not mean joints are assembled wet: Final joint dimensioning and assembly are not undertaken until each of the parts has dried to a specific moisture content. A more accurate term is dry/wet joinery—dry tenons into moist mortises. Most dry/wet joints utilize cylindrical tenons and bored

mortises. I'll briefly discuss the principles involved in dry/wet joinery, then I'll describe my techniques for applying these principles in the construction of the post-and-rung stool in the bottom photo on p. 91.

Moisture content and differential shrinkage—In green woodworking, the most important principle to remember is that wood is hygroscopic, which simply means the wood will absorb and release moisture with variations in environmental humidity. Freshly cut wood contains moisture within the cell cavities, called "free water"; and moisture in the cell walls, called "bound water." As wood dries, it first loses free water, down to about 30% MC. This is the "fiber saturation point." The cell cavities are empty, but the cell walls are still saturated. As wood dries, its dimensions remain stable until it reaches the fiber saturation point. Then it begins to shrink, check and warp as it loses bound water. Tangent to the growth rings, most woods can shrink from 10% to 15%, while on the ray plane (perpendicular to the growth rings), maximum shrinkage is only half as much, 5% to 7%. This is "differential shrinkage." Because of differential shrinkage, a cylinder shaped from green wood will eventually dry into an oval cross section, with the oval's long axis on the ray plane (see figure 1 on the facing page). Oak and other ring-porous hardwoods, commonly used by "green woodworkers," are among the species that shrink the most. For a success-

From *Fine Woodworking* magazine (July 1989) 77:60-63

ful dry/wet joint, you must take into account both of these principles: the fluctuations in the moisture content of the joint components, and the differential shrinkage that occurs during these fluctuations.

In a heated house during the winter, the moisture content of the wood in your furniture can drop to between 5% and 10%. You don't want the tenons that join this furniture to shrink under these dry conditions and come loose. When the tenons are fitted to the mortises, they should be at 5% MC to 8% MC, to ensure that they're as dry and as small in diameter as they will ever get. In contrast, the ideal moisture content of mortise components at time of assembly is about 15% to 20%. This allows for slight swelling of the dry tenon as it absorbs moisture from the shrinking mortise.

In the Eastern United States, air-drying wood in a drafty shed will lower moisture content to between 15% and 20%, ideal for "wet" mortise components. A homemade kiln, like the one described in the sidebar on p. 91, can be used to dry the tenon stock to the desired 5% MC to 8% MC. In the arid West, wood air-dries to below 10% MC, which should be within allowable tolerances for mortise wood, as long as the tenon stock is thoroughly kiln-dried. As a rule of thumb: Air-dry mortise wood; kiln-dry tenon wood.

You can account for the second principle—differential shrinkage— by paying attention to growth-ring orientation of the mortise-and-tenon components (see figure 1). Chairs tend to fall apart during winter when the dry interior environment causes the tenons to shrink. However, much of the structural damage occurs as the tenon swells during the humid summer, causing the fibers of both mortise and tenon to crumple from overcompression. With a subsequent change to low humidity, moisture content drops and the tenon shrinks; but because of the crumpled fibers, it dries to a size smaller than its original diameter, thus creating a loose joint.

When a dry/wet joint is assembled, you can compensate for this potential compression. Orient the tenon's ray plane, which is subject to the lesser amount of shrinkage and swelling, parallel to the long fibers of the mortise wood, which also will shrink less (see figure 1). This orientation is partly dependent on the purpose and the anticipated stresses that the joint will be subjected to. For instance, a chair or stool rung is stressed mostly by racking, which puts the load on the top and bottom of the tenons. There is very little force on the sides of the joint; therefore, rung tenons are positioned with the ray plane parallel with the long fibers of the chair posts. This ensures that the joint will stay tight in the racking plane. If there is any compression of the tenon from expansion during a humid cycle, it will occur in the less critical sides of the tenon. In fact, I usually slightly undersize my tenons on the sides to allow for the additional shrinkage of the mortise and the expansion of the tenon.

Differential shrinkage is also considered when locating mortises. If mortises are on one plane only, they should be bored tangent to the growth rings (into the surface perpendicular to the ray plane). Because this is the plane of minimum shrinkage, the mortised wood is less likely to split as it dries around the tenon. However, in many cases, such as on the legs of the stool in the bottom photo on p. 91, multiple mortises in one member are located perpendicular to one another. Then, a compromise position is selected so shrinkage is about equal for mortises bored in either location (see figure 1).

A moisture-resistant finish on completed furniture helps minimize swelling and shrinkage from moisture cycling. I've used tung oil thinned with turpentine on my ladderback chairs, but recent studies show that tung oil is not an effective moisture barrier. I'm now experimenting with a mixture of tung oil and polyurethane varnish.

Building a post-and-rung stool—To show how the above principles are applied, I'll describe the joinery involved in building the stool. If you begin with green wood in log form and intend to rive

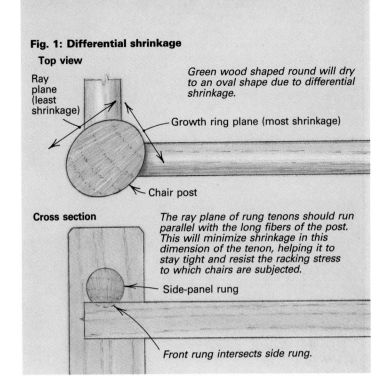

Fig. 1: Differential shrinkage

Top view

Ray plane (least shrinkage)

Green wood shaped round will dry to an oval shape due to differential shrinkage.

Growth ring plane (most shrinkage)

Chair post

Cross section

The ray plane of rung tenons should run parallel with the long fibers of the post. This will minimize shrinkage in this dimension of the tenon, helping it to stay tight and resist the racking stress to which chairs are subjected.

Side-panel rung

Front rung intersects side rung.

billets for your stool parts, you should use strong, straight-grained, ring-porous hardwoods, such as white and red oak, hickory or ash. Avoid defects; rot, bug holes and knots, or a combination of heartwood and sapwood in one piece, can all cause the wood to dry and shrink unpredictably. You can also use diffuse-porous hardwoods, such as birch, cherry and maple, but they don't split as well and must be machined or turned on a lathe.

Wet wood splits, shaves, whittles, bends and turns much easier than dry stock. So after riving, I immediately rough the parts out with a drawknife or spokeshave. I shave the parts square; then octagonal; then round, leaving them about 10% oversize in diameter to allow for shrinkage and final sizing. This translates to about ³⁄₃₂ in. per 1 in. of thickness, or ¹⁄₁₆ in. for a ⁵⁄₈-in.-dia. rung tenon. You'll note in figure 2 on the next page that the top rungs in the front and rear have an "airfoil" shape to make the seat more comfortable on the backs of legs. Then, I crosscut the parts to length, making sure that the tenons have a diameter/length ratio of about 1:1½. Shorter tenons have too little surface area to resist racking and may pull loose. The ⁵⁄₈-in.-dia. tenons for the stool should be 1 in. long. The posts are roughed down to a green diameter of about 1⅜ in. To prevent the top mortise from splitting during assembly, I let the post length run long about 1 in.

If I'm not in a hurry to use the parts, I begin by air-drying them slowly, leaving them in a shed or a corner of my shop. If you air-dry the wood in a heated room, away from the heat source, it will take about two weeks for very wet green wood to dry to 15% MC to 20% MC. A couple of days before I plan to assemble the stool, I dry the rungs on a rack located above a wood stove or in a drying kiln.

Sizing the tenons—Final shaping and sizing of the tenons is done when the rungs are thoroughly dried (5% MC to 8% MC). I size tenons with a spokeshave, then use a wood file to remove the small facets left by the spokeshave. If it's humid, I keep all rungs on the drying rack or in a plastic bag, except the one I'm working on; in humid conditions I've seen swelling occur within 30 minutes.

To test-fit the tenons as you work them to size with the spokeshave, make a gauge from a piece of dry hardwood about ½ in. thick (see the top photo on the next page). Bore three holes, using the same bit that will be used to drill the mortises, and number the holes. With a rat-tail file, enlarge the entry to hole #1, and use

Langsner uses a shaving horse to hold a rung as he shapes and sizes it with a spokeshave. The small block with the three holes is his fitting gauge. The sides of the first hole are colored, so when a tenon is rotated in the hole, the color shows where the tenon needs to be shaved more.

The notched blocks hold the post so all the mortises in one side can be bored without having to loosen the vise to move the post. A builder's line-level taped to the bit extension aligns the bit and a depth-stop clamped to the bit controls depth.

a water-soluble drawing pencil (available from art-supply stores) to coat the inside of the hole. Slightly chamfer the tenon ends with a file, to ease their fit into the gauge holes. As you insert the tenon into hole #1 to gauge your progress, the pencil marks will rub off on the tenon, showing where to shave more. When the tenon is close to size, use hole #2 for the final test fits. You'll be fitting 24 tenons for the stool, so when hole #2 gets enlarged from repeated reaming, use hole #3 to check the final fit.

You want a squeaky-tight fit on the top and bottom of the tenon. The side-to-side dimension, tangent to the growth rings, can be slightly undersize. Remove wood in small increments and test often. Final sizing is done with the file. After fitting the tenon to the mortise, I often relieve the tenon sides with a half-round file, reducing the chance of mortise split-out during assembly or later drying cycles. The shallow relief begins about ⅛ in. from the end of the tenon and ends ⅛ in. from the tenon's "shoulder" (see detail in figure 2).

On stools and ladderback chairs, the side-panel rung tenons, which bear the brunt of the fore-and-aft racking stress, can be further strengthened by interlocking with the tenons of the front and rear rungs. To accomplish this, bore and assemble the side panels first. Then bore the mortises for the front and back rungs so they slightly overlap and cut through the tenons of the side-panel rungs inside the chair post, like a log-cabin notch. To lay out the mortises on the posts, make a chair stick as shown in figure 2. The lines are not the centers of mortises. The side-panel mortises are drilled above the line, with their bottoms tangent to the line; the mortises for the front and rear rungs are drilled below the line so they overlap the line by 1/16 in.

Boring the mortises—Mortises should be bored after the wood has been air-dried to about 15% MC to 20% MC. Determine this by testing with a moisture meter or by kiln-drying a spare post along with the rungs and using it to compare relative weights to air-dried posts, as described in the sidebar. If mortises are bored in saturated green wood, they are often rough or fuzzy and as the wood dries, they take on an oval shape. In addition, mortise wood that's too wet can cause bone-dry tenons to absorb excessive moisture, leading to overcompression of the joint fibers as the tenons expand.

When mortise wood is thick enough that there's no danger of running a leadscrew out the back end, I use ordinary auger bits; in close situations, I switch to Forstner or Stanley Powerbore bits. I prefer the Powerbore bit because it's easy to sharpen, but I file the

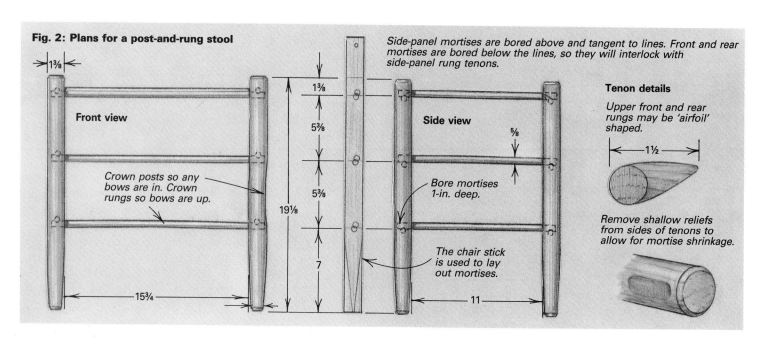

Fig. 2: Plans for a post-and-rung stool

1⅜

Front view

Crown posts so any bows are in. Crown rungs so bows are up.

15¾

1⅜

5⅜

5⅜

19⅛

7

Side-panel mortises are bored above and tangent to lines. Front and rear mortises are bored below the lines, so they will interlock with side-panel rung tenons.

Side view

⅝

Bore mortises 1-in. deep.

The chair stick is used to lay out mortises.

11

Tenon details

Upper front and rear rungs may be 'airfoil' shaped.

1½

Remove shallow reliefs from sides of tenons to allow for mortise shrinkage.

lead point to about half the factory length. A Stanley #47 auger-bit depth-stop ensures that the mortises are consistently 1 in. deep. To bore at the proper angles, I use a variety of sighting aids, including try squares and sliding bevel gauges. A drill extension makes it easier to align the bit, and a builder's line level, taped to the extension, provides a constant horizontal reference. The post, or assembled side panel, is clamped in a bench vise, as shown in the lower photo on the facing page. The simple clamping device holds the post so all the mortises on a side can be bored without having to unclamp the vise.

I bore the side-panel mortises above the layout lines with a brace or hand-held, variable-speed electric drill, and then assemble both side panels. Check each panel by eye for flatness, as shown in the photo on p. 88. You may have to twist it to eliminate any wind in the panel. Then, bore the front and rear rung mortises below the line so they will intersect the side rungs.

Although green woodworkers often assemble chairs without glue, I use it. Even though stressed surfaces in the joint mate endgrain to long grain, modern glues do provide some bonding strength. Perhaps more importantly, glue seals the endgrain of the tenon, slowing down moisture exchange within the joint. I use common white glue instead of yellow wood glue, because it sets up slower and is slipperier, thus serving as a lubricant during assembly. After the front and back rungs are glued into the side panels, you may have to "wrassel" the frame to eliminate any unevenness. With one of the legs braced on the floor, use your strength and body weight to force the frame into alignment. Check this by lining up the top rungs by eye until you have a flat seat plane. Then if necessary, scribe and saw off appropriate post bottoms so the stool stands flat.

For seating, you can use the inner bark of hickory, as shown in the photo below, or ash or white-oak splits. Woven cotton "Shaker tape" is also an option and is available, along with weaving instructions, from Shaker Workshops, Box 1028-FW17, Concord, Mass. 01742. Wrap the warp from front to rear in a continuous strip—not tight and not loose, rather slightly snug. Then, weave the weft in a checkerboard or herringbone twill pattern. □

Drew Langsner and his wife, Louise, run Country Workshops (90 Mill Creek Road, Marshall, N.C. 28753), offering summer and winter programs in green woodworking. Langsner is author of the book "Green Woodworking" (Rodale Press, Emmaus, Pa.; 1987).

This oak post-and-rung stool is an example of finely crafted furniture built with green-wood joinery techniques.

A piece of sheet metal on the bottom rack of this kiln deflects the direct heat from the electric baseboard heater below.

Drying green wood

Small drying kilns: During summer, when we're teaching week-long classes at Country Workshops, we often need to speed up the drying process for our chair parts. Over the past 10 years, I've built several small wood kilns. The first was built with cinder blocks and used a wood fire. Later, we used a 500-watt radiant heat lamp set in the bottom of a horizontal 55-gal. drum. Last summer, I built a more sophisticated kiln, shown in the photo above, with a 3-ft.-long heater in the bottom. The walls are two pieces of ¼-in. plywood that sandwich ¾-in. styrofoam insulation, assembled into a box 4 ft. by 4 ft. and 18 in. wide. Because the maximum setting on a standard thermostat is too low, the temperature is controlled by a heat-limit device mounted near the top of the box (stock #2E372 from W.W. Grainger Inc., 5959 W. Howard St., Chicago, Ill. 60648; 312-647-8900). A relay, appropriate for the amperage of the heater and the temperature control, is wired between the two. A small exhaust fan in the top of the kiln is used at the beginning of drying, when a great deal of moisture is being released. Doors at both ends of the cabinet double as adjustable dampers. Don't let the temperature rise above 160°. Charring or internal honeycombing can occur if the interior fibers dry too quickly.

With Windsor chairs, legs and stretchers present a unique drying requirement; their ends are tenons, which should be bone-dry, but they also have mortises, which should be left slightly damp. The solution is to dry the end tenons in a pot of heated sand. For heat, I use an electric hot plate, again limiting the temperature to 160°. Tenons are dry when they develop an oval cross section.

Checking moisture content: A piece of wood with 75% MC weighs 75% more than the same sample if it were completely dry (5% MC is the attainable minimum). To determine moisture content by percent, weigh a wet sample piece of wood and then dry it in an oven (under 200°) and weigh it again. Wood is "kiln-dry" when it stops losing weight. Percent moisture content equals green weight minus dry weight, times 100, divided by the dry weight.

Moisture meters measure electrical resistance between two probes inserted in the wood, but they're expensive, and most green woodworkers find them unnecessary. With experience, you can judge approximate moisture content by knowing the history of the wood after it was cut, and by sensory tests. When two pieces of dry wood are knocked together, they "plink"; wet wood "thunks." And, a piece of dry wood held to your cheek feels warm; wet wood feels cool. Try these tests with samples you know to be wet, air-dried and kiln-dried. —*D.L.*

Fox Wedging

A sly joint for a 17th-century stool

by Alasdair G.B. Wallace

A request to copy a pair of 17th-century joynt stools in brown oak offered a welcome change and challenge for me. My customer had admired a pair of 19th-century reproduction stools in an antique shop, but found the price beyond her means and equally beyond the realm of reason. Though English brown oak costs three to four times as much as domestic red oak, a quick calculation suggested that I could produce two stools for less than the price of a single 100-year-old reproduction.

Joynt stools date from the late 16th century and the advent of the technique of framing and the pegged mortise-and-tenon joint. (The term joynt comes from joined.) In addition to plain, totally unadorned joynt stools, some exhibited simple moldings and carving, while others for churches and manor houses were elaborately carved and molded. I was asked to copy the most basic stool, the product of the country carpenter.

Construction of the stool is straightforward. When preparing the stock, make the leg blanks 1 in. longer than the finished dimension to allow for trimming. You can mortise the legs before or after turning them. I prefer to turn them first so that I can fine-tune the location of the mortises relative to the turnings.

The mortises and tenons should be laid out so that the outer faces of the apron rails and stretchers will finish flush with the outer faces of the legs. For maximum strength, the tenons should be offset as shown in the drawing on the facing page, and mortises for adjacent rails or stretchers shouldn't intersect in the leg. The legs are splayed 5° from perpendicular when the stool is viewed from the ends, so those mortises and tenons must be laid out accordingly. The Jacobeans didn't glue the mortise and tenons, relying instead on pegs and the shrinkage of slightly green legs around the tenons for strength. My brown oak was bone dry, so I chose to fox-wedge the tenons to help secure the joints.

Though little-used today, the fox-wedged tenon provides an exceptionally strong joint where a through-wedged tenon would be inappropriate or impossible. A fox-wedged tenon expands the tenon within its mortise, as does a through-wedged tenon, and both require tapered mortises to accommodate the tenon's expansion. The difference between the joints is that the fox-wedged mortise is blind and the wedges must be driven into the tenon by the bottom of the mortise. A great many things can go wrong if the joint isn't laid out and cut carefully. If, for example, the tenon or wedges are too long or the mortise insufficiently tapered, the joint won't pull tight; if the mortise is too wide or the wedges too slim, the joint will be loose. Regardless of whether you glue the joints (I preferred not to), they can be further secured by pegging.

Wallace's brown oak copy of a 17th-century joynt stool, left, is held together by fox-wedged tenons. The top is attached to the apron rails with square wooden pegs. A fox-wedged tenon and mortise, above, is ready for assembly. Since the faces of the pieces are to be flush, the tenon is offset for greater strength. The mortise, right, has been too heavily undercut, causing the tenon to fracture at the end of the top kerf. The wedges and kerfs, however, are perfect.

Lay out and cut the joint as you would a standard blind mortise-and-tenon. Then taper the mortise, kerf the tenons and make the wedges following these basic guidelines:

The depth of the mortise should be about $\frac{1}{16}$ in. to $\frac{1}{8}$ in. greater than the length of the tenon.

The taper of the mortise should equal the difference between the width of the sawkerfs and the thickness of the wedges.

Begin the mortise taper at a distance of about one-fifth the depth of the mortise beneath the shoulder. (Start tapering a 1¼-in.-deep mortise about ¼ in. beneath the shoulder.) This ensures that the wedges will be driven into the tenon equally and that the tenon will be centered in the mortise.

Position the kerfs about one-fifth the tenon's width in from each of its edges (about ¼ in. on a 1¼-in. wide tenon), and cut them to a depth of about four-fifths the tenon length.

Make hardwood wedges as long as or a bit less than the length of the kerf. At its thickest, a wedge should be about twice the width of the kerf, thinner if the wood is likely to split.

I assemble the sides of the stool first, then add the end rails and stretchers. When you assemble the fox-wedged joints, make sure that the wedges are firmly in place in the kerfs, and take care not to dislodge the wedges as you insert each tenon into its mortise. To avoid jarring the wedges loose, draw the joints together with a clamp rather than driving them together with a mallet. The original stool's joints were pegged. I drove square pegs into slightly smaller round holes, then flushed them off with a chisel. To attach the top, I used the Jacobean method of driving square pegs through it into the apron rails. Nails, pocket screws or buttons can do the job, too.

Everyone in the business of reproduction has his or her own secret recipe for stain. These range from unlikely concoctions of manure, ashes and soot to commercial stains. Don't be afraid to experiment. I used a manure/ash/soot combination, painting it on liberally, filling cracks and hollows and leaving it for three or four months. Brushing the mixture off revealed a deep brown surface. Thorough wiping in areas of high wear and some judicious sanding achieved the antique effect my client desired. A beeswax, turpentine and lampblack mixture completes the finish. Apply it over five wiped-on coats of 1-1 white shellac/methylhydrate which seals the wood and gives it life and depth.

My customer's wish that the stool look old presented me with an ethical dilemma. Judging by the wealth of "authentic" joynt stools I saw on a recent trip to England, the Jacobean carpenter was much more prolific than we realize or current high prices have tempted their modern counterparts to augment the Jacobean output. I was able to satisfy the customer's desire for a piece that looked authentic by staining and distressing. By carving my name and the date on the back face of an apron rail I ensured that no one would ever be duped by my deception. □

Alasdair G.B. Wallace makes furniture in Lakefield, Ontario.

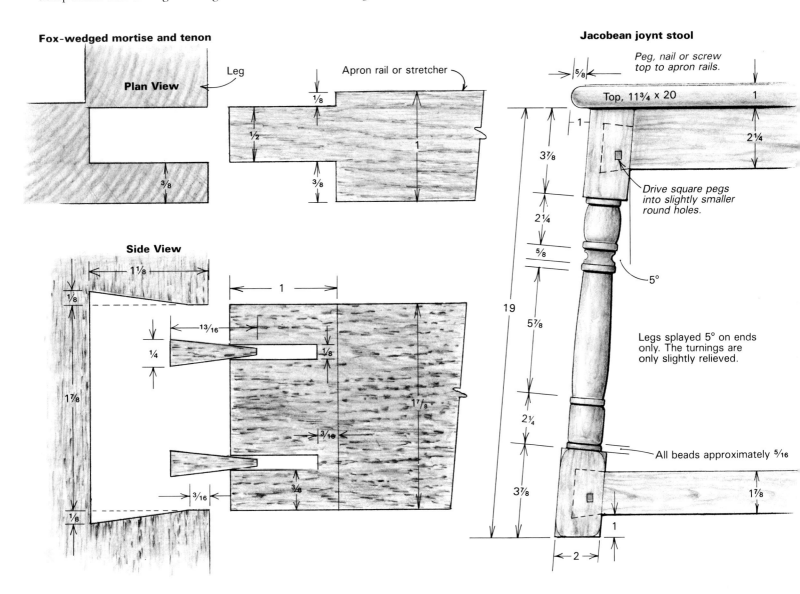

Fox-wedged mortise and tenon

Plan View — Leg — Apron rail or stretcher

Side View

Jacobean joynt stool

Peg, nail or screw top to apron rails.

Top, 11¾ x 20

Drive square pegs into slightly smaller round holes.

Legs splayed 5° on ends only. The turnings are only slightly relieved.

All beads approximately $\frac{5}{16}$

Fig. 1: Cabriole leg anatomy and shaping overview

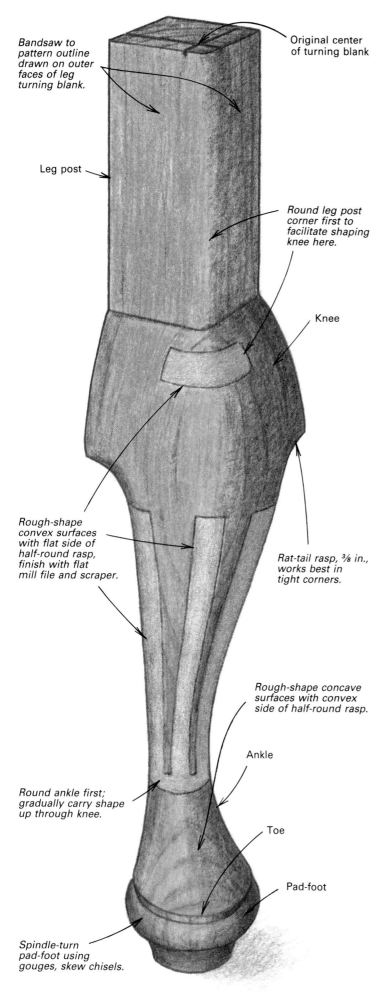

Bandsaw to pattern outline drawn on outer faces of leg turning blank.

Original center of turning blank

Leg post

Round leg post corner first to facilitate shaping knee here.

Knee

Rough-shape convex surfaces with flat side of half-round rasp, finish with flat mill file and scraper.

Rat-tail rasp, ⅜ in., works best in tight corners.

Rough-shape concave surfaces with convex side of half-round rasp.

Ankle

Round ankle first; gradually carry shape up through knee.

Toe

Pad-foot

Spindle-turn pad-foot using gouges, skew chisels.

Shaping a Cabriole Leg
An easy job with files and rasps

by Eugene E. Landon

Many woodworkers are afraid of cabriole legs. There's something intimidating about all those graceful interconnecting lines. And making matching pairs seems to require a touch of genius. In point of fact, however, cabriole legs are a breeze. I had my young helper, Joel Crabtree, feeling guilty for awhile thinking I must have worked incessantly through the night to produce sets of legs for six chairs. Each morning he would find yet another completed set. When he finally discovered I was doing a leg in 20 minutes or so, he felt more sheepish than guilty.

I'm sure craftsmen of the period (1730-1795) worked as quickly. The simultaneous existence of plain and ornately carved styles reflected the European origin and local taste more so than the skill of the woodworker. Economics sometimes dictated the extent of carving; each carved area was charged for separately. Shaping the plain legs for a Queen Anne or Chippendale chair, which I'll describe later, requires only rudimentary skills in spindle-turning and in the use of files, rasps and scrapers. Figure 1 identifies the parts of the leg and will give you an overall idea of how it is made. The dimensions are for the late Queen Anne, early Chippendale chair shown on p. 96, but the legs can be adapted to different chairs, tables and other furniture pieces.

If you have doubts about your ability to make cabriole legs, I invite you to glue up a blank from a cheap, soft wood, such as pine, then go at the job with abandon. There really are not any subtleties or secrets.

Preparing the blank—The leg blanks are 17½ in. long (to allow some excess at both ends for later trimming) and 2⅝ in. square. To ensure strength, choose wood without much grain runout. The leg I'm shown making in the photographs is cherry of the worst-working sort—rock hard and brittle. It probably came from a leaning tree. Even so, the job isn't difficult.

Make a leg template according to the dimensions in figure 2 on p. 97, and trace it onto what will become the two outside surfaces of the leg. Mark the center of the ends of the blank at this time, as a reference for mounting it on the lathe later. Then, carefully bandsaw to the outlines on both sides, using the offcuts from the first cuts to support the leg for the second cuts. You'll get the

Drawings: Lee Hov

The development of a cabriole leg: First, the template at bottom is traced onto two sides of the squared stock. In his right hand, the author holds a blank that has been bandsawn following the template lines. Next, the foot is turned on the lathe. The top surface of the square section just above the turned foot forms the toe. In his left hand, Landon holds a finished leg that has been rasped, filed and scraped. An experienced worker can do the whole job in 20 minutes.

most precise cuts if you tape the offcuts in place using shims of paper or veneer to fill the bandsaw kerf. After bandsawing, what was the center point in the leg-post end of the leg is now offset. The leg axis extends from this point down through the center of the foot (see figure 2). This clever axis alignment is what allows the leg to be conveniently shaped on the lathe.

Your leg should now look like the template shown at the bottom of the photo above and like the leg I'm holding in my right hand. Chuck this in the lathe with the foot at the tailstock and turn the foot according to the dimensions given in figure 2. Note that the top surface of the square section (just above the turned foot) forms the toe. You should just nick this as shown; if you try to turn any higher up the ankle, you'll ruin the lines of the leg. Your sample should now look like the second leg from the top in the photo.

Rasping and filing—The easiest way to shape cabriole legs is with rasps and files. The initial cuts are heavy ones and are made using a half-round rasp: the convex side for concave curves, the flat side for convex curves. I also use a ³⁄₈-in. rat-tail rasp on occasion; it's particularly good for removing small high spots on the top concave surface of the foot (just back from the toe) and underneath the knee. These areas are mostly endgrain, and the wider rasp is more difficult to control through the transition to the long-grain areas.

A 10-in. or 12-in. flat mill file and a round file will remove the rasp and bandsaw marks. A scraper, made from a length of old power-hacksaw blade, will then remove the file marks. The trick to rasping and filing is to smoothly push or pull the tool in a gentle arc to gradually develop the desired shape. If you hold the handle of the rasp in your right hand and its tip in your left, it will cut on the push stroke. Reverse the rasp in your hands and it will cut on the pull, or "draw," stroke (hence the name: draw-filing). Keep the teeth clean, and don't let the rasps and files rub against each other, as this will dull them quickly.

Position the work in a bar clamp held in a vise, as shown in the photos. Since the narrowest part of the leg is at the top of the foot, establish the basic shape here first. Use this as a reference to gauge your progress in developing the shape for the rest of the

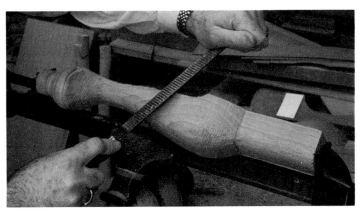

The leg is clamped in a vise, above. Landon has already shaped the top surface of the foot and is shown here using the convex side of a half-round rasp to round the corners of the leg. The goal is to remove enough wood from each of the four corners to make the ankle round. The profile of the curve at the ankle should extend up the full length of the leg.

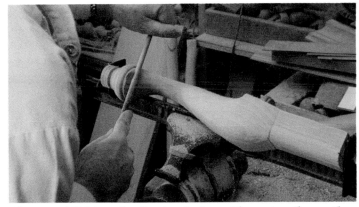

After establishing the basic shape with rasps, the author quickly removes the tool marks with fine files. The key to successful filing is to move the tool smoothly in a gentle arc and gradually develop the final shape. Drawfiling works well here: If the file's handle is in your right hand, you push; if it's in your left hand, you pull. Rotate the leg gradually as you refine the shape, and work in whatever direction that's necessary to avoid tearout.

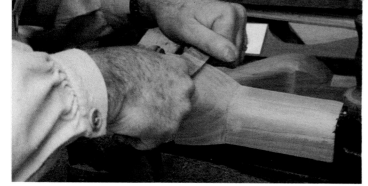

Above: Bandsaw marks remaining on the flat surfaces at the upper part of the leg are removed with a flat mill file. Rounding the post corner first creates a step in the top of the knee and gives you enough room to shape the knee properly. Below: Landon's favorite scraper, made from a length of power-hacksaw blade, polishes the fine file marks away. A light touch with supermarket-variety green Scotch-Brite, which traditional-minded Landon refers to as 'sharkskin,' will yield a uniform surface ready for finishing. The occasional tiny scraper chatter marks on the final surface resemble those found on 18th-century work.

leg. Begin by rasping the top of the foot down into a fair curve that blends into the ankle. At the ankle itself, the goal is to remove each of the four corners in turn until the ankle is round. The profile of the curve at the ankle extends through the length of the leg. It is easy to check the width and uniformity of the curve by eye as you proceed.

Begin the shaping by rotating the leg by 90°, working each corner in turn. It may take several complete revolutions before you are satisfied with the rough shape. Continue this procedure, but reduce the rotation angle to first 45°, then 22 1/2°, and so on until the profile is shaped fair. Orient the leg as you wish, working in whatever direction that's necessary to avoid tearout.

At the outer corner of the top of the knee, it will seem at first that there is not enough wood to allow a curve; rasping one would lower the front of the post. This problem, however, takes care of itself if you round the outer corner of the post first, which creates a step in the top of the knee. Because the area is endgrain, I generally shave it with a chisel for better control, but rasps and files will work here, too.

I finish the legs using a scraper, as mentioned, followed by green Scotch-Brite (available in your local supermarket). The final surface, with its occasional tiny scraper chatter marks, looks just like the surface I frequently find on 18th-century work. Set the legs aside for the moment; you'll have to do some fine-tuning later, after the legs are assembled into the chair frame. □

Eugene Landon builds reproductions of period furniture in Montoursville, Pa. You'll find additional suggestions for carving in his article on pp. 116-119. Mack Headley's instructions for carving the shell on pp. 98-102 may also be helpful.

Photo below: Terry Wild

Above is the original chair from which the templates and dimensions were taken for the drawing on the facing page.

Building a Chippendale chair

Now that you know how easy it really is to make a cabriole leg, you may be itching to give it a try. On the facing page are the measured drawings you'll need to make the chair shown in the photo above. The first step is to scale the templates up to full-size and cut them out. Because chairs are almost always built in sets, make the templates from a durable material. Label them clearly, as in years hence, you may want to use them again. Write down angles, thicknesses and other technical notes on the templates as well.

After cutting the joints, assemble the chair in sections, which will ease the problem of getting it square. If you try to glue up a whole chair at once, the job may get out of hand. Begin by gluing up the rear posts, the crest rail and the rear seat rail. Take care that everything is plumb, flat

Fig. 2: Chair plans

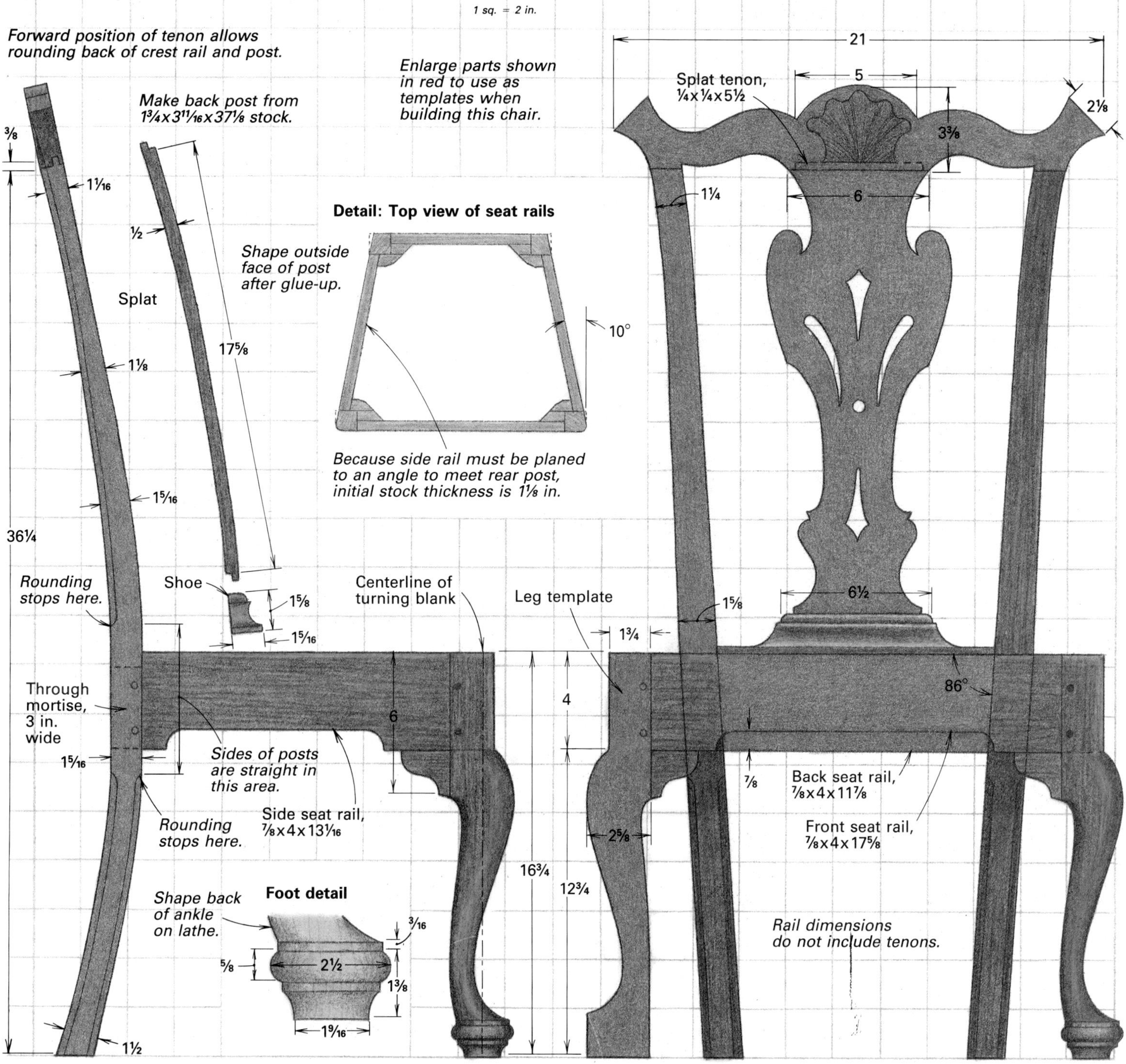

1 sq. = 2 in.
Forward position of tenon allows rounding back of crest rail and post.
Make back post from 1¾x3¹¹⁄₁₆x37⅛ stock.
Enlarge parts shown in red to use as templates when building this chair.
Splat tenon, ¼x¼x5½
21
5
2⅛
3⅜
6
1¼
⅜
1¹⁄₁₆
½
Splat
Detail: Top view of seat rails
Shape outside face of post after glue-up.
10°
17⅝
1⅛
Because side rail must be planed to an angle to meet rear post, initial stock thickness is 1⅛ in.
1⁵⁄₁₆
36¼
Rounding stops here.
Shoe
1⅝
1⁵⁄₁₆
Centerline of turning blank
Leg template
1¾
1⅝
6½
86°
Through mortise, 3 in. wide
4
6
1⁵⁄₁₆
Sides of posts are straight in this area.
Rounding stops here.
Side seat rail, ⅞x4x13¹⁄₁₆
⅞
Back seat rail, ⅞x4x11⅞
Front seat rail, ⅞x4x17⅝
2⅝
16¾
12¾
Shape back of ankle on lathe.
Foot detail
³⁄₁₆
⅝
2½
1⅜
1⁹⁄₁₆
Rail dimensions do not include tenons.
1½

and square. Note that the shoe, or saddle, which is mortised to receive the tenon on the bottom of the splat, is not glued in place until the back is assembled. You want the splat tenon to fit tightly into the shoe. If the splat were glued in place, it would most likely split because of seasonal wood movement. Therefore, cut its tenons after the rest of the back has been glued up solid. As a last resort for a splat that turns out too short, you can modify the shoe's height to compensate. Also, before fitting the shoe, it's easiest to glue the back glue blocks in place against the back rail, then plane them flush with the front surface of the back posts after the glue has dried. If you see a chair with some other glue-block arrangement, chances are it isn't original.

When the back is dry, the remaining rails and the legs can be glued in place. Once you know the back is straight and square, you can devote your full attention to squaring the rails and legs. Dry-fit the pieces first, just in case you have to modify the shoulder lines or adjust the mortises and tenons. When all is correct, mark the bottoms of the legs, remove them, and then cut them to length. After the assembly is dry, saw off the excess length from the top of the front legs.

The final step in construction is to fine-tune things: Reshape the outsides of the leg posts so they angle back in line with the side seat rails. I use rasps and files for this job as well. At the same time, reshape the top of the knee to follow suit. Lastly, you'll need to chisel a notch in the top of the post for the corner of the seat frame, which should be cut and planed to fit.

—E.L.

Carving a Scallop Shell

Gouge's sweep determines the curves

by Mack Headley, Jr.

Fig. 1: Laying out the shell

A. Divide height into 9 units (red) and draw arcs to define lobes and wing corners. Divide height into 5 units (blue), draw arc to define hinge and line to locate outer rays.

B. Outline perimeter with imprint of gouges shown.

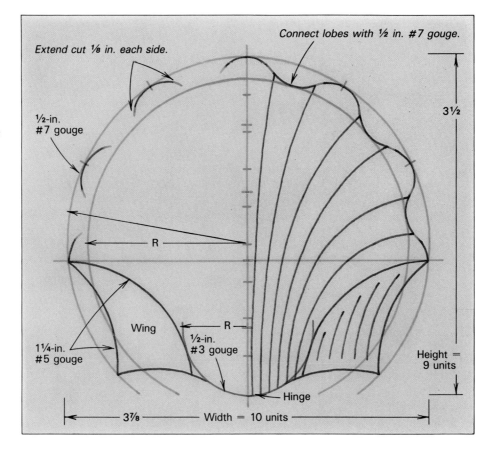

Extend cut ⅛ in. each side.

Connect lobes with ½ in. #7 gouge.

½-in. #7 gouge

3½

R

Wing

1¼-in. #5 gouge

½-in. #3 gouge

R

Hinge

Height = 9 units

3⅞

Width = 10 units

C. Sketch in lines to define convex and concave rays. Save for reference. Make concave rays slightly narrower than convex rays.

The shell was a very popular detail on English and Colonial furniture throughout the 18th century. Carved on drawer fronts, knees of cabriole legs, and the crest and seat rails of chairs, the shell was appreciated as more than just decoration. The study of nature was fashionable at the time and artisans attempted to analyze, and capture in their designs, the symmetry and proportion they found in natural forms. Classicism was also in vogue, so symbolic meanings (the Greek goddess Aphrodite arose from the sea on a scallop shell) would have added a dimension to its popularity which is hard for us to appreciate today. Yet the shell's appeal as a decorative detail endures.

In this article, I'll go through the step-by-step development of a shell. This particular shell is a style common on Pennsylvania furniture. I've chosen to carve an applied shell—one that will be glued onto a flat surface. You can apply the carving techniques to carve shells directly on drawer fronts or crest rails.

Carving gouges are made in various widths and curvatures. The curvature, or sweep, is designated by a number from 1 to 11. The higher the number, the more pronounced the curve. Curves are carved by selecting gouges with the appropriate curvature and transferring their shapes to the wood.

Make a full-size drawing of the shell on paper or wood, following the layout shown above. The perimeter is defined by the imprints of the gouges shown. These same tools will later be used to carve the shell. The sweep numbers given correspond to my gouges. Because sweeps are not standardized, however, you may find that your gouge doesn't exactly match the curve in the drawing. In that case, choose another gouge to get the right shape.

This shell measures 3½ in. high and 3⅞ in. wide, based on proportions of 9 units high by 10 units wide. By using these proportions, you can scale the shell up or down to suit your needs. The lines between the rays are drawn freehand, pivoting off the knuckle of the little finger to control the curve. Save the final drawing as a reference for laying out the rays on the carving.

Mack Headley, Jr. is master cabinetmaker at Colonial Williamsburg, Va. A videotape of Headley carving the shell in this article is available from Taunton Press.

1 With dividers, lay out the perimeter of the shell on the back side of a ⅝-in.- thick board, as shown in the photo at right. For a beginner, it might be more comfortable to start with a paper pattern traced from your drawing, although I'm inclined to stay away from paper patterns because of the bloated character caused by the thickness of a pencil line. Outline the perimeter with the gouge imprints shown.

The next step is to saw out the blank on a bandsaw or with a coping saw. Saw slightly outside the gouged outline of the wings and hinge, and around the arc that defines the limits of the convex rays. It isn't necessary to saw in and out around the lobes because it's easier to remove this material with a gouge.

Lay out the perimeter of the shell on the back side of the board. Then outline the perimeter with gouge imprints (right).

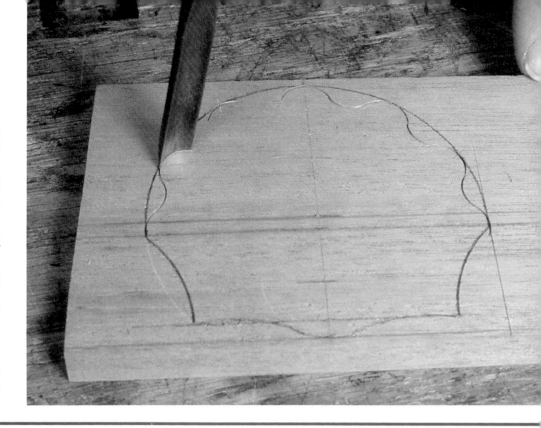

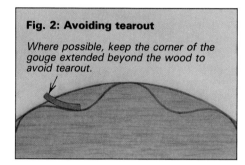

Fig. 2: Avoiding tearout

Where possible, keep the corner of the gouge extended beyond the wood to avoid tearout.

2 Next, with the appropriate gouge, cut right to the line. Angle the gouge so the bevel is vertical, and cut straight down ³⁄₁₆ in. The force comes from the forearm and body. Lean into the tool and push down with your weight, as shown in the photo at right. Lever out the chip at the bottom of the cut. These bordering cuts establish the edge around the bottom of the shell, as shown in figure 3.

Remove the wood from the concave rays first. Be careful that the corners of the gouge don't get under the grain at points where the outline runs diagonally across the grain. The danger of tearout is greatest at the tip of the center ray, where the cut follows the grain, and least at the tips of the outer rays, where the cut is across the grain. Try to keep the corner of the gouge extended beyond the limits of the wood as much as possible, as shown in figure 2.

You can remove the wood at the side of the wings with little chance of tearout. If you have a lot of wood to remove or you are working with especially hard wood, shear across the grain diagonally with a skewed cut.

After sawing around the perimeter, cut to the imprint line with the appropriate gouge. Angle the tool so the bevel is vertical, then lean into the tool and push down with your weight. Cut down ³⁄₁₆ in. and lever out the chip.

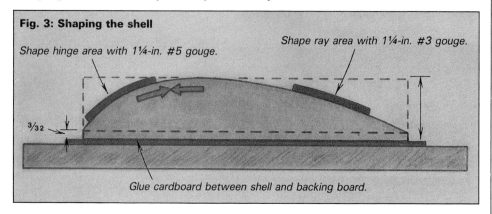

Sculpt the shell surface by transferring the shape of a 1¼-in. #5 gouge to the hinge area and a 1¼-in. #3 gouge to the ray area. The #5 cuts (top) follow the grain while the #3 cuts sweep from the center ray down to the wings on each side (above, left and right). The gouge should lie evenly on the finished surface.

Fig. 3: Shaping the shell

Define the wings by cutting straight down with a 1¼-in. #5 gouge (top) and levering out the chip (above).

Ride the heel of a ¼-in. #7 gouge on the shoulder left by the #5 gouge to create a radius at the bottom of the shoulder.

3 After you've outlined the perimeter, glue the shell, layout facedown, to a board about 14 in. long, with a piece of cardboard in between. I use hide glue, but any water-soluble glue will work.

The next step is to sculpt the surface of the shell. The curvature at the hinge area is formed by a 1¼-in. #5 gouge, cutting with the grain as shown in the top photo. When the #5 gouge lies evenly over the hinge portion, shape the flatter portion of the shell with a 1¼-in. #3 gouge.

With these cuts, your wood will begin to reveal itself. Unless your stuff has very even grain, you'll have to adjust your cuts to the direction of the grain. Begin the cuts with the 1¼-in. #3 gouge, working from the tip of the central ray out toward the outer rays at the wings. These cuts, sweeping diagonally across the grain, should work cleanly across the most distorted grain patterns. Blend the cuts from the #3 gouge into the curve from the #5 gouge. The surface is finished when the #3 gouge lies evenly over the surface of the shell up to the junction of the #5 curve.

4 Remove most of the extra wood at the wings with the 1¼-in. #5 gouge. With the tool held vertically, cut straight down to within ¼ in. of the back of the shell and lever out the chip. Then, ride a ¼-in. #7 gouge along the base of the vertical shoulder that you just cut, working from the hinge to the tip of the outer ray, to create a radius at the bottom of that vertical shoulder. Ride the heel of the gouge at a low angle against the shoulder and raise it until it begins to cut. Reduce the wing surface to a ³⁄₃₂ in. thickness with a ½-in. #2 gouge.

Pivot off your knuckle to control curves when drawing the rays (top). Define the rays with parting tool cuts (above). Adjust spacing by leaning the tool.

5 After the wing areas are completed, draw the rays on the sculpted surface of the shell. Follow your layout drawing and practice the technique of pivoting on your knuckle to control the curves. With a V-parting tool, make shallow cuts along these lines to separate the rays, working from the high center point of the shell toward the edges. This is an opportunity to read the grain of your wood, and to determine from which direction final cuts need to be made. The edge of the V bordering the concave rays will be saved, as shown in figure 4. Give special attention to the cuts that go across the grain diagonally. A very sharp V-parting tool will make these cuts with minimal tearout, but if tearout does occur, come in from the other direction and clean it up. The area of greatest difficulty will be at the hinge portion, where the cuts run straight across the grain, $\frac{3}{32}$ in. apart. Be careful not to tear out the wood between these cuts. To prevent tearout at the edge, stop the cut just short of the edge and complete it from the other direction. You could also make a vertical cut with a straight chisel. After the shallow cuts are made, deepen them to a strong $\frac{1}{16}$ in. at the rays, tapering to a strong $\frac{1}{32}$ in. at the hinge. As you deepen these cuts, this is your last chance to adjust them sideways for good spacing and flowing curves.

6 The next step is to shape the areas between the parting tool cuts into convex and concave rays. Because the rays diminish in width from the tip to the hinge, several different gouges will be needed to shape the full length of each ray, as shown in figure 4. The transition areas, where the curve produced by one gouge meets the curve from another, will need to be blended to get a smooth, flowing line. Strive to produce a finished surface with your tool so there's little, if any, need to sand.

Begin with the convex rays, starting about $\frac{3}{4}$ in. from the tip and working out toward the edge with a $\frac{1}{2}$-in. #3 gouge. Be careful not to tear out the edge when you're cutting across the grain. Cut down to the bottom of the V left by the parting tool and ride the side of the gouge against the shoulder left by the parting tool cut, as shown in figure 4. If the corner of the gouge cuts into the facet, you will ruin your work, so be careful. At its tip, the ray should show the full curve of the gouge. Shape the first $\frac{3}{4}$ in. of all the convex rays with the same tool, then switch to a $\frac{1}{4}$-in. #4 gouge to shape the

Shape tips of convex rays with a ½-in. #3 gouge, carefully avoiding tearout on cross-grain cuts (above). Left hand helps control the tool on concave rays (below).

Cut from the bottom upward with a ⅟₁₆-in. #11 veiner to carve the veins in the wings.

The finished shell is ready to be separated from its backing and glued on a piece of furniture. The curves and flats are designed to catch and play with light and shadow.

next 1 in. or so of each convex ray. Lastly, switch to a ⅛-in. #6 gouge to shape the remaining section. Cut in the direction of the hinge on this last section.

Shaping the concave rays will also require a series of gouges. Again, be careful when the gouge exits across the grain and at points where the gouge cuts against the grain on the diagonal. You don't need to shape the concave rays at the hinge area, where they are spaced only ³⁄₃₂ in. apart. The parting tool cut alone will give the desired visual effect in the hinge area.

7 The last detail will be to cut the five small veins on the wings with a ⅟₁₆-in. #11 veiner. These break up this large, flat surface, and accent the linear quality of the hinge area. The cuts should run parallel to the side curve of the wing and be spaced about ⅛ in. apart. Enter the wood with the veiner perpendicular to the surface to capture the full curve of the tool as it enters the wood. As with the parting tool, you may want to make a shallow cut and adjust the spacing by leaning the tool to the side. The veins should be a shallow ⅟₁₆ in. deep. Dragging the veiner back through the cut burnishes and polishes the surface.

Some areas may need a light sanding with worn 220-grit sandpaper, folded to get into corners. Be careful not to round off the crispness of sharp corners and ruin the definition they should give when the finish is applied.

To remove the shell from the backup board, slip a thin knife or palette knife between the layers of cardboard and gradually work it under the shell until it is free. The excess paper can be removed by lightly wetting it with water to soften the glue. Your shell is now ready to be glued in place. ◻

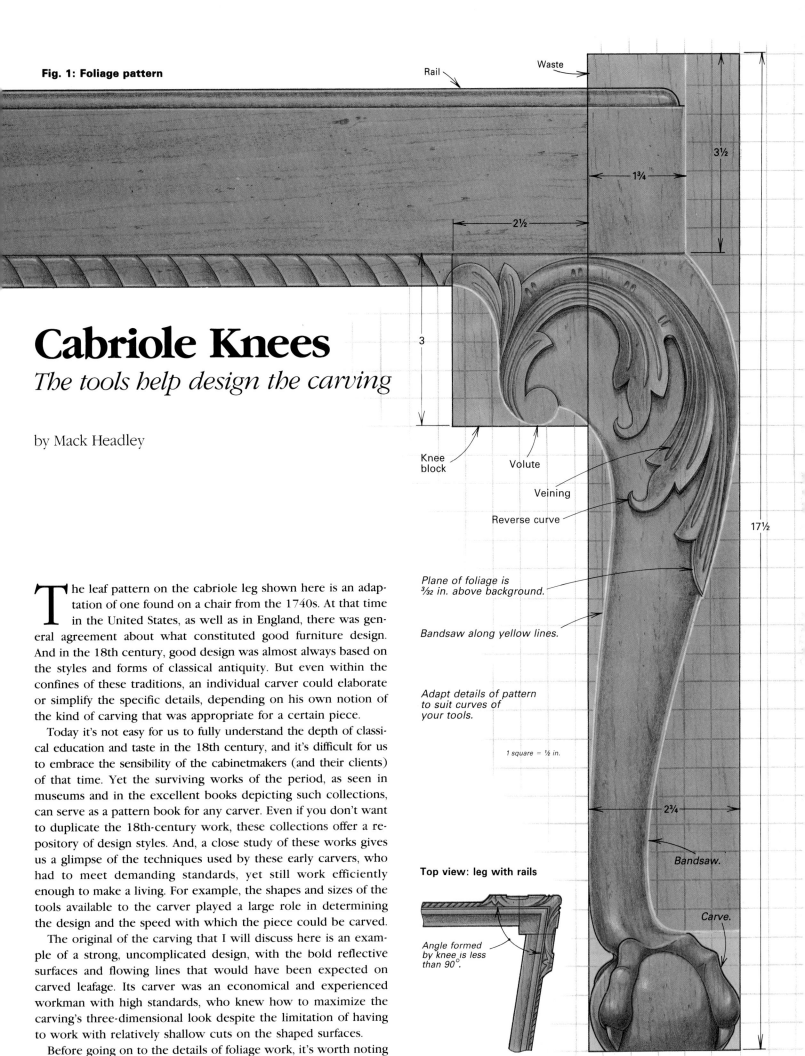

Rail

Waste

3½

1¾

2½

3

Knee block

Volute

Veining

Reverse curve

17½

Plane of foliage is ³⁄₃₂ in. above background.

Bandsaw along yellow lines.

Adapt details of pattern to suit curves of your tools.

1 square = ½ in.

2¾

Bandsaw.

Carve.

Top view: leg with rails

Angle formed by knee is less than 90°.

Cabriole Knees
The tools help design the carving

by Mack Headley

The leaf pattern on the cabriole leg shown here is an adaptation of one found on a chair from the 1740s. At that time in the United States, as well as in England, there was general agreement about what constituted good furniture design. And in the 18th century, good design was almost always based on the styles and forms of classical antiquity. But even within the confines of these traditions, an individual carver could elaborate or simplify the specific details, depending on his own notion of the kind of carving that was appropriate for a certain piece.

Today it's not easy for us to fully understand the depth of classical education and taste in the 18th century, and it's difficult for us to embrace the sensibility of the cabinetmakers (and their clients) of that time. Yet the surviving works of the period, as seen in museums and in the excellent books depicting such collections, can serve as a pattern book for any carver. Even if you don't want to duplicate the 18th-century work, these collections offer a repository of design styles. And, a close study of these works gives us a glimpse of the techniques used by these early carvers, who had to meet demanding standards, yet still work efficiently enough to make a living. For example, the shapes and sizes of the tools available to the carver played a large role in determining the design and the speed with which the piece could be carved.

The original of the carving that I will discuss here is an example of a strong, uncomplicated design, with the bold reflective surfaces and flowing lines that would have been expected on carved leafage. Its carver was an economical and experienced workman with high standards, who knew how to maximize the carving's three-dimensional look despite the limitation of having to work with relatively shallow cuts on the shaped surfaces.

Before going on to the details of foliage work, it's worth noting

Left, a template is made by cutting the outlines with the tools that will be used for the carving. Right, a line of stop cuts, to prevent chipping, is made around the penciled template out- *line in the same manner as the template itself is cut. Here, the background is being leveled down in a series of cuts to full depth. Stop cuts are deepened as necessary.*

that a knee carving such as the one shown in figure 1 need not be restricted to chairs: It would work well on a tea table and could be adapted to the long, curved knees of a tripod table. In all these cases, the majority of the curves in the leg flow along the level of the carving's background. Thus all curves appear to be continuous beneath the foliage, and the widest part of the knee below the carving is thinner than it would be on an uncarved leg. There is plenty of bulk in this area to ensure a strong leg, however, and the curve can be gently shaped to blend into an ankle about the same thickness as the ankle on an uncarved leg.

The actual knee-carving process can be broken down into five steps. The same steps can be applied to other types of carving as well. First, a full-leg template is cut, and the design is marked out. Second, another template or pattern for the carving is made and transferred to the leg. I cut the templates and patterns with my carving tools to ensure that these tools can form all the shapes in the design. I have a fairly good selection of tools in my kit, as discussed below, so this isn't generally a limitation; actually, the tools are a great aid in controlling both the design layout and its execution. The third step is to cut vertical stop cuts on the leg around the perimeter of the design and carve out the background areas. Fourth, the main shapes of the leaves are incised and the surfaces carved smooth. Fifth, the veining and other detailing is cut.

Drawing foliage with tools—In the initial planning stages, it is important to envision the effect you wish your carving to have. Drawing is the best way to define these shapes, thus reducing the chance of careless blunders or dead ends during the actual carving. Drawing skills are also important to the carver, because it can be difficult to fit templates and patterns around curved surfaces. Usually the pattern can be used to establish the main lines, but the details must be drawn directly on the wood.

The flow of the foliage should complement the curves of the knee, as outlined on the full-leg template, which is used to draw the lines for bandsawing the blank. The first step, therefore, is to

draw the leg template full-size and then draw the foliage upon it to establish the general form and flow of the leaves. The foliage pattern generally begins with the somewhat tedious copying of carved foliage depicted in 18th-century design books. Copying is easier if you lay out the designs on grids of various proportions, yet the leaves must still retain the flow and appear correctly balanced. As a general principle, lines and veins should emanate from a logical point of origin, such as the main stem of the leaf, and flow smoothly, fanning out to their full spread with a balanced progression and then reducing toward the tips.

The shapes I use in drawing the foliage conform to the sweeps of various gouges in my kit. I rely on a few broad gouges of related sweeps to help establish the broad shapes, a few narrower gouges whose curves flow comfortably into the wider ones and several smaller tools for detailing. My basic kit includes 12mm and 30mm #3 sweep gouges; $7/16$-, $1/2$-, $3/4$-, 1- and $1\frac{1}{4}$-in. #5 gouges; $1/4$- and $1/2$-in. #7 gouges; a $1/8$-in. #8 veiner and a $3/16$-in. #9 gouge. Flat chisels of various widths, as well as a scraper or two, are handy for smoothing background areas and working in tight spots. If a line doesn't exactly conform to a gouge's sweep, or if I want to expand or contract a curve, I can roll the gouge around the curve like a wheel, steering it as I go. Working *with* a set of tools rather than *against* it is, along with sharpness, a key element in successful carving.

Rounding the leg—After bandsawing the basic leg shape, I round the surfaces with a spokeshave to bring out the flow of the leg. Shaping the leg below the area to be carved provides a reference surface to work from in shaping the foliage area, which must be proud of the main line of the leg. With cabriole legs, the carving should blend with both the leg's vertical curve and its horizontal plane.

The point of the knee begins flat at its junction with the upper post of the leg, and wood is gradually removed in a broad, convex curve. Hold a crisp line down the top two-thirds of the area to be

From *Fine Woodworking* magazine (September 1988) 72:57-61

The main elements of the individual leaves are separated with a gouge whose curvature matches the desired profile. Because of the curves of the pattern, at times, one half of the cut may be with the grain while the other half is against it. The solution is to take light cuts on the side that is cutting well, changing direction as necessary.

carved, then make a transition to a ⅛-in. half-round for the lower third. You want the foliage area to stand about ⅛ in. above the leg surface at the tip of the lowest central leaf. The fullest point of the knee is lowered ⅛ in. on each face in a gradual convex curve beginning at a point about two-thirds of the leg width back from the front of the knee. Extra wood must be left for carving the foliage at the top of the leg, where it meets the post, and for carving the volute at the back of the leg. The leg at its widest point, including the projection of the carved area, should be in proportion to the chair or other piece of furniture supported by the leg.

Leaf template—In addition to the customary whole-leg template used to trace the lines to be bandsawn, I recommend you make another template or pattern to transfer the carving design to the wood. The carver who made the original leg would have been so familiar with this design that he could work without a pattern. After all, even if he produced only one set of a dozen chairs of this pattern, the symmetry of each knee would have required him to repeat the leaf's sculpture and detail 24 times. If you don't have the dexterity developed through numerous repetitions of the same pattern, though, you'll find that a template will be invaluable in helping you avoid mistakes.

As previously discussed, you should cut out the template using your carving tools, as shown in the top, left photo on the facing page. If the pattern is based on a two-dimensional drawing, as appears to be the case with much 18th-century design, the pattern will have to be adjusted to account for the extra 3⁄16 in. or so added by the curve from the protrusion of the knee to the leg post. This can be accounted for by transferring the major horizontal elements from the pattern to the frontal curve, then sketching in extended vertical lines to complete the outside shape. The shaping of the front of the leg removes any reference points for orienting a template, but you can line it up by eye.

After sketching in all the details, double-check the lines against your tools to be sure they still fit (see the top, right photo on the facing page). When all is well, use hand pressure alone to outline the carving with the appropriate gouge shapes. The cuts should be perfectly vertical or slightly undercut. These stop cuts will allow the background to be carved away without chipping the border lines of the leaves. In tight corners, you can also make the stop cuts by smoothly slicing with the point of a knife. In the initial stages, don't worry about the surface of the background; concentrate on preserving the border of your leafage. After reaching the depth of the initial gouge cuts, make another series of stop cuts. To lower the background the full 3⁄32 in. so the surface appears to flow into the line of the lower leg, you'll have to go around the whole design at least twice. Because of the knee's shape, changes in grain direction are inevitable. Work with or across the grain whenever possible. Keep tools sharp.

Prepare the final background using flat chisels of varying widths. The widest chisels possible, in a given area, will ensure the most uniform, even surface. Final smoothing of the background can be done with narrow cabinet scrapers. You should not be too finicky. Traditional carvers often left some chisel marks on background surfaces. In addition, a scraped surface is not as reflective as the surface left by a crisp chisel cut. You can minimize the chatter marks commonly seen on a scraped surface by making alternating diagonal passes with the tool. This technique will prevent you from accentuating the marks left by the previous pass.

Carving the leaves—After the background has been carved to depth, sketch the main flow lines of the leaves, and use a gouge to bring out each leaf's overall contours, as shown in the photo above. To give the strongest impression of movement, make a deep concave cut in each leaf, along the outside of its arc from the volute, as shown above. While cutting these low areas on each of the three major leaves, preserve the full height of the leaf above the background at the extreme inner edge of each arc. Cutting to the full depth of your raised work at the peak of each arc, the concave cuts should diminish to half the raised depth as

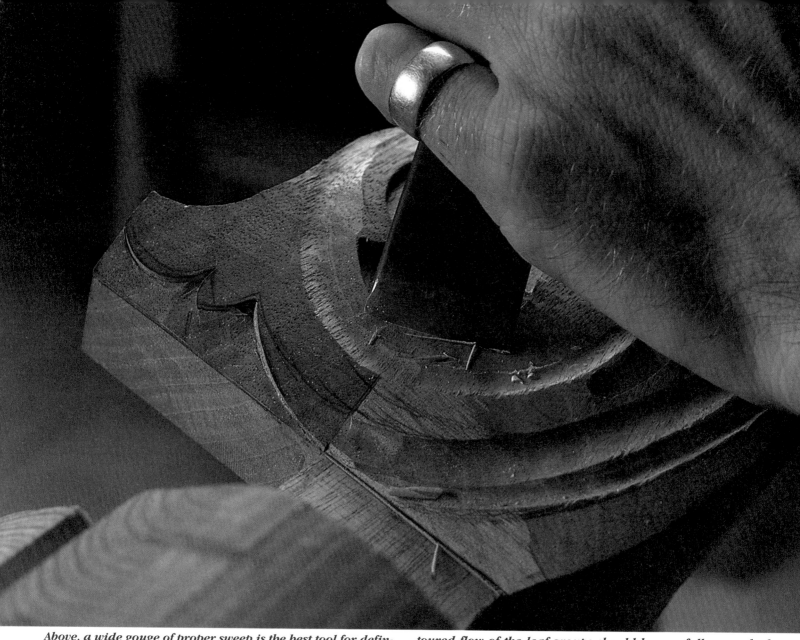

Above, a wide gouge of proper sweep is the best tool for defining the knee shape, even when working in cramped areas such as here—the background at the top of the knee block. The light yet broad slices level such areas uniformly. Below left, the con- toured flow of the leaf groups should be carefully smoothed (here with a scraper) before detail carving begins. Below right, a gouge, used bevel up, finishes up a diminishing curve that was begun by wider ones in the set.

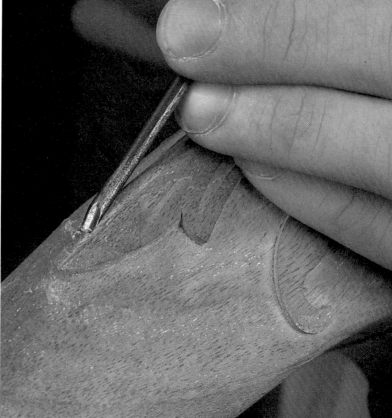

the cuts end at the leaf tips and begin on the kneeblock. The concave cuts of the two leaves at the highest arc should diverge from a single cut at their beginning, at the top of the kneeblock, to two separate cuts for the center and lowest inside leaf.

Challenging changes in grain occur as the concave cuts move from the top of the knee downward. Regardless of which direction the cuts are made, half of the gouge cuts will be against the grain because of the way the pattern's curve meets the grain direction. A sharp tool will minimize the tearout, but it'll probably be necessary to cut from both directions to get a smooth surface. Skewing the tool slightly will also produce a cleaner cut, because the tool can slice instead of wedge into the wood. In any case, the juncture of the two cuts should meet at the low point of the curve. The veining of the leaves will later help remove any awkward transitions.

A broad, convex gouge cut should run from the full-raised height on the inside arc of each leaf to meet the bottom of the concave cut, with a clean transition between the two curves. The broad convex surface will catch light on a broad plane, while the quick convex curve will either reflect a fine line of light or throw a deep shadow, depending on the direction of the lighting. Throughout the process, the carver should strive for fluid gouge cuts, which produce the brightest, clearest and most continuous reflective surfaces. The best surface can be achieved by matching the gouge to the desired curve. Use the widest gouges possible at all times, as shown in the photo at left. The cut of a single gouge can be extended by cutting while holding the gouge on the diagonal, which will narrow the width of the cut and increase the arc of the curve.

The eye of the volute should be shaped as shown with a broad convex curve. Individual gouge cuts are also made to give the tip of the two internal leaves the impression of flipping back on themselves. This is accomplished by a concave cut on the inside of each leaf's hooked bottom with the continuation of the leaf's major broad convex curve preserved at the leaf's very tip. The shaping of the lowest lobe of the volute should be a continuation of the convex arc that runs around the innermost arc. The two small leaves at

the top of the kneeblock should be relieved with medium-sweep concave cuts that terminate ⅛ in. to 1/16 in. short of the leaves' uppermost points, preserving the full background depth.

Make sure the contoured surface is as smooth as possible. Although the detail carving to come will cut much of this surface away, enough of it will remain to define the overall flow. If you try to smooth this later, the carving may end up looking uncertain.

When the flow of the leaves has been established, the veining and other details can be cut in, as shown in figure 1 on p. 103 and in the two middle photos below. The veins should emerge from the volute and slowly separate as they move toward the end of the leaves. The sculptural effect of the leaves turning to the outside of their arc and flipping under at their tips can be reinforced by holding the major weight of the veining high on the arc of the leaves. The veins should end just short of the tip of each leaf, with the central vein of the two major central leaves just entering the leaf-tip area. This lowest central vein is flanked by a slightly higher vein on the outside of the arc and by the highest vein on the inside arc. The arrangement of the inside and outside lobes of the leaves again emphasizes the impression of movement.

Finishing up — Sandpaper isn't much help in producing even, reflective surfaces and crisp outlines and shadows. Sanding will usually round off the transition of details and give an amorphous and doughy character to the work. Until you've had enough practice in sharpening and tool use to cut the wood cleanly with gouges alone, you can blend any slight surface irregularities with cabinet scrapers. Fine files, rifflers or shaped-hardwood burnishers are also useful for polishing carved surfaces. The broad surfaces of carvings on exposed knees and the backs of chairs have usually worn from use, producing a level of polish probably not given, but likely anticipated, by their original carvers. □

Mack Headley is a master cabinetmaker at Colonial Williamsburg in Virginia. His article on shell carving is on pp. 98-102.

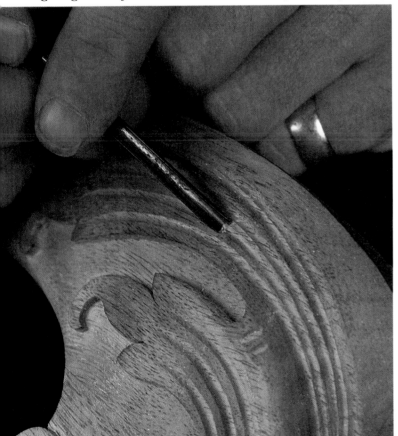

Below left, veining is cut into the contoured surface with an appropriate gouge. The same concerns regarding grain direction apply as with larger tools. Below right, strong side lighting on the finished knee shows not only the crispness of

light and shadow possible in low-relief carving, but also the general planes and curves that underlie the detailing. Defining and smoothing these shapes was done before any of the fine-detail carving began.

Crowning Glory
Carving pineapple and flame finials

by Ben Bacon

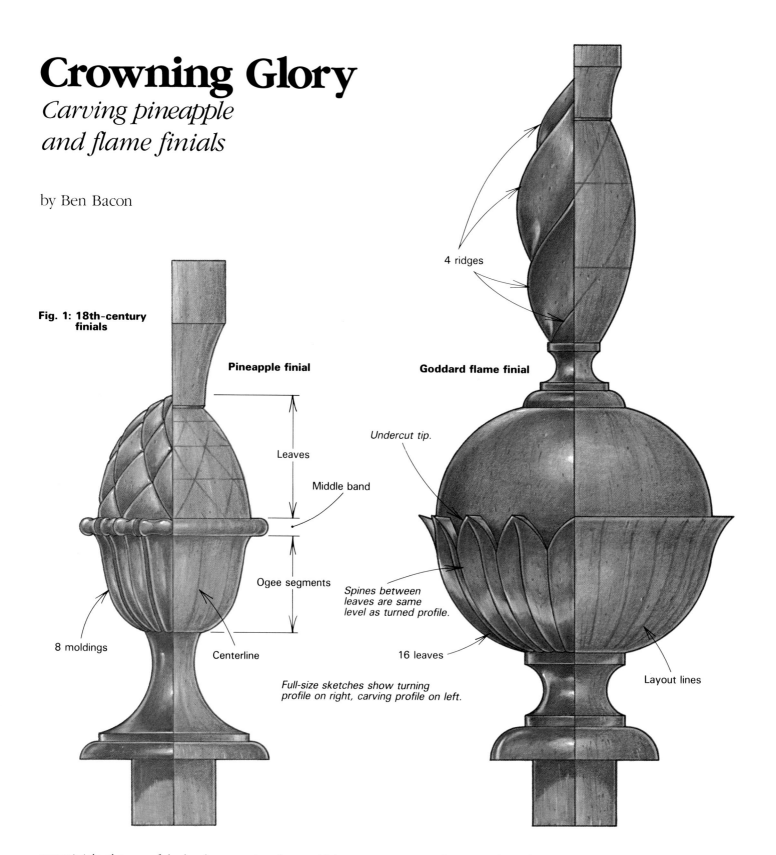

Fig. 1: 18th-century finials

Pineapple finial

Leaves

Middle band

Ogee segments

8 moldings

Centerline

Goddard flame finial

4 ridges

Undercut tip.

Spines between leaves are same level as turned profile.

16 leaves

Layout lines

Full-size sketches show turning profile on right, carving profile on left.

Finials, the graceful, slender summits of many 18th-century furniture classics, are perfect for practicing the simpler aspects of carving, although the expression "simple carving" is something of a paradox. All carving, from the plainest to the most complex, requires the same methodical process of research, drawing, modeling, roughing out, and detail work. Finials are particularly good for beginners to develop these techniques because they are familiar objects—small, easy-to-make, and they incorporate a variety of elements, from decorative leaves to fanciful, spiraling tongues of flame. They also are painless to discard and to start again should things go wrong.

Before you begin, you must learn about what you want to carve to produce a working drawing. This sounds tedious, and it usually requires several trips to libraries, museums and dealers' showrooms, but, if you skip this step you'll likely flounder, get discouraged and quit the project. Since we are more concerned with carving here, I've done the research for you, and given you a drawing of two typical American finials, figure 1.

One finial is a flame, a Goddard-Townsend favorite that was frequently carved on Rhode Island chests, clocks, and highboys. The other is a pineapple finial, which was used in many different forms all over the East Coast. Both finials are designed to cap off a piece of furniture, so the dominant element of each is its uppermost section—the flame and exposed pineapple. Beneath

From *Fine Woodworking* magazine (March 1986) 57:36-40

these, each has a circular band of leaves or moldings. These decorative elements visually break-up the surface of a finial so it doesn't look merely turned, but they are regular enough not to detract much from the more important top decoration.

The first step is to turn the basic shape on a lathe. Both finials are made of South American mahogany, but walnut, maple, or cherry would be suitable. Don't get carried away with your turning—leave enough wood to do the carving. Because carving is a subtractive process (rather than an additive one, like cabinetmaking), it's easy to forget that most carvings are the remains of larger pieces of wood. As you work, you must visualize the finished carving, as well as the block needed to produce it. This is easy to see in turned work—find the greatest diameter of any carved section, as shown in the drawing on the facing page, and turn to that diameter. Also, leave enough waste at the top for clamping.

The pineapple is divided into three sections—the lower, molded half, the middle band, and the upper leaves. The molding consists of eight ogee moldings around the circumference, each segment itself divided in half. To lay out the molding, set dividers and mark the circumference on the middle band into eight equal sections. Each mark locates the centerline of one segment. Draw in the centerlines from the middle band down to the bottom of the finial, making sure that the gaps between the lines taper evenly as you draw down the globe-shaped turning. Begin carving on these centerlines by running a 3mm V-shaped parting tool down each line to make a series of 2mm-deep channels, as shown at top right. Note how the finial is clamped to the bench between pairs of bandsawn softwood supports. Clamping is mandatory. Most carving techniques require both hands on the tool. Generally, one hand is the power hand, supplying most of the force of the tool to the handle (or, wielding the mallet for heavier work), and the other hand is the controlling hand, the fingers spread over the metal, guiding the cutting edge. If the work is clamped securely, all the force will be transmitted through the tool to the wood, rather than into launching the work across the room. It's also impossible to cut your hands if both of them are behind the cutting edge. Be cautious—a 30mm gouge slicing across your wrists or fingers can do as much damage as a tablesaw.

You should be able to carve three or four of the centerlines before unclamping and rotating the piece. Repeating your cuts this way is the fastest way to carve, because you spend less time hunting for and picking up different tools than you would if you carved each section individually. After you've cut all the centerlines, take a #2 3mm gouge to round over both sharp edges left by the parting tool, as shown in carving sequence in figure 2, leaving two soft curves that will form the ridges of the ogee.

Again working from the centerline, use dividers to mark the two bands that will delineate the outer edges of each segment. The bands fall either side of the dividing line between segments, which is midway between the carved centerlines, as shown in figure 2. After these straight lines are drawn, use U-shaped fluters to carve a hollow down each band line. Begin with a #7 4mm, but switch to progressively smaller fluters as the molding tapers. Here I would use a #9 3mm, followed by a #8 2mm. The edge of the hollow forms the side of the band, so be sure to make smooth, even cuts, keeping the outside of the tools (the side away from the centerline) just on the line you've drawn. Once this is done, and all your lines are neat and even, take a small gouge (#2 or #3, 2mm and 3mm spade tools, described on the following page, work well for maneuvering in these tight spots), and round over the inside sharp edge of the cut, as shown at center right, leaving

Carve a 2mm-deep channel down each centerline, top photo, with a V-shaped parting tool. The finial is clamped to the bench with wooden blocks, bandsawn from softwood so they won't dent the carving. To complete the molding, use small gouge, above, to round over the sharp inside edge of the fluter cut.

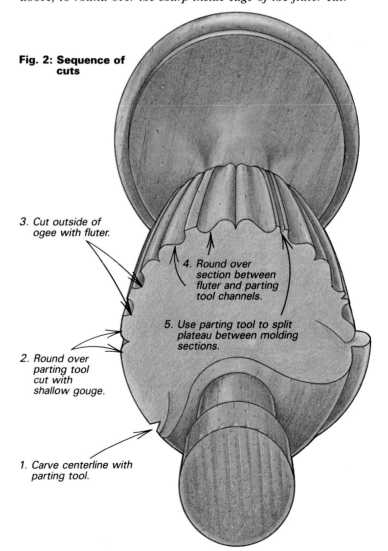

Fig. 2: Sequence of cuts

3. Cut outside of ogee with fluter.

4. Round over section between fluter and parting tool channels.

5. Use parting tool to split plateau between molding sections.

2. Round over parting tool cut with shallow gouge.

1. Carve centerline with parting tool.

Photos: Robert Aberman; drawings: David Dann.

the sharp outside edge. Now, repeat the entire carving sequence on the middle band. Make sure your cuts are crisp and that you have no rough tool marks or torn wood fibers where the band meets the molding or the pineapple.

The moldings are now complete, but need to be separated. Take the parting tool and run it down between the bands, splitting them into two distinct and equal parts, as shown at top left. Then take ¼-in. and ⅜-in. chisels (I used cabinetmakers' bevel-edge chisels) and deepen the V cuts, leaving a very sharp, straight division between the moldings.

The next step is to carve the leaves on the top. First, saw off the excess wood at the top and carve the top with a #5 20mm gouge to the shape shown in figure 1. Then, to make sure that all the pineapple leaves on each level are the same size, draw bands of diminishing width around the finial, corresponding to the tips of the pineapple leaves. Next draw in the individual leaves, as shown in the plan, making sure that they diminish in size as they reach the top of the finial.

Clamp the finial dowel to the bench between bandsawn blocks, with a softwood support block directly beneath the pineapple. The first cut is with a 6mm parting tool between the leaves. Then, using #2 and #3 3mm spade tools and 8mm fishtail gouges, round over the four sides of each leaf, leaving the center proud, as shown in the photo at left. Sand the leaves, if

After separating each ogee molding into two parts by running a parting tool down between the bands, above, use ¼-in. and ⅜-in. bevel-edge chisels to deepen the V-shaped parting-tool cuts. Next, outline the pineapple leaves with a parting tool, then round over the four sides of each leaf with a shallow gouge, left, leaving the center of each leaf proud. Finally, sand the leaves.

Spade tool from a fishtail

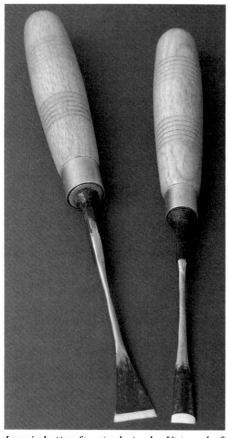

Less is better for spade tools. Upper shaft indicates how much fishtail is reground.

A good spade tool is, without doubt, the most useful tool a carver owns. It has a very thin shaft, usually no more than 3mm to 5mm square, a flared cutting edge, and can be maneuvered into tight spots where no other tools can go. The thin shaft is less likely to contact delicately carved elements than that of a heavier tool, and, therefore, causes far less damage, while giving the cutting edge maximum movement when you cut behind, under and around forms, such as the foliage work on picture frames or on the drawer fronts of some lowboys and chests-on-chest.

Although spade tools are great for maneuverability, their design does have some inherent problems. The thin shaft makes the tools weak, especially in relation to the force that such a broad cutting edge transmits. This makes the tools unsuitable for heavy or mallet work. The flared end is usually never more than ¾ in. long, so a frequently sharpened tool has a very short working life. These reasons may be why the tools are no longer manufactured.

Since you can't buy new spade tools, and it's becoming increasingly difficult to find old ones, your only alternative is to make them yourself or to convert them from other tools. The easiest method is to adapt them from commercially available fishtail gouges, which are much heavier than spades. A true spade looks like a triangle on a stick. Carefully grind away the excess metal from about 1 in. behind the cutting edge to about 3 in. Then grind away directly behind the cutting edge to make the tool flare from the shaft at a greater angle. Some tools have an angle as great as 60°, but I think 75° to 80° is sufficient. As with all adaptations, the end product is not ideal. Removing metal directly be-

hind the cutting edge will often cut into the inner shape of the tool, distorting the interior grind and ultimately altering the actual shape of the tool's cutting edge.

You can avoid these problems by making your own tools from scratch. Annealed bar stock steel is ideal for very fine spades with a 5mm to 6mm cutting edge, like those shown at left. In the days when umbrellas were engineering marvels of bone, ivory and rosewood, the interior framing was steel the ideal thickness for spade tools. Grinding the tool out of bar stock steel is a lot more work. If you want a tool with a 6mm-wide cutting edge, you have to buy 6mm-wide steel and grind about 1.5mm off each of the four sides to get a 6mm cutting edge and a 3mm shaft. Once you get the outside shape you want, grind the cutting edge to the desired radius. Most spade tools are in the #2 to #7 range, but you can make any curve you want. As with all cutting tools, you want to make the cutting edge as thin as possible, while maintaining a strong edge. You will need to harden and temper the tool, then form a tang by grinding the back of the tool to a point, like an awl. Clamp the tool in a vise with wooden sides, tang side up, and tap a handle onto the tang with a few gentle blows from your mallet.

Though it takes time and effort to form a precise, thin cutting edge, you will be rewarded by the number of times the tool helps you solve carving problems. You'll use and sharpen it so much, you'll notice that the cutting edge will get shorter and shorter, until it merges with the shaft. Like a wine from a vintage year, you'll enjoy returning to it again and again, and all too soon you'll find your favorite tool will be gone. —B.B.

necessary, then run down the groove between the leaves again with the parting tool, to make sure that the leaves are distinct. The finial is now complete, ready to be mounted.

The Goddard flame is carved in much the same way as the pineapple. Start with the leaves, evenly marking out the 16 tips with dividers and drawing centerlines down the leaves. You want to carve each centerline so it is lower than the leaf's edge. Run a 6mm parting tool down the centerline to make a 5mm-deep V-channel, shown below, top left, then round over the sides toward the center with shallow gouges (#3 8mm, #3 12mm, #2 3mm, #2 5mm). For a crisp, gently rounded cut, hold your gouge upside down with its bevel up, as shown in the photo below, right. Note that the definition between two leaves comes from the sharp spine created at their juncture as you round each edge toward its centerline. To be effective this line must be sharp, straight and even, so take care when rounding over. No wood is removed from the actual spine, so it remains at the same level as the original turned profile. Once the definition between the leaves is good, give the leaves a strong, straight centerline by running the parting tool down the center, straightening the line and removing any bumps or ridges.

The tops of the leaves are distinct from one another and curve slightly away from the ball. Carving this type of decoration re-

quires two steps, traditionally called "relieving" and "setting in." In relieving, you remove as much waste wood as possible between the leaf tips with a parting tool, carving straight into the wood, removing a V-shaped wedge that corresponds to the flaring away of the leaf tips. "Setting in" is the process of removing small amounts of wood to refine the desired shape and achieve a sharp edge. Once the waste is removed by relieving, you have enough room to manipulate your tools for these delicate finishing cuts, which are very similar to the fine paring cuts used by cabinetmakers to fit joints.

Once you've removed the waste with parting-tool relief cuts, take gouges that fit the shape of the leaf tips (#2 or #3 gouges, 5mm, 8mm), and set in the tips, bottom left, undercutting them slightly so that the leaf edges don't appear thick and clumsy. The same gouges are good for refining the surface between the tips to make the curve of the top section flow smoothly between and under the leaf tips. Don't make your setting-in cuts too deep, or you'll leave unsightly tool marks in the finished surface that are impossible to remove unless you recarve the surface.

Saw the tip of the finial off, carefully reshape the top, and draw the flame, which is composed of four ridges and four hollows. First, draw one spiraling line freehand on the flame blank until the flow of the line is smooth and regular. Then add two concentric bands to divide the blank into three equal horizontal seg-

Cut a deep channel down the center of each leaf with a parting tool, top left, so that the midsection is lower than the edges. Next, round over the sides of the leaf with bevel-up gouge, above. There's no hard division between leaves, just a sharp spine created as you round each edge toward its centerline. Finally, undercut each edge with a gouge matching the leaf-tip shape, left, so it won't look heavy.

The wood between the ridges of the flame is removed with a sharp fluter or 5mm gouge, top photo. If wood begins to tear out, reverse the cutting direction by moving your hands, as above, rather than wasting time by walking around the bench.

ments. With the dividers, separate each band into four equal parts, beginning where the spiraling line crosses the band. It's simple to then join these reference points to make four evenly spaced spiraling lines.

The greatest problem in carving the flame is keeping the sharp ridge between the hollows from breaking out. Because you're carving a spiral tapering at both ends, the grain direction changes constantly. In some places you'll be carving long grain; in others you'll be carving across the grain. Use sharp tools—a large fluter or 5mm #9 gouge—to remove the wood from the hollows, leaving the 3mm-thick ridge, top left. Keep a keen eye for wood breaking off ahead of the tool. When this happens, reverse the direction of your cut, as shown at left. For speed and efficiency, most good carvers work ambidextrously, allowing them to easily reach any part of the work without maneuvering their bodies. Achieving this type of skill, however, requires a year or two of practice. Then, use the same tools to achieve a thin, sharply defined peak, running in a smooth spiral from top to bottom, without waver or wobble. It is vital not to carve the very top of the ridge, if you do you'll distort the outline of the flame, introducing dips and irregularities where you should have a clean, spiraling line that conforms exactly to the shape of the original turning. Once you've worked all the ridges, sand the hollow of the flame, using 120- to 180-grit paper. Recut where necessary to refine the sharpness of the ridge, then you should be done.

I hope the finials give you a habit-forming taste of carving. After carving these finials, you should be ready to research and develop your own forms. More than anything, carving is a matter of practice, and more practice, to acquire the drawing and tool-handling skills that distinguish an accomplished craftsman. □

Ben Bacon is an American carver who is now working in London, where he has remained after completing a five-year apprenticeship in carving, gilding and framing.

The final touch

Woodcarvers generally create one of four distinct surface textures when they complete a carving—they either leave the tool marks showing, sand the surface, file everything smooth, or decorate the surface using metal punches. The choice of technique depends largely on your skill, what's being carved (flat relief, foliage, deeply carved foliage, figures, chair work, or architectural ornament), and how the work is to be finished (polished with some type of oil or covered with gold leaf, for example).

A straight-from-the-tools finish gives clearly defined details and great visual clarity, but requires a great deal of skill to do it right. You must use your tools accurately and cleanly to produce a crisp surface free of distracting facets and torn wood fibers. Some workers also object to the slight irregularities of the cut surface.

Sandpaper is most often used where you want smooth, regular surfaces, but don't need great definition. Sanding is usually necessary when you plan to use a glossy, clear finish that would highlight the inevitable small facets and marks left by tools.

Figure carvers prefer rifflers, small shaped files, because they feel the filed surface has a great subtlety and fineness of finish that cannot be achieved with tool or paper.

For backgrounds in relief work, a variety of different shaped metal punches (circles, double circles, stars, points, diamonds, for example) are used to literally punch the wood, creating a decorated surface that disguises the general unevenness of the surface.

The tool-mark texture and sandpaper are the only relevant methods for beginning carvers, so I will concentrate on these. Many books advise carvers to reject sandpaper altogether and rely solely on tools for the finish texture, but I think this is a misconception based on a failure to understand that sandpaper and carving tools are both instruments for removing wood. Carving tools remove wood quickly and accurately, with sharp definition. Sandpaper removes wood relatively slowly, but leaves a uniform, smooth surface that lacks sharp definition. Once you understand this difference, you can analyze what kind of surface you want, and then decide which of the two

methods will best achieve this surface.

Carving tools are the only medium when your goals are sharpness and crispness. In foliage work, flat relief work, and most carved decoration on carved and gilt furniture, where crispness is paramount, sandpaper should never be used, and care should be taken to achieve a fine, clean finish with the tools alone. Sanded foliage looks muddy and clumsy. But, if you're going to carve a surface that will be highly polished, one where the small facets that tools leave would mar the look and flow of the carving, then sanding is not only acceptable, but advisable. On the flame finials, for example, sanding the broad flutes between the ridges on the flame is the fastest way of achieving a smooth, regular, mark-free surface. It could be done with tools, but it would take far longer and probably look worse. But, if you sand the fine divisions between the ogee bands on the pineapple finial, you will end up with an indistinct mess.

In short, don't compensate for clumsiness with carving tools by using paper, but don't be afraid to use sandpaper where it is needed. As in all woodworking, suit the tools to the job at hand. —*B.B.*

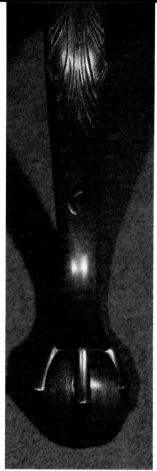

Because of the large diameter of Pine's mahogany interpretation of a Philadelphia-style tripod, the author dished the top with a router instead of on the lathe. Hand tools then leveled the surface and carved the piecrust design. The ball on the shaft can be left plain or be carved. In either case, it should be turned to the diam-

eter shown in the measured drawing on p. 114—the carving is so shallow that no allowance is necessary for it. The ball-and-claw foot and knee carving are hallmarks of high-style work, but less ambitious tables with pad feet and plain legs can succeed in capturing the uncluttered look of the best Queen Anne.

Tip-and-Turn Tables
Philadelphia detailing produced the masterpieces

by David Ray Pine

O f the many tripod tea tables made in America in the 18th century, those built in the Philadelphia area are considered by many experts to be the most desirable. The basic design and proportions are very successful when left unadorned ("in the Quaker taste"), but these tables lend themselves equally well to the highly embellished forms that are more often associated with Philadelphia Chippendale furniture.

The tripod table that I built and will describe here is often called a piecrust table, in reference to its scalloped molded top. Tables of this type—regardless their top's shape—are often called "tip-and-turn" tables, since the top of such tables can be swung to a vertical position and/or rotated on its "birdcage" support, much like a lazy Susan (see details in figure 2). The birdcage seems to have been popular only in the Pennsylvania region. New England

and Southern tripod tables often tip, but seldom do they turn.

Figure 1 shows the dimensions of my table. If this project tempts you but seems too ambitious, there are many ways in which the design can be simplified. In *Fine Points of Furniture* ($12.95 from Crown Publishers, 34 Engelhard Ave., Avenel, N.J. 07001), Albert Sack shows some two dozen variations on the tripod table. Many have pad feet and plain turned tops with slightly raised rims, and there's at least one with a simple flat top with a half-round edge. Still others have fixed tops that neither tilt nor turn.

I won't concern myself much with turning or carving in this article, but will describe the general order of how to make a tripod table, including important considerations that might not be too evident if you haven't made one before.

Construction begins with turning the shaft. Take special care

Fig. 1: Philadelphia piecrust table

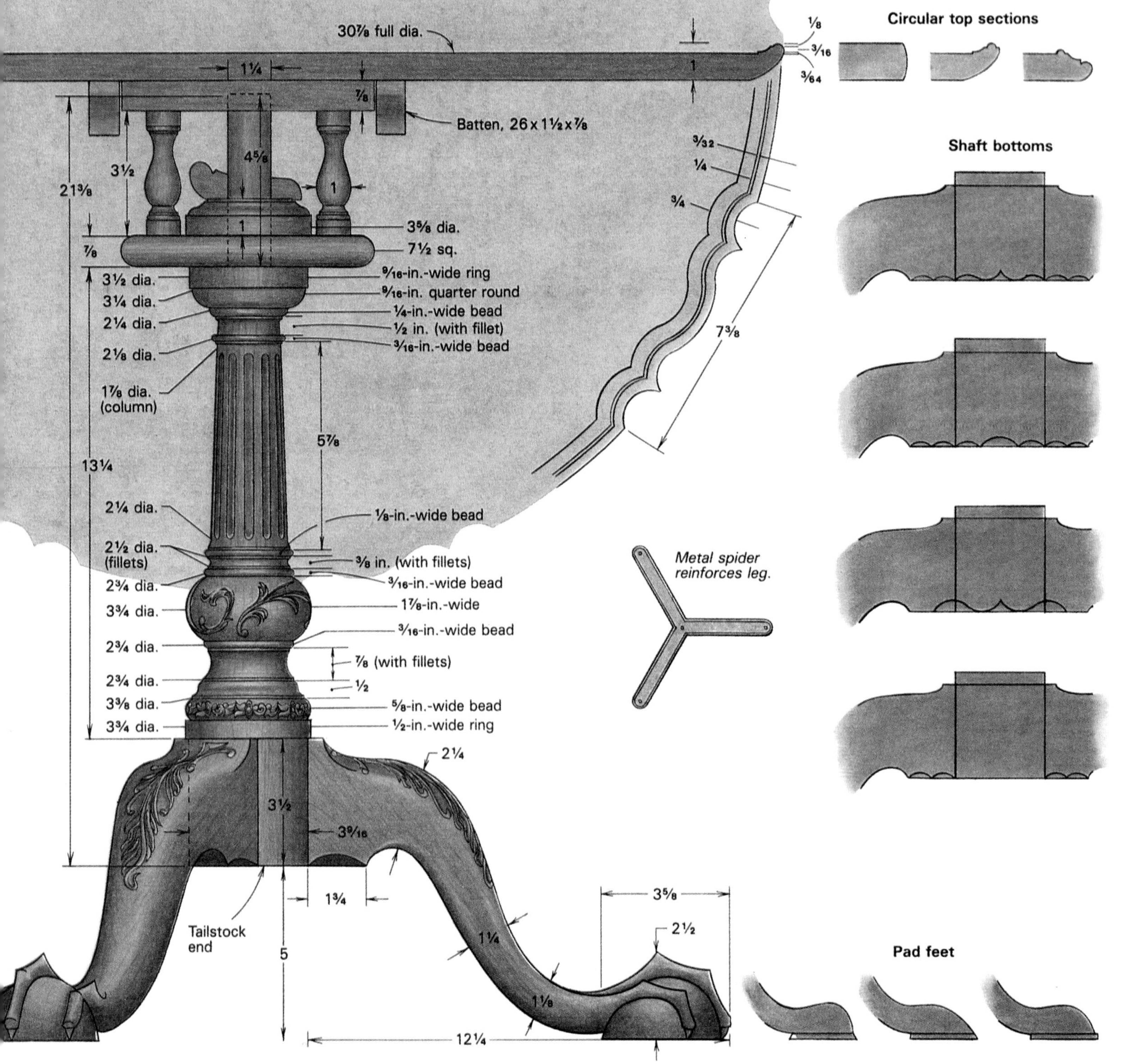

30⅞ full dia.
1¼
⅞
1
Batten, 26 x 1½ x ⅞
4⅝
3½
21⅜
1
1
3⅝ dia.
⅞
7½ sq.
⁹⁄₁₆-in.-wide ring
⁹⁄₁₆-in. quarter round
¼-in.-wide bead
½ in. (with fillet)
³⁄₁₆-in.-wide bead
3½ dia.
3¼ dia.
2¼ dia.
2⅛ dia.
1⅞ dia. (column)
5⅞
13¼
2¼ dia.
⅛-in.-wide bead
2½ dia. (fillets)
⅜ in. (with fillets)
2¾ dia.
³⁄₁₆-in.-wide bead
3¾ dia.
1⅞-in.-wide
³⁄₁₆-in.-wide bead
2¾ dia.
⅞ (with fillets)
2¾ dia.
½
3⅜ dia.
⅝-in.-wide bead
3¾ dia.
½-in.-wide ring
2¼
3½
3⁹⁄₁₆
1¾
Tailstock end
5
1¼
1⅛
12¼
3⅝
2½
⅛
³⁄₁₆
³⁄₆₄
Circular top sections
³⁄₃₂
¼
¾
7⅞
Shaft bottoms
Metal spider reinforces leg.
Pad feet

in turning the area of the shaft where the legs will join. This section must be perfectly cylindrical—any taper will affect the stance of the legs. Turn both ends of the shaft and the ledge where the birdcage will rest flat and square to the axis of the shaft. Wait until the legs are fitted to the shaft before doing any carving or fluting. This will decrease the likelihood of damaging fine details while driving legs into and out of their sockets.

Choosing stock for the legs is next. Note that while each leg requires 3-in.-thick stock for the ball-and-claw foot, the leg is only 2 in. thick where it enters the shaft. With pad feet, you can get away with 2-in.-thick stock. After sawing the legs to shape, plane the end for the dovetail square to both the foot and the sides. I have a set of flat bits for my tablesaw's molding cutterhead that are ground to 14°, and I use them for cutting sliding dovetail pins. The pins can be cut with a crosscut blade on the tablesaw instead.

The shoulders of the dovetails can either be carved to fit around the shaft or left flat with the shaft faceted to match. Old tables were done both ways—then as now, it seems to have been a matter of preference for each maker. I've used both methods, and prefer to flatten the shaft for each leg, as shown in figure 3. It's easier for me to achieve a good fit at the shoulder, and I believe it makes the dovetails somewhat stronger, as there is more wood surrounding the pins because the angle is not so acute. (Lance Patterson of Boston has used the other approach—making legs to fit a round base—to good effect in building a music stand.)

Drawings: Lee Hov

I like to align one leg with the grain rings exposed on the ball of the shaft and space the others equidistant from that one. This "master leg" will be at the front of the table (if a round table *has* a front!). Fit each leg to its socket by trial and error, paring waste away until the leg slides snugly up to the shoulder. It's a good idea to mark each dovetail pin and its socket to avoid mixups.

Now, finish shaping the legs and carve the feet. Carve the master leg last, so you can "put your best foot forward." Do any carving on the shaft now, then glue the pedestal up.

After the glue hardens, the bottoms of the legs should be pared even with the end of the shaft. Often, the bottom edge of the portion of shaft between the legs and the bottom edge of each leg itself are decorated with scallops. This scallop pattern is cut at an angle, so that it runs out a little way under the base of the table. The photo and drawings show the idea.

The best tables are reinforced at the bottom of the shaft with a three-legged iron "spider," which is screwed to the bottom of the shaft in the center, and to each leg somewhere beyond the dovetail joint. On some tables, the spider is bent to conform with the curve of the leg and can run several inches down each leg. The dovetail joints are the table's weakest point, and a sudden jolt, as from an armload of books, can cause the shaft to split out between two of the legs. The spider spreads the stress evenly around the base of the table. If you don't know a blacksmith who can forge a spider for you, you can cut one out of heavy ³⁄₃₂-in. sheet metal. Either way, the edges are best beveled back so they're less likely to show. Alternatively, the spider can be inlaid.

The two battens that help hold the tabletop flat will eventually be screwed to the underside of the top. The top tips up by rotating on dowels worked on the top edge of the birdcage (see figure 2). These dowels are captured in holes bored tangentially to the top edge of the battens. On old tables, battens often taper from the center to the ends; sometimes, they have an ogee or a lamb's tongue sawn on the ends. Make the battens before the birdcage. If you plan to make a small table that neither tips nor turns, make a single wide batten to fit a wedged through tenon at the top of the shaft. This tenon can be round or square—either is

correct. On old tables, battens always run cross-grain (to prevent warping), and there is no provision for wood movement. On a new table, it makes sense to slot the screw holes in the battens.

The birdcage consists of a top and a bottom plate, held together by four turned balusters. The plates are generally square in shape (very rarely is one circular) and about twice the size of the shaft's largest diameter. Most often, the top plate is square-edged, but, on better tables, the bottom plate has a half-round worked on all four of its edges. Work the dowels on the top plate by bandsawing waste away, then rounding them over by hand until they slip-fit in their batten holes. Bore both plates for the balusters' tenons simultaneously if you're planning on through tenons, which can be wedged. Blind tenons are, perhaps, neater in appearance, but they require a lot of measuring for location and depth. The central hole for the shaft should pierce the bottom plate, but stop about ¼ in. deep in the underside of the top plate.

The length of the balusters (between tenon shoulders) should be about the same as the diameter of the table's shaft. It's a curious fact that the birdcage balusters keep their characteristic vase shape (except English birdcage balusters, which are columnar in shape), regardless of whether the shape of the shaft is vasiform or has the flattened ball and column. Thus, the balusters aren't necessarily miniature copies of the shaft. The balusters' through tenons should be cut off about ¹⁄₃₂ in. too long—this leaves enough surplus to trim after glue-up. Split the tenon ends with a chisel and drive the wedges immediately after glue-up, aligning them cross-grain so they don't split the plates.

The bottom plate of the birdcage is sandwiched between a ledge on the shaft and a loose, lathe-turned ring that's held in place by a wedge through the shaft. There's often a notch cut into the flat on opposite sides of the top of the ring. The wedge engages these twin notches and keeps the ring from rotating when the top is turned, which would wear away the finish and eventually the bearing surface. With the ring and birdcage in place, mark the location of the wedge on the shaft. This should be at right angles to the master leg. Cut the tapered slot for the wedge and make the wedge several inches longer than necessary. For the

Fig. 2: Birdcage and battens

Fig. 3: Cutting dovetails and sockets

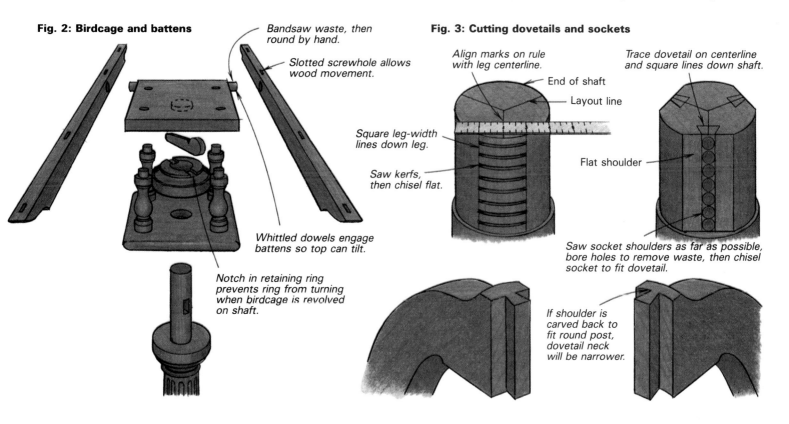

Bandsaw waste, then round by hand.

Slotted screwhole allows wood movement.

Whittled dowels engage battens so top can tilt.

Notch in retaining ring prevents ring from turning when birdcage is revolved on shaft.

Align marks on rule with leg centerline.

End of shaft

Layout line

Square leg-width lines down leg.

Saw kerfs, then chisel flat.

Trace dovetail on centerline and square lines down shaft.

Flat shoulder

Saw socket shoulders as far as possible, bore holes to remove waste, then chisel socket to fit dovetail.

If shoulder is carved back to fit round post, dovetail neck will be narrower.

tabletop to revolve properly, the wedge should bottom out in its slot while just removing all slop from the ring and birdcage. The bottom of the slot must line up exactly with the top surface of the ring. If the slot is too high, the tabletop will rattle around; if the ring is too thick, the wedge will bind things up and the top won't turn at all. When you have things just right, trim the wedge to length and shape its ends.

Tops are generally done as faceplate turnings, as described by Gene Landon in the article beginning below. Dished tops have a tendency to cup after the center is wasted away, either because of unbalanced tension or due to moisture within the wood. It's a good idea to temporarily attach the battens as soon as the top is dished, to keep the top from moving. Stock for any dished top should be at least $^{15}/_{16}$ in. thick, but stock more than $1\frac{1}{8}$ in. thick will look too heavy, even on a large table. The total height of the raised rim is usually $^{5}/_{16}$ in. to $\frac{3}{8}$ in., which looks taller than you'd think after it's shaped up.

The molding on old tables doesn't usually have much of a perk or fillet at the surface of the top—just enough to define the edge of the cove. In contrast to Landon's method (see below), I dish the top first, truing out any cupping as it occurs. Next, I true and turn the top surface of the rim, with the back of the rim last. It's a good idea to do all the lathework in one session, as the top will probably move overnight, causing the edge to wobble. This can make sanding difficult, and makes further turning a real problem.

The scallop on a piecrust top consists of a serpentine curve flanked by a small semicircle on both sides. These scallops repeat from 8 to 12 times (always an even number) around the top, and are separated by small segments of the circular edge. As a rule of thumb, the scallops are about twice the length of the segments, though this does vary on old work. When laying out a top,

draw the whole width of the molding out, as what looks good on the outside edge may appear too cramped on the inside perimeter. The width of the molding is usually between $\frac{5}{8}$ in. and 1 in., and radii of arcs and curves increase and decrease accordingly. Usually, tops are laid out with a serpentine curve topmost when the top is tipped, rather than a plain segment.

I'm uncomfortable turning a top bigger than about 24 in. on my homemade lathe. An alternative method, which I used to make this table, is to use a router and flat bit to waste the center away. First, bandsaw the piecrust perimeter. Then begin routing in the middle of the top, and make a spiral cut toward the outside edge. As you approach the rim, use a block (thicknessed equal to the depth of cut) to help support the router base. Rout as near the inside line of the piecrust mold as possible, then remove the marks left by the router bit using a plane and a scraper. Pare to the inside line of the molding using appropriate gouges, then lay out the line of the bead. I use a compass set to the bead's diameter and slide it around the top with the point hanging over the scalloped edge.

Set the bit depth to cut the stepdown from the topmost bead, then rout it using the same support block as before. Conceivably, you could rout a portion of the cove using templates, but I doubt that it would be worth it. It's easy enough from this point to finish the job using carving tools.

The birdcage can now be installed between the battens. Attach the catch (part H-43 or H-48 from Horton Brasses, P.O. Box 120, Cromwell, Conn. 06416) to the top and inlet its keeper into the birdcage top if you haven't done so already. A little final sanding should be all it takes to get the table ready for finish. □

Ray Pine makes furniture in Mt. Crawford, Va.

Turning and Carving Piecrust
Traditional methods still pay off

by Eugene E. Landon

A piecrust top looks intimidating, but even a beginner can carve one with sharp tools and some attention to the order of events. You don't need many carving tools—a $\frac{3}{8}$-in. #5 gouge (or one suitable for the shape of cove to be carved), a #2 gouge about the same width and a medium-size flat chisel will suffice. I've probably turned and carved three or four dozen piecrusts, and can tell you that the job is very satisfying. Be sure, however, that your wood and your glue joints are sound. I once had a knot catch the tool while turning a 30-in. blank, and the exploding top left permanent marks on both my shop and my memory.

Tops come in a variety of sizes. The one shown here is medium size, about 20 in. in diameter. Feel free to scale the design up or down. You expect a mahogany tabletop of any size to be one piece—mahogany was once available in very wide planks indeed—but walnut tabletops larger than 12 in. in diameter are generally glued up from two or three boards.

Old tabletops were made from air-dried wood with about a 15% moisture content. In modern houses, they shrink quite a bit

as central heating brings the wood's moisture content down to about 8%. One hallmark of a genuine lathe-turned antique top is that it's no longer round. So, for this reproduction, I'm using air-dried walnut from the stack out behind my shop, rather than wood from my kiln. With luck, it'll shrink about as much as the original table, which is $\frac{3}{8}$ in. out of round. This shrinkage will take a year or so to occur.

The process begins by gluing up the blank, bandsawing it round and attaching a glue block to which the lathe faceplate can be screwed. I don't use paper in the glue-block joint because I don't want any chance of repeating that memorable explosion. It's easy enough to saw off the bulk of the block when the turning is done—run the tabletop horizontally over the tablesaw to make a series of side-by-side kerfs in the block, chisel off the waste, then plane the bottom of the table flat.

Gene Landon works wood in Montoursville, Pa. The original of the table shown here is at Independence Hall, in Philadelphia.

1. With my lathe turning at its slowest speed, about 700 RPM, I flatten the back and round the outside edge with a gouge, then clean the surface with a skew used as a scraper. This produces dust from the endgrain areas, but pretty good shavings from the long grain.

2. I traced a portion of the tabletop, which the curators at Independence Hall in Philadelphia were kind enough to let me do, and took careful measurements. Here, with a parting tool, I'm marking the inner extent of the piecrust—the center of the top will be dished out flat up to this line. If you look closely, you can make out the slight step at the outside rim, made with the point of a skew. This is my gauge line for the final thickness of the rim.

3. Here's an early stage of dishing, using a gouge. As wood is removed, the top will warp slightly because the uneven tensions in the wood are finding new balances. This causes the rim to go out of a flat plane, which is desirable—the final carving will not look too mechanical, but will have a little up-and-down wander.

4. I turn the cove with a carbide-tipped scraper (soldered up for me by my favorite local machine shop) that has a profile like a flat little fingernail. This narrow profile allows me to fine-tune the shape of the cove until it exactly matches the profile of the gouge I'll use for the carving, as shown in the next step.

5. Check the profile of the cove by stopping the lathe and pressing the gouge—in this case a ⅜-in., #5 sweep—into the cove at the same angle as when you will be carving. The fit shown here is just right and matches the original table. Piecrusts superficially look alike, but each carver makes the cove to match his particular tools.

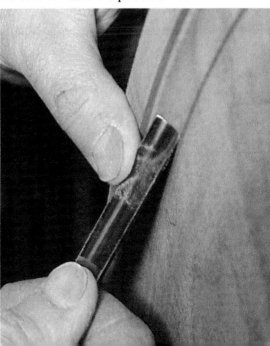

6. With the top cut to final depth, tool marks can be removed by scraping. I made this tool from a power-hacksaw blade—there's a clear view of it in photo 15. It has a slightly convex edge, and I use it with the burr left by the grinding wheel.

7. With a template made from the tracing of the top, you can step around the circumference. Note that each small scallop comes the same distance from the step at the top of the cove. This distance will be the width of the outer bead when the carving is complete. One reason I don't make a lot of drawings is that I document each reproduction with photos of the original; I also make rubbings of carvings and other relief details when possible.

8. Bandsawing the profile is about as nerve-racking as this project gets. The scallops are at the limit of what this ¼-in. blade can turn. Be sure before you start that you can cut the tight radius, or else everything up to this point is wasted labor.

9. After filing the profile smooth, mark the width of the outer bead with calipers or a compass, then make vertical "stop cuts" using gouges of the appropriate sweeps to match the curves. These cuts define the inner border of the bead and prevent it from splitting off when the adjacent surface is lowered. I prefer narrow gouges for this job, because wider ones require so much pressure that they may split the bead off anyway. Where the grain is short, I use an X-Acto knife for the stop cut. However, with a bead as narrow as this one, be prepared to glue some chips back on (I use model-airplane cement).

10. Using a #2 gouge, which will make cleaner cuts than a flat chisel, rough a level surface from the bead to the top of the turned cove. Deepen your stop cuts if the chips aren't coming off clean next to the bead, but don't go so deep that the cuts will show in the finished carving. If the gouge digs in, cut from the other direction.

11. With the gouge from photo 5, gradually work the profile of the cove out toward the rim, leaving enough wood beneath the cove to allow for the stepdown to the tabletop. I've chosen this photo out of sequence so that you can see what the finished step will look like (see lower right corner of photo). The tool action for the roughing cut is worth practicing—it's a combination of turning a screwdriver and prying up a paint-can lid. This slices and scoops uniform, controlled chips. Work with the grain as much as possible. Where the coves meet, a skew chisel or a knife can make a neat miter stop cut, but it's a tough job to carve the cove up to the miter—the wood gets in the way. When it gets impossible to get the gouge into position, switch to a #2 gouge and use the corner of it, working at whatever angles it takes, to slice and scoop out the final shape of the cove. Some cuts will have to be made vertically. Expect the miters to take some time. Be patient worrying away the wood and the result will be just fine.

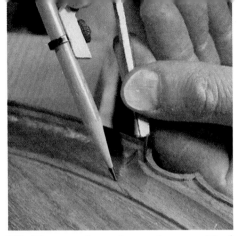

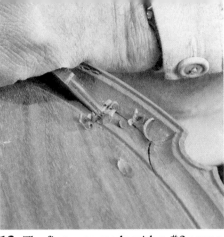

12. The next four photos show a critical part of the carving, extending the flat top up to the cove. Marking out is done with a compass, then stop cuts are made with chisels and gouges. Be careful not to make your stop cuts too deep, or they will mar the look of the top. The trick is to work the flat down gradually.

13. The first cuts, made with a #2 gouge, can be fairly bold, similar to the way in which the roughing cuts were made when carving the cove. But be somewhat cautious. There's a real danger of going too deep and making a depression between the flat top and the cove. This will absolutely ruin the look of the table.

14. I've switched to a flat chisel here for paring away the gouge marks. Note the size of the chips and try to match them with your own tools. You must work in thousandths-of-an-inch—if you can't produce chips of this size, your chisel is dull. Check frequently with a small straight-edge to be sure you don't go too deep.

15. Final leveling and polishing comes from scraping. The tool is pushed and the touch is very light. Up to this point in the process (including the turning), I've reground the edge three times to refresh the burr. The fuzz in front of the tool is not so much dust as it is super-thin shavings.

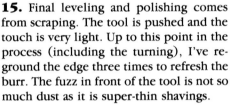

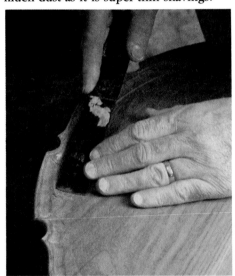

16. Here's the idea on the back. Rough out with a coarse rasp, then finish up with ever-finer rasps and files until the wood shimmers. You'll probably find that the back has warped as a result of the dish on the other side. This is no problem, because the surface ought to be planed flat anyway, when the glue block is removed.

17. I still have a way to go yet, and the sun is going down, but I'll have plenty of time tomorrow to finish the carving. Even with just this small section done, I think it's astounding how sculptural and strong a piecrust looks, especially when you consider that the carving stands only ¼ in. proud of the top. Those old carvers really knew how to catch light and shadow, didn't they? They set the standards for us all. □

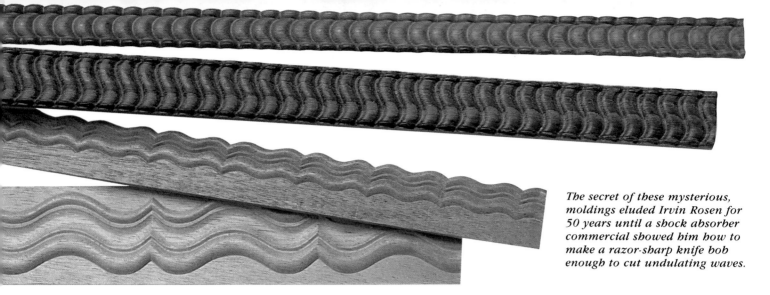

The secret of these mysterious, moldings eluded Irvin Rosen for 50 years until a shock absorber commercial showed him how to make a razor-sharp knife bob enough to cut undulating waves.

Ripple Molding
Reinventing a 19th-century mechanical marvel

by Carlyle Lynch

My friend Irvin Rosen was just a youngster in 1925 when he encountered a woodworking mystery that would haunt him for nearly 50 years. He was helping his father restore an 1830s-vintage clock embellished with a precisely cut ripple molding that he had never seen before. Rosen was impressed that neither his father nor his grandfather, both experienced craftsmen, could imagine how the molding had been made, though they were certain it had been cut with a machine, not handcarved. Rosen vowed to learn the secret of the mysterious molding. It took him nearly 50 years, and his quest led him to reinvent a woodworking machine that had been lost more than a century ago.

Rosen's machine is a motorized scraper. A lead screw connected to the motor drives a heavily weighted, razor-sharp cutter back and forth along a strip of mahogany or rosewood in a methodical carving/scraping motion. As the cutter assembly moves along the molding stock, a metal finger attached to it follows a special template to give the carriage a regular undulating motion that corresponds to the ripple pattern of the molding. It's a time-consuming process, taking several hundred passes to cut even a small piece of molding. Rosen suspects the original moldings were cut in a similar way, but he can't prove it. All the original ripple molding he's found has been on clocks made at the Jonathan Clark Brown factory in Bristol, Conn. Brown's factory burned in 1853, and his machine was destroyed. No patent, sketch, or description of it has ever been found.

I didn't meet Rosen until after he had invented his machine, so, on a recent visit to his home in the tiny hamlet of McKinley, Va., I asked him how he did it, with so little information to go on. Rosen is a slightly built, soft-spoken man loaded with what some call "native ability," that combination of sound knowledge of tools, a lot of common sense, and no fear of work. He needed

that kind of character. Before retiring as woodworking teacher at the Virginia School for the Deaf in Staunton, he spent much of his free time working on the molding—sketching, building, trying every idea he could conceive. But, after three years of almost constant thought and work following his retirement, he hadn't figured it out.

Then, after one especially tiring and discouraging day, he sat down after supper to watch the television news and saw a commercial advertising shock absorbers. A car was speeding over a series of railroad ties, its body moving smoothly forward, while its wheels danced a blurred staccato over the ties. There it was! Make the cutter dance up and down. He had already been experimenting with linear scrapers, so he began working to combine their back-and-forth motions with the shock absorber action. After experimenting with various types of tracks, templates and guides, he found the right combination.

The machine Rosen devised, shown on the facing page, center, is a fairly simple device. The motor drives a variable-speed pulley keyed to a long, horizontal lead screw mounted in pillow blocks. A nut on the shaft propels an angle-iron frame fastened to a carriage that straddles two angle-iron rails. The molding stock is clamped between the rails under the carriage, which, in turn, holds a vertically mounted cutter against the molding blank. A weight on the carriage forces the cutter against the strip while the turning shaft slowly propels the carriage forward, down the length of the shaft. As the cutter moves along the molding stock, a metal finger under the carriage bears against a rippled template fastened to one side of the track, causing the carriage to bob up-and-down (or left-to-right), as shown on the facing page. When the cutter reaches the end of the shaft, it flips a switch that reverses the motor, beginning the cycle in reverse. In this way, the machine can run unattended for hours. It takes about 200 passes, and

From *Fine Woodworking* magazine (May 1986) 58:62-64

Irv Rosen's machine-made ripple molding re-creates the original charm of antique steeple clocks made in Connecticut during the 1800s. Details, facing page, highlight the unerring precision and crisp cuts produced by his molding machine.

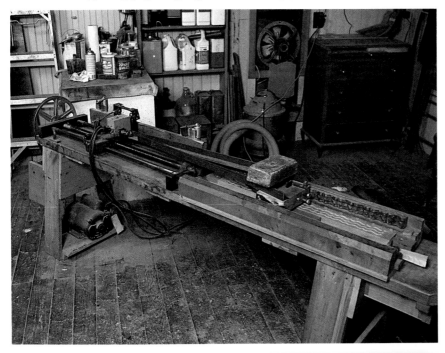

Ripple molding develops slowly from several hundred passes of a razor-sharp cutter, which is pulled back and forth over the molding stock until the desired depth of cut is reached. The rotating lead screw, foreground, first pushes the angle-iron carriage and the cutter down the length of the molding. A heavy weight on the cutter keeps it in contact with the wood during each pass. At the end of each pass, a switch reverses the motor and the rod pulls the carriage assembly back. The cutter, beveled on both sides, is shaped to match the molding profile being cut.

To form a left-to-right waving pattern, the cutter assembly follows a ripple template attached to the side rails of the machine.

Handscraped waves

by Trevor Robinson

When my wife and I go to art museums, she claims I spend more time looking at the picture frames than at the pictures. That's an exaggeration, but I'll admit that I've long been fascinated with the ripple or wave patterns on some 17th-century wooden frames. I didn't have a clue about making the molding until I found a reference to a device called "a waving engine" in Moxon's *Mechanick Exercises*, first published in 1678. Moxon lived in Holland during the period when those Dutch frames were made, so it's likely he learned about the technique there. By the middle of the next century, the waving engine was obsolete.

I patterned my waving engine after Moxon's, but had to make many modifications to turn his sketches into a working machine. The machine is basically a scraping device. The key to the undulating cut is a scalloped guide board, called a rack, and a tapered guide bar mounted in a box-like frame under a cutter. You attach the molding stock (mahogany is my favorite) to the rack, then run the rack through the cutter frame. As the rippled lower face of the rack rides up and down on the guide bar, the molding stock is carried into, then away from the cutter, producing a wave-like scraping cut. The cutter is a $\frac{3}{16}$ in. or thicker piece of steel with a 45° bevel behind its cutting edge. At the beginning of the cut, the guide bar edge is set level with the top of its slot and the cutter is clamped down so it's just touching the workpiece. Then the guide bar is raised slightly, and the rack pulled through and pushed back. After cutting the waves along the whole length of the stock, the guide bar is raised again, and the process repeated over and over until the molding has been cut to its finished depth. Each cut has to be very light. The depth of cut is controlled by a wing nut and threaded rod to advance the guide bar. The 21 to 1 taper on the guide bar means that as the bar moves into the frame, its top rounded edge rises slightly, but remains parallel to the engine base, ensuring a square cut. With a screw of 24 threads-per-inch, one full turn of the wing nut raises the molding 0.002 in., resulting in a cut of the same depth. Most of the time, raising the molding 0.004 in. gives satisfactory results, but initially you can cut twice that depth. The best finish cuts are obtained by making shallow 0.001-in. or even 0.0005-in. cuts. A simple calculation will show that if your molding is to be ¼ in. deep, you will be pulling and pushing it through the cutterhead about 60 times. I think that's the reason the waving engine became obsolete! □

Trevor Robinson, a professor of biochemistry at the University of Massachusetts in Amherst, makes musical instruments as a hobby and is intrigued by unusual ways of working wood.

Fig. 1: Hand-powered waving engine

Make rack from hard maple or other smooth hardwood. Each side of rack has differently spaced grooves.

Molding

Bolted-steel bar secures cutter.

Adjustable fence

Handvise grips rack.

Wingnut

Weight dampens vibration on long molding stock.

Setscrew for adjusting height of wheel support.

Slot houses vertical guide for side-to-side moldings.

Rack runs over rounded edge.

Turning handle advances cup washer and guide bar.

Fixed fence

Push and pull handles to move rack.

T-shaped track guides molding.

1A: Section view

Work piece

Upright

Threaded rod embedded in upright.

Guide bar

---

three hours, to mold a 25-in. strip of mahogany, and twice that long for rosewood. The variable-speed pulley lets Rosen control the speed of the cutter. The wider the molding and the harder the wood, the more slowly the cutter has to move.

Rosen has copied all the J.C. Brown moldings he's found. With another carriage, one that moves from side-to-side between the curved template and a strong spring, he makes "pie crust" molding, which resembles that on carved pie-crust tabletops. He has also discovered a way for his machine to make curved and circular moldings, but that part of his invention is still under wraps.

Rosen, himself an expert clock restorer and builder, now sells ripple moldings to craftsmen all over the world. Since that fire in 1853, steeple clocks, still a popular pattern of American shelf clocks, have been quite plain little things with little more than half-round pilasters decorating their cases. Now, thanks to Rosen's determination and curiosity, builders can give their reproductions all the compelling pizzazz of the Brown originals. □

Carlyle Lynch, a designer, cabinetmaker and retired teacher, lives in Broadway, Va.

Three Tips for Mounting Hardware

Hinging a Jewelry Box

by Sam Bush

Mounting hinges on a small box can be frustrating. It's exacting work that comes at the end of the project, when you'd like to be done. Here are a few ideas I find helpful for hinging a box of the card-file type, where lid and box must align well.

I prefer using unswaged brass butt hinges because they're attractive and readily available. It's handy if the hinge-leaf width is the same as the box-side thickness, since this avoids having a closed mortise with a fragile back wall. Two hinges are enough for boxes up to 12 in. long; for longer boxes, I might use three.

For high-quality work, mortise the hinge leaves into both the box and the lid. A little off the pace but still okay is to mortise the entire hinge into only the box, screwing the top leaf right to the lid so it stands proud of the surface. Either way, clamp the lid to the box as shown in the drawing so the ends accurately line up, and lay out the hinges by eye, adjusting so they're equidistant from the ends. Now mark the length of the mortises with a knife drawn against the ends of the hinges or by just nicking and then using a square.

If the mortises are to be cut with chisels, lay out the depth and width with the marking gauge set as shown. Depth lines should be inside and out if the mortise is open. Chisel cautiously, with the tool's bevel facing up so that the chisel's flat back will leave a flat mortise. Be careful not to go *too* deep, or you'll end up with bound hinges that spring the lid open at the front.

I prefer to cut the mortises with a mortise bit in a router and clean them up with a chisel. I set the router for depth and its fence for width right from the hinge, then test it on a scrap. If I'm making a double mortise, I cut the scrap in half and close it over the barrel of the hinge to test the

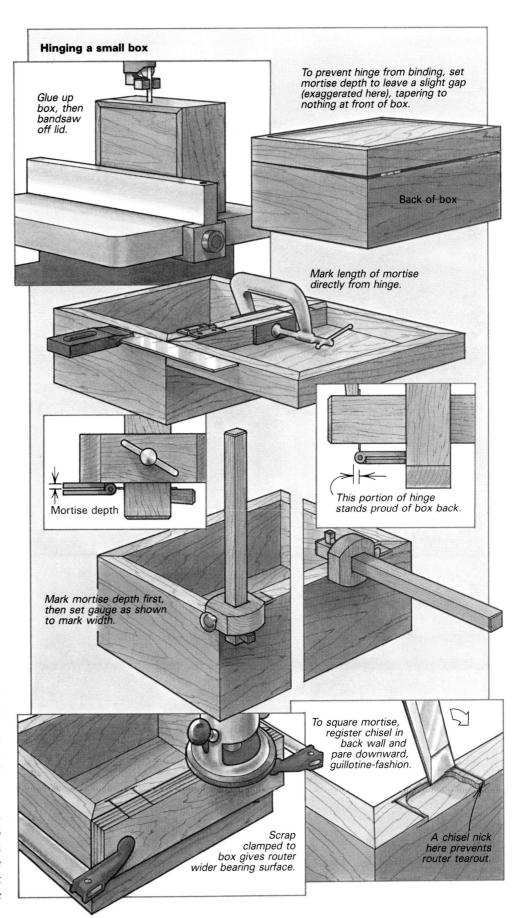

Hinging a small box

Glue up box, then bandsaw off lid.

To prevent hinge from binding, set mortise depth to leave a slight gap (exaggerated here), tapering to nothing at front of box.

Back of box

Mark length of mortise directly from hinge.

Mortise depth

This portion of hinge stands proud of box back.

Mark mortise depth first, then set gauge as shown to mark width.

To square mortise, register chisel in back wall and pare downward, guillotine-fashion.

Scrap clamped to box gives router wider bearing surface.

A chisel nick here prevents router tearout.

Drawings: David Dann

depth. Single or double, it's the barrel, not the leaf thickness, that governs depth. I make the mortise a touch shallow, which leaves a tiny gap at the back of the box but ensures that the front will close nicely.

When routing the mortises, be sure you're going *in between* the end lines, not off to one side. It's a good idea to nick the grain at the right end of each mortise with a diagonal chisel cut so the exiting router bit doesn't break it out. Generally, the router is well supported by the side and end of the box, but you could clamp on a piece of wood, parallel and straight-edged, to improve the bearing surface, at the expense of some clumsiness and having to reset the router fence. Squaring up the mortise with a chisel is easy if you lay the chisel against the routed back wall and pivot it down into the corners, guillotine-fashion. This cut is with the grain, so not too hard. Make a cut or two on the end knife lines, and the mortises are done.

At this point, the hinges theoretically fit right into the mortises and are ready for screws. Drill tiny lead holes for the screws, or you'll surely twist off a soft brass screw head—an incredible nuisance. The holes should be smaller than the screw diameter and as deep as the screw length. Also, they need to be *on-center*, since the tapered screw-head seating in the tapered hinge hole will otherwise pull the hinge off-location. An accurate center punch is nice for locating lead holes, but I prefer an awl, partly out of stubbornness but also so I can use the hinge's tapered seating to my advantage.

For example, when mounting the hinges on the box, which I do first, I mark the holes a *tiny* bit off-center to the inside to draw the hinge leaf in tight. Then I drill and install the top screws one at a time, closing the box after each one to check the alignment. If things aren't right, I influence the lid toward perfection by *slightly* off-centering the next screw. This is especially helpful on the lid of a single-mortise type box.

If, after all this, there's still an alignment problem, the addition of thin wooden liner strips, projecting only ⅛ in. and rounded at the top, usually solves it and gives nice friction to the closure, too. Why didn't I say this in the beginning? I like this detail so well, I often make boxes with lift-off lids and skip the hinges altogether! □

A longtime instructor, Sam Bush runs a specialty woodwork business in Portland and is head of the Guild of Oregon Woodworkers.

Gauge Speeds Knife-Hinge Installation

by Larry Brusso

I think that knife hinges are the most attractive way to hang a fine cabinet door, and they're appropriate on any well-made piece of furniture, contemporary or traditional. I make straight knife hinges for overlay doors and L-shaped ones for flush doors. Installed properly, they give a door a satisfying, friction-free swing.

Unlike most commercial knife hinges, which have leaves riveted together by the pin, mine separate into two parts. This lets me use a simple gauge to position them precisely. Knife hinges look best if they're mortised into both the cabinet and the door and positioned so the pin is half covered by the door's edge. The pin leaf of the hinge is mortised into the top and bottom of the carcase. It's extremely important to get the pins in the top and bottom in the same plane and in the same relationship to the carcase sides. If you don't, the door on which you lavished so much attention will hang like an old garden gate. I find it inconvenient to cut mortises in an already assembled cabinet, so I clamp up the case dry and use the gauge shown to position the pin leaves. Then I knife their outlines, disassemble the case and chisel the mortises. The case can be glued up with the pin leaves in place.

To fit an overlay door once the pin leaves are installed, first trim the door about ⅛ in. shorter than the opening and position it so its hinge edge, with the door in the closed position, butts against the pins. Then mark each pin location on the door's edge by knifing a line on each side of it. Set the bottom door leaf first by lining up its hole with the two knife marks. Position the leaf lengthwise so the hole is half covered by the door's bottom corner, then knife around the leaf and cut its mortise. Install the top door leaf similarly, but position it lengthwise so the hole is slightly less than half covered. That way, you can lengthen the mortise a little at a time until the edge of the door lines up with the edge of the carcase.

To hang the door, screw the bottom door leaf in place, but leave the top one off. Slip the bottom leaf over its pin, holding the door as if it were open. Tilt the door toward you slightly and hold the top door leaf on its pin with your fingertip. Now tilt the door back, carefully sliding the leaf into the mortise. Check the door's alignment and lengthen the mortise as necessary before driving the screws.

The same procedure works for flush doors hung on L-shaped hinges, save for two differences. To mark for the door leaves, you have to snake the door inside the cabinet and position it such that its front edge butts against the pins. And you must be very sure to set both hinges correctly on the first try, because you cannot adjust the mortise length afterward to move an L-shaped hinge. □

Larry Brusso, of Pontiac, Michigan, makes and sells knife hinges.

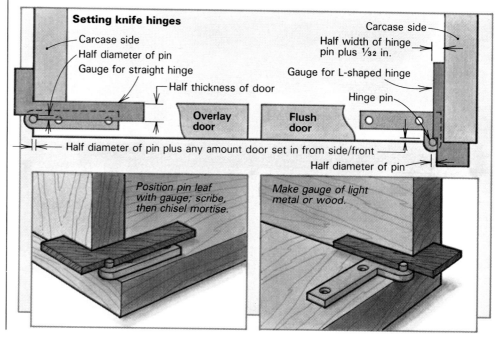

Setting knife hinges

Carcase side
Half diameter of pin
Gauge for straight hinge
Half thickness of door

Carcase side
Half width of hinge pin plus ¹⁄₃₂ in.
Gauge for L-shaped hinge
Hinge pin

Overlay door   **Flush door**

Half diameter of pin plus any amount door set in from side/front

Half diameter of pin

Position pin leaf with gauge; scribe, then chisel mortise.

Make gauge of light metal or wood.

Locking Up a Chest

by Simon Watts

In olden days when chests doubled as strongboxes, a sturdy lock was essential. Some chests were even fitted with multiple locks whose keys were guarded by different people, ensuring that the case could not be opened without witnesses. Although you may not need *quite* that much security, locks are still handy for keeping chests, jewelry boxes and toolboxes from being casually explored. This series of drawings shows how to mark out and set a chest lock.

Begin by marking the centerline of the top front edge of the chest with a pencil. Square this line across, continuing it down the inside face. Place the lock on this centerline and mark the wood on both sides with a knife (**A**). Knife these lines square across the edge and down the inside of the chest. Now set a marking gauge to the width of the top plate of the lock and gauge a line along the upper edge of the chest to show where wood must be removed. Reset the gauge and mark the lower edge of the lock plate on the inside of the chest. Mark also the center of the keyhole by setting a gauge to the vertical distance between the center of the keyhole and the top surface of the lock plate (**B**).

Now deepen the gauge marks with a chisel and pare the waste for the top plate, using your thumb and index finger as a stop to prevent the chisel from slipping and cutting too far (**C**). Drill out the keyhole a fraction bigger than the key, using a wood backing to prevent tearout (**D**). Set a gauge to the thickness of the back plate and scribe a line on the top-plate mortise, then chisel to the scribed line to mortise the back plate.

Mark the outline of the body of the lock with a pencil (no great accuracy is required here since the lock's plates hide this part) and remove the waste with saw and chisel (**E**). Try the lock in place (**F**) and chisel where needed to fit the body so the lock plates are snug in their mortises. If necessary, shape the keyhole with a small rattail file to fit the key. I screw the lock in place, engage the striker plate in it and turn the key to lock it in place. Some plates have projecting tangs that position

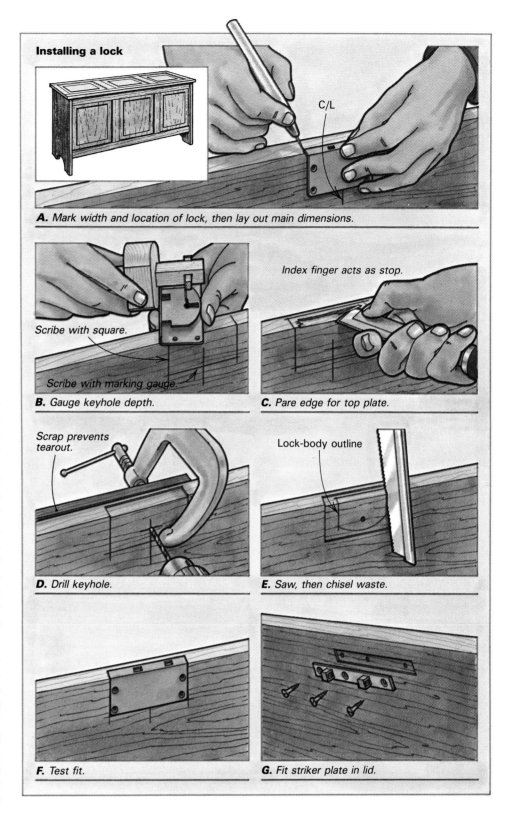

Installing a lock

A. Mark width and location of lock, then lay out main dimensions.

Scribe with square.

Scribe with marking gauge.

B. Gauge keyhole depth.

Index finger acts as stop.

C. Pare edge for top plate.

Scrap prevents tearout.

D. Drill keyhole.

Lock-body outline

E. Saw, then chisel waste.

F. Test fit.

G. Fit striker plate in lid.

the striker in the lid when it is gently closed (**G**). If yours doesn't, put the screws in the striker points-up, close the lid and bear down lightly. When you mortise the striker into the lid, leave it a fraction proud so the lid contacts the chest at this point only.

The final step is to attach the pierced brass escutcheon plate. This is either screwed or nailed with escutcheon pins to the face of the chest over the keyhole (some locks have a keyhole-shaped brass insert set into the face). Fit this type of lock only to a chest with a lid that's of frame-and-panel, plywood or veneer construction. Otherwise the wood's seasonal shrinking and swelling will move the striker out of alignment and the lock will fit properly only during the season in which you installed it. □

Simon Watts is a woodworker and author of Building a Houseful of Furniture *(Taunton Press, 1983).*

Index